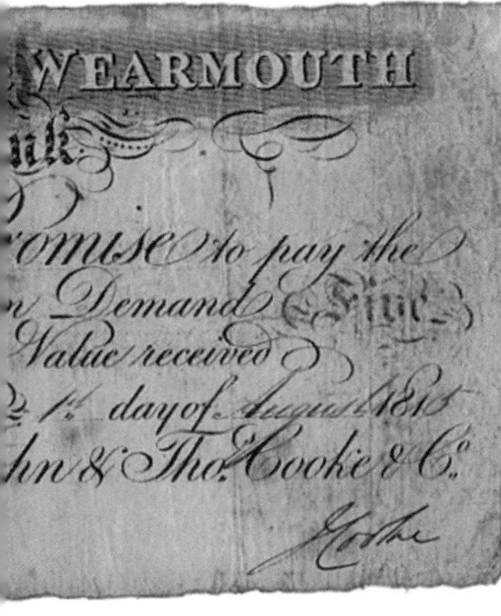

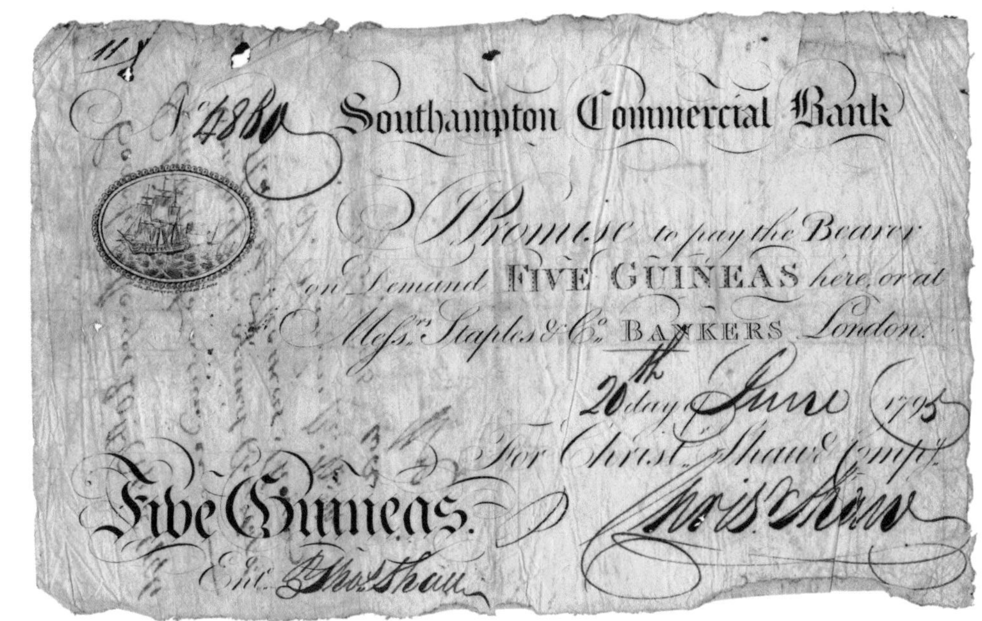
Southampton Commercial Bank
I Promise to pay the Bearer
on Demand FIVE GUINEAS here, or at
Messrs. Staples & Co. BANKERS London.
20th day June 1795
For Christr. Shaw & Compy.
Five Guineas.

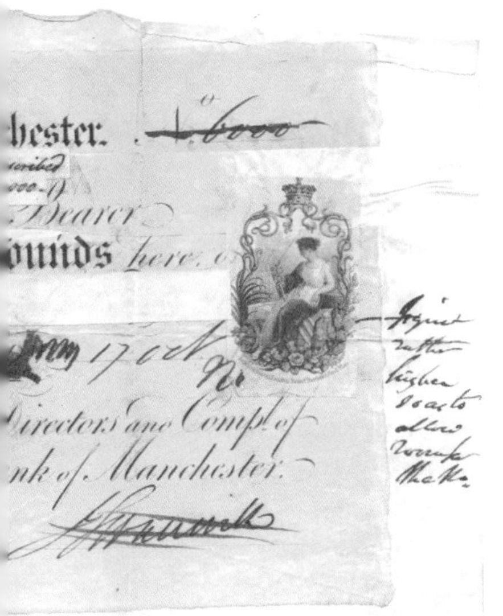

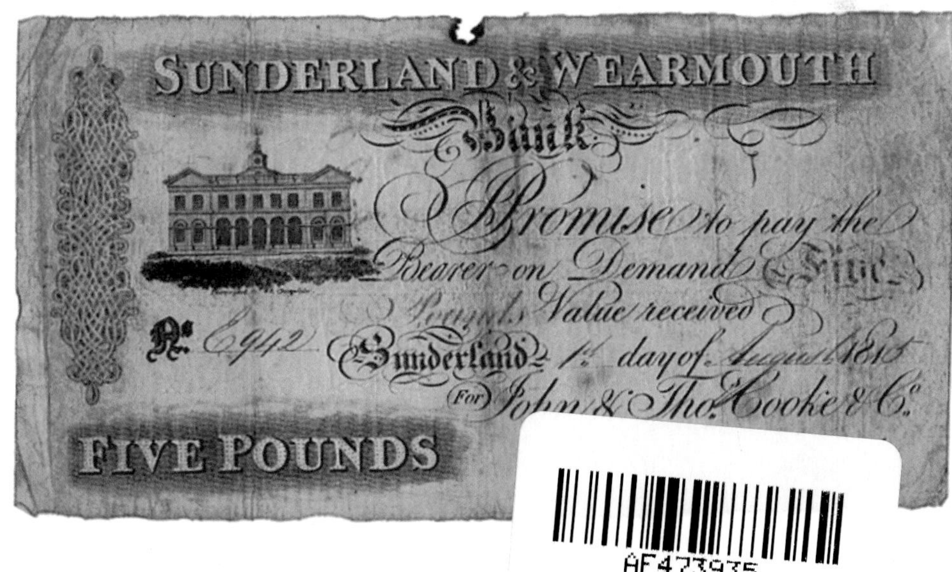
SUNDERLAND & WEARMOUTH
Bank
I Promise to pay the
Bearer on Demand Five
Pounds Value received
No. E942
Sunderland 1st day of August 1815
For John & Thos. Cooke & Co.
FIVE POUNDS

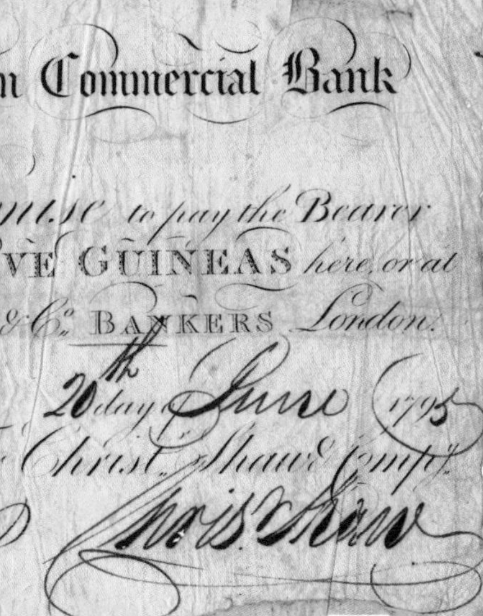

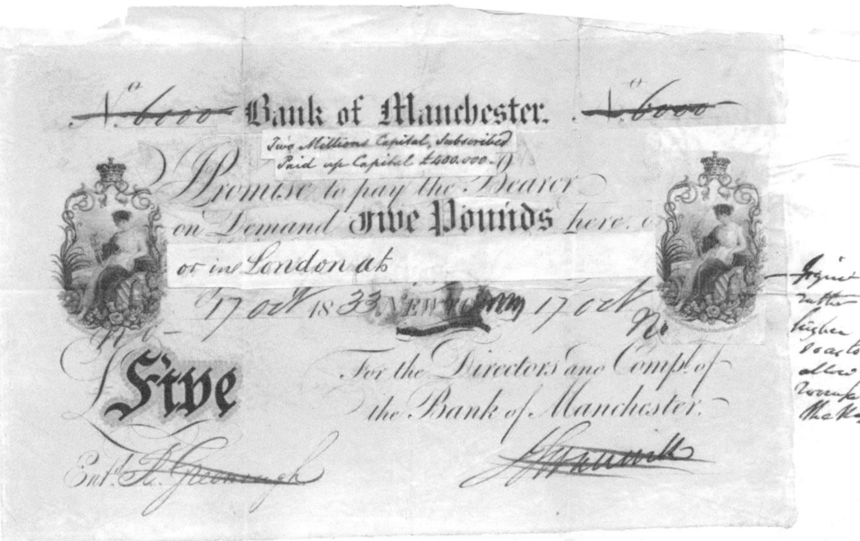
Bank of Manchester.
Two Millions Capital, Subscribed
Paid up Capital £400,000
I Promise to pay the Bearer
on Demand Five Pounds here, or
or in London at
Five
For the Directors and Compy. of
the Bank of Manchester.

SHOW ME THE MONEY

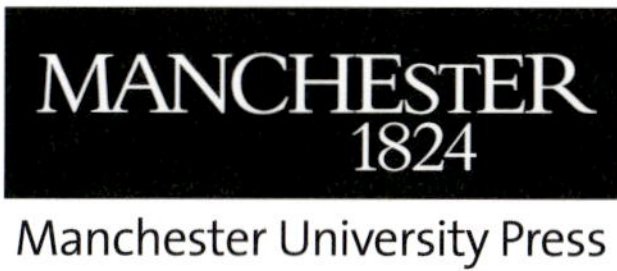

Manchester University Press

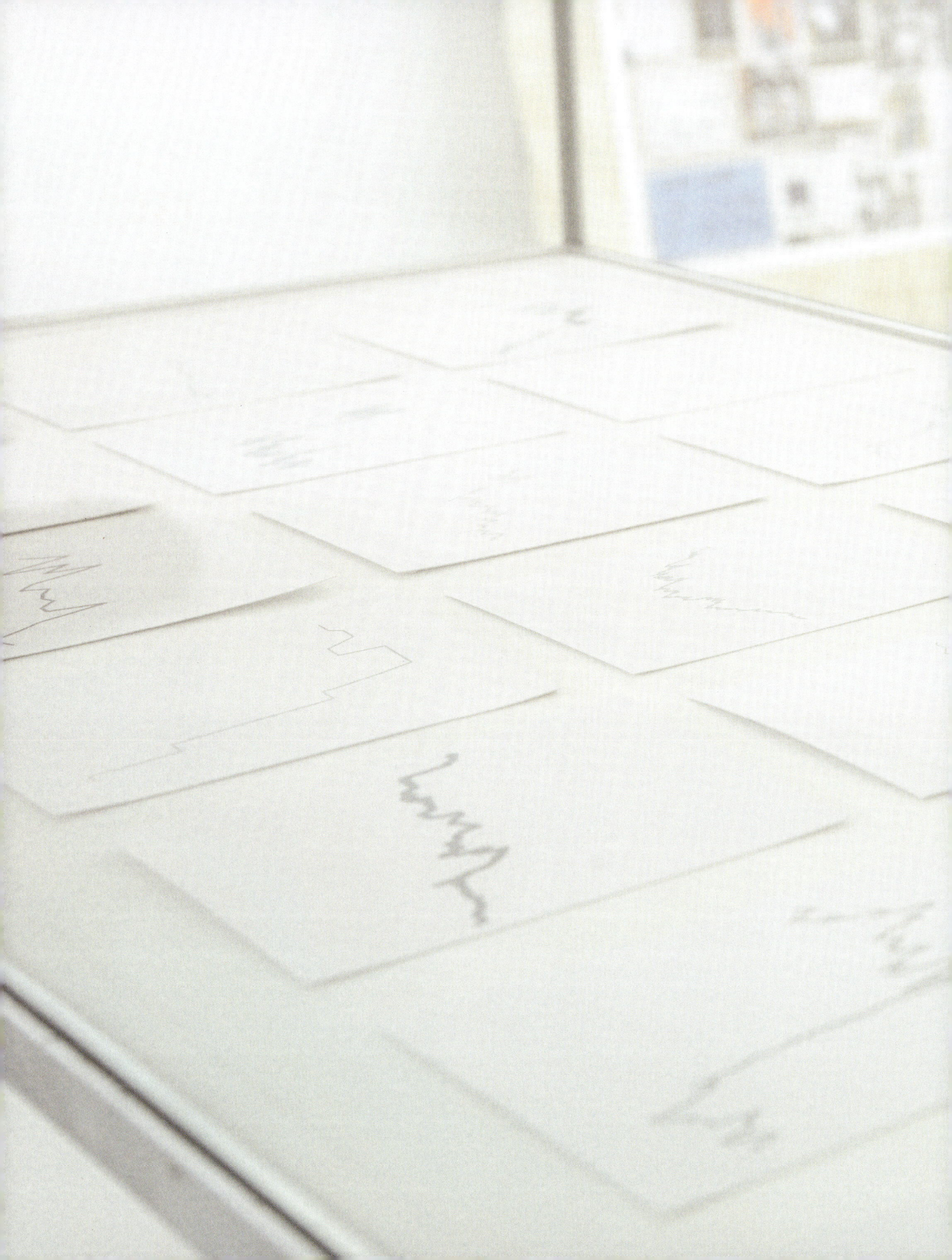

SHOW ME THE MONEY
The image of finance, 1700 to the present

Edited by Paul Crosthwaite, Peter Knight and Nicky Marsh

Manchester University Press
Manchester and New York

distributed in the United States exclusively by Palgrave Macmillan

Published by Manchester University Press
Oxford Road, Manchester M13 9NR, UK
and Room 400, 175 Fifth Avenue, New York,
NY 10010, USA
www.manchesteruniversitypress.co.uk

Distributed in the United States exclusively by
Palgrave Macmillan, 175 Fifth Avenue, New York,
NY 10010, USA

Distributed in Canada exclusively by
UBC Press, University of British Columbia,
2029 West Mall, Vancouver, BC, Canada V6T 1Z2

British Library Cataloguing-in-Publication Data
A catalogue record for this book is available from the British Library

Library of Congress Cataloging-in-Publication Data
applied for

ISBN 978 0 7190 9625 9 hardback

First published 2014

Designed by www.axisgraphicdesign.co.uk

Printed by Gutenberg Press Limited, Malta

Cover:

William Hogarth, *The South Sea Scheme* (1721)

'Babsonchart of United States Business Conditions'. 28 January 1929, in Roger W. Babson, *Business Barometers Used in the Management of Business and the Investment of Money* (Babson Park, MA: Babson Statistical Organization, 1929).

Show me the money is supported by
the Arts and Humanities Research Council (AHRC)

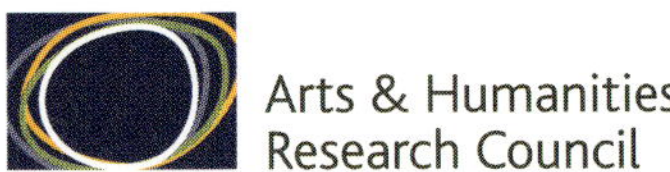

Contents

Contributors

Chapters

Paul Crosthwaite is a Lecturer in English Literature at the University of Edinburgh. His publications include *Trauma, Postmodernism and the Aftermath of World War II*, and, as editor, *Criticism, Crisis and Contemporary Narrative: Textual Horizons in an Age of Global Risk.* He is currently working on a book entitled *Speculative Investments: Finance, Feeling and Representation in Contemporary Literature and Culture.*

Peter Knight is a Senior Lecturer in American Studies at the University of Manchester. He is the author of *Conspiracy Culture* and *The Kennedy Assassination*, and is currently completing *Reading the Market: Genres of Financial Capitalism in Late Nineteenth-Century America* (for Johns Hopkins University Press).

Nicky Marsh is a Professor in the English Department at the University of Southampton. She has published on contemporary women's poetry, and is the author of *Money, Speculation and Finance in Recent British Fiction.* She is currently writing a book on the cultural and fictional responses to the emergence of a number of 'new markets' from the 1950s to the 1990s.

Alistair Robinson is the Director of the Northern Gallery for Contemporary Art in Sunderland and has curated influential exhibitions such as *Rank: Picturing the Social Order, 1516–2009.*

Isabella Streffen is an artist who recently completed doctoral research into military visioning technologies and their use in fine art practice. She works across media to examine and respond to fundamental problems of politics, perception, technology and narrative. She is currently an AHRC Postdoctoral Research Associate on the *Show me the money* project, and an Early Career Research Fellow at Oxford Brookes University.

Think pieces

Justin Fox is the author of *The Myth of the Rational Market: A History of Risk, Reward, and Delusion on Wall Street* (HarperBusiness, 2009). He is a former columnist at *Time* magazine, and is currently editorial director of the Harvard Business Review Group.

Andy Haldane is Executive Director for Financial Stability at the Bank of England, and is one of the most prominent public voices on the credit crisis.

Ben Lewis is an art critic and documentary maker, whose works have appeared in *The Independent* and on the BBC.

Bill Maurer is a cultural anthropologist at University of California, Irvine who conducts research on law, property, money and finance. He is Director of the Institute for Money, Technology and Financial Inclusion.

Alex Preston, a former City banker, is a journalist and is the author of *This Bleeding City* (Faber, 2010), a novel about the 2008 banking crisis.

Acknowledgements

This book and the exhibition it accompanies would not have been possible without the support of many individuals and organisations. Much of the initial thinking towards the project took place as part of the Arts and Humanities Research Council (AHRC)-funded 'Culture of the Market Network', based at the University of Manchester. The AHRC generously extended its support for this work with 'follow-on funding' to allow for the staging and publication of *Show me the money*. We are very grateful to the AHRC for its vital role in bringing this project about. Further financial support came from the Faculty of Humanities at the University of Manchester and the School of Literatures, Languages and Cultures at the University of Edinburgh, and we thank colleagues there too. The project was also assisted significantly by the generosity of the Arts Council.

We also wish to express our deep gratitude to staff at each of the host venues for the exhibition: the Northern Gallery for Contemporary Art in Sunderland; the Chawton House Library in Alton, Hampshire; and the People's History Museum in Manchester. We enormously appreciate the support (financial and otherwise), enthusiasm and dedication of staff at these fine venues and we are very conscious of the fact that, without this commitment, *Show me the money* certainly would never have become a reality.

Sincere thanks also go to the many artists and bodies that granted permission for the inclusion of works in the book and/or exhibition. They are identified individually elsewhere in this volume, but we take this opportunity to thank them collectively for their kind support of this project. We are likewise grateful to the leading commentators on financial issues (our 'notables', as we like to think of them) who responded enthusiastically to our invitation to contribute think pieces on their views of 'the market' to this book: Andy Haldane, Bill Maurer, Justin Fox, Alex Preston and Ben Lewis.

We are also indebted to all at Manchester University Press for their commitment to bringing this book to fruition under tight time constraints, as well as to the Press's anonymous reviewers, whose comments have helped us to improve the project in numerous ways. Special thanks to the book's designer, Alan Ward, for his work.

Finally, thanks to our colleagues at the universities of Edinburgh, Manchester and Southampton, and to our families, for their interest, patience and forbearance. There are some debts that money can't repay.

Introduction

Paul Crosthwaite, Peter Knight and Nicky Marsh

The failures in the global financial system that occurred in 2008 were experienced as a crisis because they were confusing and chaotic. The causes and implications of the event appeared to be too complex, too impenetrable and too surprising to be understood. The Queen herself – estimated to have lost £25 million in the crash – was reported to have asked, when visiting the London School of Economics that autumn, 'if this crisis was so large' then how 'did everyone miss it?' As the works presented in *Show me the money: The image of finance, 1700 to the Present* suggest, financial processes are often difficult to see not in spite, but precisely *because*, of their vast size. Finance – money, investment, credit, debt – is the air we breathe, and it is difficult, if not impossible, to get an objective view of an atmosphere that envelops us so completely.

Another pillar of the Establishment, Rowan Williams, then Archbishop of Canterbury, suggested in 2010 that 'economics [is] too important to be left to economists'. The artists, photographers, illustrators and other graphic practitioners who have shaped the visual culture of finance showcased in this book draw the attention of those who view and study their works to many aspects of financial systems that mainstream economists – with their emphasis on the rationality, efficiency and equilibrium of markets – would prefer to deny or ignore. These works highlight the cultural, emotional, libidinal and even mystical factors that animate financial markets, and often propel them far from a state of equilibrium. Above all, they tell a story that has always been known to anyone exposed to the world of finance (which is all of us), but is easily missed: a story that shows that finance has a history of ever-repeating and ever-expanding crises, which are abstract and global, yet also visceral and local.

The cultural and aesthetic artefacts included in this volume, however, do not merely reflect, or even simply interrogate, the realities of financial exchange, but also play an active role in constituting those realities. From satirical cartoons and lists of 'prices current' in the eighteenth century, to newspaper illustrations, tickertapes and stock charts in the nineteenth, to conceptual artworks, network simulations and digital trading platforms in the twentieth and twenty-first, visual media have shaped how professionals and lay people alike perceive and act in the market; and since the market is nothing more than these perceptions and actions, they have shaped the market itself, too. Hence, if the image- and object-makers represented in this volume provide certain kinds of challenges to the forms of economic knowledge propounded by economists, then (we would venture to suggest) the art critics and cultural historians who analyse the visual culture of finance offer their own counterweights, by demonstrating how markets are both mediated and, at least partially, *made* by visual and verbal rhetorics, and protocols of representation, genre, narrative and iconography.

As used in this book, the term 'finance' today encompasses the issuance and exchange of money; markets for stocks, bonds, currencies, commodities, derivatives and property; financial institutions, including investment, 'high street' and central banks, building societies, insurers and hedge funds; and a financial 'class' made up of investors, CEOs, rentiers and others whose wealth derives primarily from these markets and institutions. We trace the origins of the contemporary financial world back over three centuries, to 1700, because this date roughly coincides with the culmination of the defining development in the early history of modern finance: the English 'Financial Revolution', signalled most visibly by the foundation of the Bank of England in 1694, and responsible, as a result of the numerous new speculative credit instruments that it spawned, for events including the South Sea Bubble of 1720, in many ways the archetypal financial boom and bust.

As the economist Giovanni Arrighi has argued, the Financial Revolution inaugurated a transatlantic system of capital accumulation, centred on Britain, which dominated global trade and commerce for well over a century.[1] Since the nineteenth century, the world economy's centre of gravity has shifted westwards, towards the United States, but the world-system has remained first and foremost transatlantic, and London and New York continue to be the planet's pre-eminent financial centres. Accordingly, this book places a particular emphasis on visual responses to British and American financial history, while also making substantial reference to the visual archives of other nations that have vied with Britain and the United States for financial supremacy over the last three centuries, and those that are set to do so during the twenty-first century.

The perspectives on these visual materials offered in the following chapters build on a set of approaches to finance that have been grouped under the term 'cultural economy'. Distinguishing itself both from a conventional 'political' economy and (all the more so) from the narrowly mathematical form of economics practised in the mainstream of the discipline, cultural economy stresses the vital role of 'cultural' factors (broadly defined) in the functioning of financial systems. One branch of cultural economy, the 'social studies of finance', for example, has highlighted the status of financial models as cultural (that is, manufactured, negotiated, contested) artefacts, rather than as strictly technical or scientific statements, and demonstrated their tendency not simply to objectively record, but to 'performatively' generate, patterns of financial exchange.[2] Other important work has been ethnographic in orientation, and has drawn attention to the ways in which notionally abstract and impersonal financial structures are shaped by the distinctive cultures of particular institutions – their values, customs, codes of initiation and affiliation, behavioural norms and so on.[3] There also exists an abundance of scholarship dedicated to charting the mutually constitutive relationship between finance and literature – as domains commonly defined by the meaning and value of writing – in periods ranging from the early eighteenth century to the present.[4] There have, however, been very few attempts to grasp the integral importance of visual culture to both the operation of finance itself and a critical questioning of some of its assumptions and practices.[5] One of the key aims of this book, then, is to make, at the very least, a substantial contribution to rectifying this omission.

At the same time, the scholarly work in this volume seeks to sharpen the political edge of a cultural economy-style approach to finance. While cultural economy has been very effective in demonstrating that finance is the product of cultural forms of every kind, it has not always fully articulated why this matters politically. Our response to the latter question is that if visual representations, for example, have highly consequential economic effects, then the ideological assumptions encoded in such representations matter profoundly, and the field of representation emerges as a primary site of political struggle. The task of the cultural economist is, then, to chart this field and identify the representational strategies via which dominant power structures have been entrenched, and those which offer opportunities for contestation and transformation. To return to the starting point of this introduction: the status of the global credit crisis as a 'cultural' crisis (a crisis of knowledge and representation) is inextricable from its status as a political and economic crisis – a crisis of capitalism – in which the reigning theories of how a neoliberal, hyper-financialised form of capitalism is supposed to work were cast into disarray, and the idea of the financial system as existing for the benefit of society at large revealed as a fiction, as top bankers slipped away with huge payoffs, while ordinary citizens were cast out of their homes and jobs. If cultural economy is to register fully the vast inequalities that are the ultimate consequences of the 'culture of finance' it must position itself as an ally of political economy, and not as an alternative to it.[6]

The various forms taken by the visual culture of finance are arranged in this book around five themes. Chapter 1, 'Debt and credit', explores how its two titular terms – the yin and yang of finance, at once antonyms and synonyms of one another – have been negotiated in visual culture since the English Financial Revolution. The works covered in this section are acutely aware of their status both as meditations on the entanglements of debt and credit and – in view of their often substantial market value – as potential credit vehicles in their own right. Chapter 2, 'Framing finance', also traces its narrative back to the early days of the modern financial economy, examining successive attempts to visualise 'the market' in both its totality and its particularity, and to find a visual language for the strange and ineffable flickerings and flutterings of increasingly abstract financial entities. Chapter 3, 'Animal spirits', traverses the last three centuries of financial history once more, in order to tell a third story about changing constructions of the market, one in which psychological factors loom especially large, whether in the guise of the scheming, avaricious speculator pulling the strings behind the scenes; in the form of the mass, 'animal' hysteria of the panicked crowd; or via the idea of the market as itself a kind of 'being', with an omniscient 'mind' of its own. Chapter 4, 'The money shot', explores the way that as money and financial instruments have become increasingly abstract and dematerialised, contemporary artists have investigated the visceral, affective and thoroughly material aspects of money in all its modern guises and disguises. The chapter concentrates on the tropes of burning and falling; the staging of disappearances and reappearances; and the promises and implied lies of contracts. However, it also tells the unbelievable story of the art collection of the Royal Bank of Scotland, a parable for the way that the value of artworks and financial instruments can literally disappear overnight, leaving only a few ghostly traces of what formerly seemed so real. Chapter 5, 'Booms and busts', focuses on financial upheaval since the early 2000s, addressing artworks that highlight and subvert some of the prevailing orthodoxies in contemporary financial discourse, from the taken-for-granted associations between market undulations and the sublime landscapes of the natural world, to the purposefully opaque jargon surrounding the derivative instruments implicated in the 'credit crunch', to the dominant ideology of 'socialism for the rich and capitalism for the poor'.

These chapters are interleaved with short essays or think pieces by five notable commentators on finance, who approach the field from very different perspectives. We asked these writers to reflect, quite simply, on what the idea of 'the market' means to them. The results provide penetrating and provocative counterpoints to the chapters they accompany. Andy Haldane, Executive Director for Financial Stability at the Bank of England, tackles our brief head-on, explaining that his image of today's financial markets is both radically different from, and yet at some essential level still closely related to, the Greek agora or the provincial marketplace. The anthropologist Bill Maurer, meanwhile, turns our question on its head, arguing that the real challenge is not to see but to *hear* the market, understood not as a system of representations but as a network of more or less 'noisy' channels and junctions. Tracing the development of modern finance theory, Justin Fox, financial journalist and Executive Editor of the Harvard Business Review, paints a troubling picture of the financial marketplace as a terrain almost entirely devoid of people, and asks, who, then, are such markets for? Conversely, people are at the centre of novelist Alex Preston's survey of recent fictional accounts of the credit crisis, as he makes a plea for errant financiers to be understood not as pantomime villains but as complex, if flawed, individuals. Finally, the art critic Ben Lewis traces the intriguing parallels and dubious intersections between contemporary financial markets and the market for contemporary art.

The images, objects, narratives and artworks that make up this book and exhibition explore the ways in which finance has become a dazzlingly sophisticated and globally interconnected phenomenon that requires us to think anew about the ways in which we understand time and space: money is instant; it is everywhere and nowhere. *Show me the money* highlights the ways in which art and culture have allowed us to explore the increasingly abstract and self-referential nature of finance, the complexity of its operations that are virtually impossible for those on the outside to envisage. Yet the three locations of the exhibition also suggest ways in which this overarching narrative of finance is complicated by the particularities of place: finance may be everywhere, but its meanings and effects vary markedly from one site to another.

The exhibition opens in the Northern Gallery for Contemporary Art in Sunderland, a location well within the ambit of one of the iconic casualties of the credit crunch, Newcastle-based Northern Rock (which merged with Sunderland's North of England Building Society in 1994 and operated offices in the city), and a place coming to terms with the abandonment of a host of grand redevelopment projects in the wake of cuts imposed following the financial downturn. It then moves to the lovingly restored family home of Jane Austen, the Chawton House Library in Alton, Hampshire. This is the place where Austen completed her mature novels (including *Mansfield Park*, *Sense and Sensibility* and *Persuasion*), where her brother was involved in the failure of the local bank (whose losses included the £13 profit from *Mansfield Park*) and where the Governor of the Bank of England, Mark Carney, unveiled Austen as the new face of the £10 note in 2013. The final destination for the exhibition is the People's History Museum in Manchester. The history of Manchester and its environs, from the speculative manias and working-class struggles against unrestrained capitalism that accompanied the area's industrial development to the contemporary crisis in the Co-operative Bank, presents another distinctive narrative of the relationship between high finance and locality. Each of these locations, then, suggests a different perspective on money, the market, debt, credit and the other themes of the exhibition. We hope that the variety of material contained in *Show me the money* – the book and the exhibition – will multiply these perspectives, demonstrating that the 'image of finance' is always dependent on where you happen to be standing.

Notes

1 See Giovanni Arrighi, *The Long Twentieth Century: Money, Power, and the Origins of Our Times*, 2nd edn (London: Verso, 2009).

2 See, for example, Michel Callon, Yuval Millo and Fabian Muniesa (eds), *Market Devices* (Oxford: Blackwell, 2007); Donald MacKenzie, *An Engine Not a Camera: How Financial Models Shape Markets* (Cambridge, MA: MIT Press, 2006); Donald MacKenzie, Fabian Muniesa and Lucia Siu (eds), *Do Economists Make Markets? On the Performativity of Economics* (Princeton, NJ: Princeton University Press, 2007).

3 See, for example, Mitchel Y. Abolafia, *Making Markets: Opportunism and Restraint on Wall Street* (Cambridge, MA: Harvard University Press, 1996); Karen Ho, *Liquidated: An Ethnography of Wall Street* (Durham, NC: Duke University Press, 2009); Caitlin Zaloom, *Out of the Pits: Traders and Technology from Chicago to London* (Chicago: University of Chicago Press, 2006).

4 See, for example, Patrick Brantlinger, *Fictions of State: Culture and Credit in Britain, 1694–1994* (Ithaca, NY: Cornell University Press, 1996); Colin Nicholson, *Writing and the Rise of Finance: Capital Satires of the Early Eighteenth Century* (Cambridge: Cambridge University Press, 1994); Sandra Sherman, *Finance and Fictionality in the Early Eighteenth Century: Accounting for Defoe* (Cambridge: Cambridge University Press, 1996); Mary Poovey, *Genres of the Credit Economy: Mediating Value in Eighteenth- and Nineteenth-Century Britain* (Chicago: University of Chicago Press, 2008); Alexander Dick, *Romanticism and the Gold Standard: Money, Literature and Economic Debate in Britain 1790–1830* (Basingstoke: Palgrave Macmillan, 2013); Francis O'Gorman (ed.), *Victorian Literature and Finance* (Oxford: Oxford University Press, 2007); Gail Turley Houston, *From Dickens to* Dracula*: Gothic, Economics and Victorian Fiction* (Cambridge: Cambridge University Press, 2005); Andrew Lawson, *Downwardly Mobile: The Changing Fortunes of American Realism* (Oxford: Oxford University Press, 2012); Walter Benn Michaels, *The Gold Standard and the Logic of Naturalism: American Literature at the Turn of the Century* (Berkeley, CA: University of California Press, 1987); David Zimmerman, *Panic! Markets, Crises and Crowds in American Fiction* (Chapel Hill, NC: University of North Carolina Press, 2006); Nicky Marsh, *Money, Speculation and Finance in Contemporary British Fiction* (London: Continuum, 2007).

5 Notable exceptions to this general neglect are studies of contemporary financial advertising as it has appeared in print (Christian De Cock, James A. Fitchett and Christina Volkmann, 'Myths of a near past: Envisioning finance capitalism anno 2007', *Ephemera: Theory and Politics in Organization* 9:1 (2009), 8–25; Christian De Cock, Max Baker and Christina Volkmann, 'Financial phantasmagoria: Corporate image-work in times of crisis', *Organization* 18:2 (2011), 153–72) and on screen (Robert Goldman and Stephen Papson, *Landscapes of Capital* (Cambridge: Polity, 2011)). Though they lack the present book's historical scope and its broad approach to the visual culture of finance, several recent volumes are also notable for their attention to contemporary artistic responses to financial issues: Franziska Nori and Piroschka Dossi (eds), *Art, Price and Value: Contemporary Art and the Market* (Milan: Silvana Editoriale, 2008); Gregory Sholette and Oliver Ressler (eds), *It's the Political Economy, Stupid: The Global Financial Crisis in Art and Theory* (London: Pluto, 2013); Katy Siegel and Paul Mattick, *Money* (London: Thames and Hudson, 2004).

6 For a more detailed discussion of the politics of cultural economy, see Paul du Gay and Michael Pryke, 'Cultural economy: An introduction', in du Gay and Pryke (eds), *Cultural Economy: Cultural Analysis and Commercial Life* (London: Sage, 2002), 1–19; Philip Mirowski and Edward Nik-Kah, 'Markets made flesh: Callon, performativity and the FCC spectrum auctions', in MacKenzie, Muniesa and Siu (eds), *Do Economists Make Markets?*, 190–224; and Peter Knight, 'Introduction: Fictions of finance', *Journal of Cultural Economy* 6:1 (2013): 2–12.

Debt and credit 1

Nicky Marsh

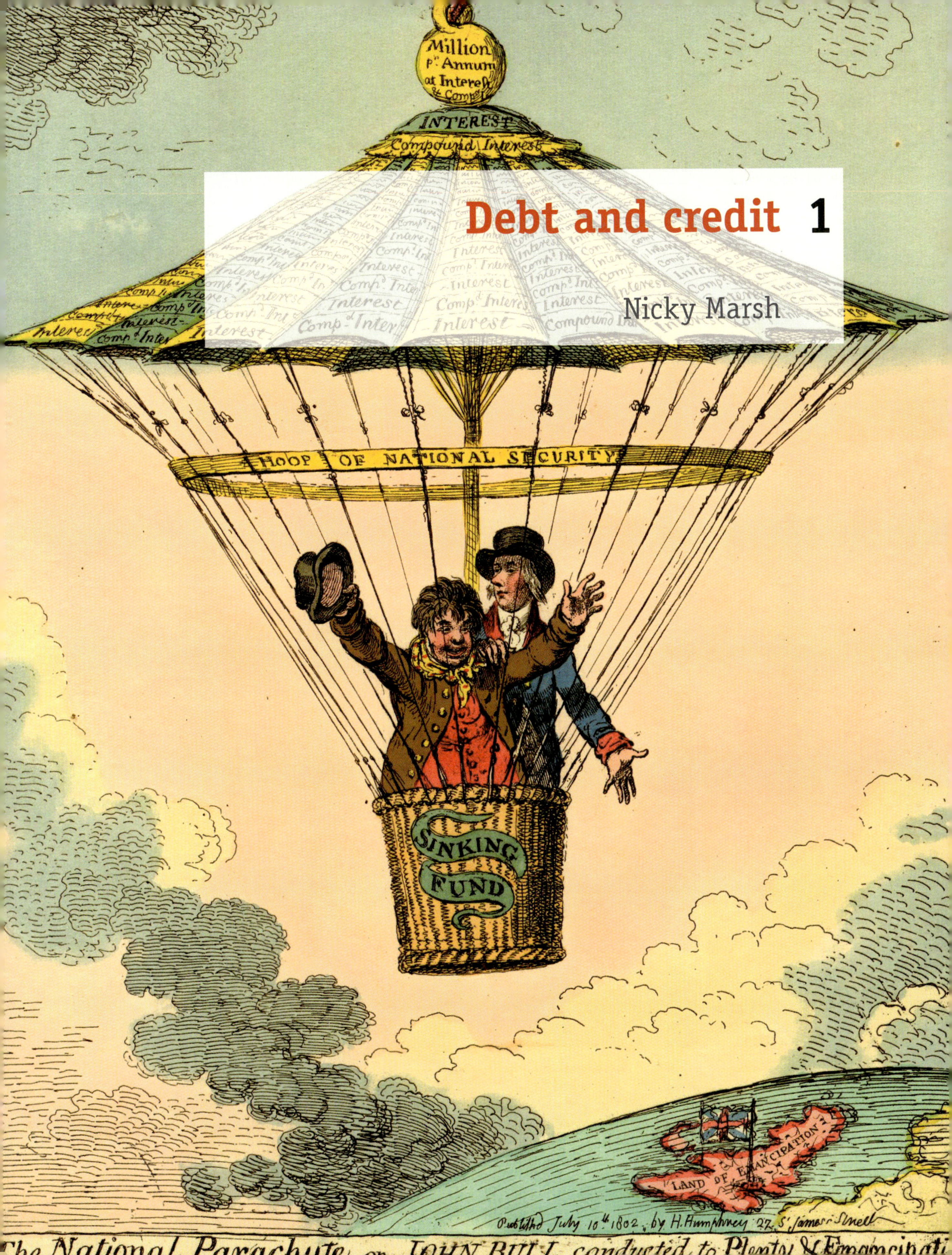

Debt and credit

Nicky Marsh

Show me the money: The image of finance begins at the start of the eighteenth century, the high point of England's Financial Revolution in which the central constituents of the modern nation's financial system – a central bank, a national debt, and the forms of taxation, bonds and paper monies that could sustain them – all came into being.[1] Modern credit was realised from a debt: the newly inaugurated and private Bank of England was charged with managing the national debt and did so by issuing paper money and Government bonds and the processes of abstraction that have become synonymous with modern finance, as wealth circulates through representations that become increasingly independent from their material origins, began. Public debt was thus 'misrecognised' in the moment of its creation, Patrick Brantlinger has suggested, when it was 'fetishised through public credit' as a form of 'wealth', and this confusion between credit and debt, and the ways in which it has been played out through the very different languages of the public and private, is embedded in the visual history of finance.[2]

In the wake of the 2008 crisis critics from a wide range of contexts have become attentive to the significance of this long-standing conflation of debt and credit, as they function as both synonyms and antonyms, and have attempted to return meaning to their independent functions. This tendency found its fullest form in the anthropologist David Graeber's impressive *Debt: The First 5000 Years*. Graeber represents debt as a necessary consequence of sociality, arguing that viewing it in solely negative terms involves accepting individualism as axiomatic and rejecting that co-operation and interdependency can also be the foundations of society. For Graeber debt is a way of organising rather than simply negating social relations: 'debt is what happens' when 'two parties cannot walk away from each other, because they are not yet equal. But it is carried out in the shadow of eventual equality.'[3] The implications of credit have been explored by Richard Dienst, Fred Moten and Stefano Harney, who argue that credit represents the financialisation of debt's social possibilities. Dienst, for example, suggests that while debt 'comprises every socially articulable expression of the gap between what we have, what we need, and what we want', credit, the drawing of profit from this gap, destroys the social. He draws upon Marx to underline the destructive nature of credit, suggesting that credit is 'a corrupt Absolute Idea developing itself in ever higher spirals of alienated activity within a hollowed-out community.'[4] The same logic is apparent in Moten and Harney's dialectic of credit and debt, in which credit is described as a 'means of privatization and debt a means of socialization. So long as debt and credit are paired in the monogamous violence of the home, the pension, the government, or the university, debt can only feed credit, debt can only desire credit. And credit can only expand by means of debt. But debt is social and credit is asocial. Debt is mutual. Credit runs only one way.'[5] This division between creditor and debtor is central to our political moment: as Maurizio Lazzarato has convincingly argued, this relationship has usurped that between capital and labour as the central polarity around which society is organised.[6]

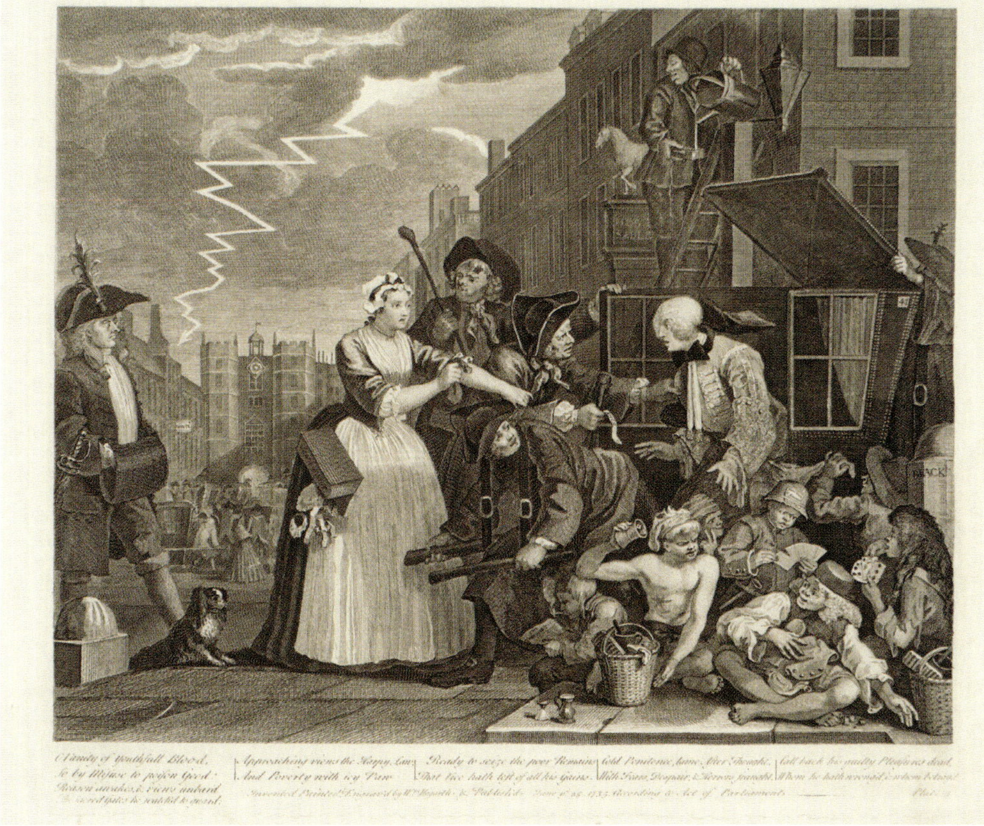

Figure 1
William Hogarth (1697–1764), *A Rake's Progress*, plate 4 (1735). Etching and engraving on paper.

This chapter traces the ways in which these suggestive contradictions and social dynamics of debt and credit have been represented in art and visual culture more generally. Starting with William Hogarth's allegorical depictions of the Financial Revolution and ending with the re-emergence of allegory in the revolutionary work of those associated with the Occupy movements, it examines the recurring spatial and visual forms that have been given to debt and credit. It explores how credit and debt's tilted scales, represented by a base downward iconography for debt and a giddily ascending one for credit, are often interrogated in visual culture as it makes apparent the contradictory and unequal social relationship between the two. The chapter also explores how art has offered a persistent critique of this dyad, a political critique of our misreading of the social implications of debt and credit and an aesthetic critique which aims to find an alternative, as well as a parallel, for finance within the art object. This latter contestation gives rise to a second, intertwined, argument that suggests contemporary art has provided us with an alternative understanding of credit and debt, as it has sought to counter its own status as a speculative commodity by re-positioning itself instead as site of collectivity and activism.

William Hogarth's 1735 *A Rake's Progress* offers one of the most iconic narrative images for the relationship between debt and credit and provides a useful opening visual vocabulary for understanding the dialectic between the two. The seven plates that comprise the series make clear that the descent into the debtor's prison was a mental and physical as well as a moral one involving the loss of character from which credit could be drawn. Jenny Uglow's biographical reading of Hogarth, for example, suggests that the fourth plate in the series, *Arrested for Debt* (Figure 1), registers a familial trauma of debt: it was the plate that Hogarth 'returned to most, darkening and deepening it, as if the sudden shock of his father's arrest had never left him – and making it seem like a judgement on the whole fashionable world' and in the revised later plates the judgement becomes biblical, the 'sky is black, split by a jagged fork of lightning'.[7]

Yet Hogarth is not Tom, the protagonist of *A Rake's Progress*, and the series suggests something more complex than a condemnation of the indebted gambler, cast from prison to madhouse. Tom, as Uglow also notes, is both a predator and a victim. In the opening plate he is at once 'the impoverished heir of parental neglect', fathered by a miser who 'gave his son no nourishment but gold, a hard and fatal metal' and the abuser of women, buying off Sarah Young, his apparently pregnant fiancée, with his new-found riches.[8] Hence Tom's rejection of his father's miserly ways are associated with a destructive excess that aligns him with the paternal figure, suggesting not only an obvious rejection but also a continuity, an 'Instruction from Example Bred' as the caption attached to the first plate suggests.[9] The relationship between the miser and the spendthrift, as Walter Benn Michaels has noted in a very different context, is more similar than it is different, as both use money to destroy money. 'Going the miser one better', Michaels suggests, 'the spendthrift tries to buy his way out of the money economy. If the miser is always exchanging his money for itself, the spendthrift tries to exchange his for nothing and so, by staging the disappearance of money's purchasing power, to stage the disappearance of money itself'.[10]

Tom's ability to make money 'disappear' can be read in the context of Hogarth's ongoing fascination with the Financial Revolution. Alongside the literal gambling debts that Tom incurs is an anxiety about the 'paper credit' so recently issued by the Bank of England, which, as Ronald Paulson has noted, Hogarth associated with 'illusion and danger and [the] suspicion of skullduggery'.[11] Hogarth was rightly fearful of the counterfeiting that paper money made possible; his own livelihood was secured by the Engravers' Copyright Act – otherwise known as 'Hogarth's Act' – and *A Rake's Progress* was held back until the day in which the act went into effect.[12] Hogarth's more specific suspicion of the ephemeral nature of printed money emerges in the very first plate: an early reader, for example, deems it 'unnecessary' to 'explain every little mark of usury and covetousness' that it displays and comments only on 'the striking articles' from the father's notebook: 'Put off my bad shilling.'[13]

Hogarth's critique of Tom Rakewell's private debt in *A Rake's Progress* was thus also a critique of the conflation between debt and credit that was central to the Financial Revolution, as credit money emerged as a way of managing and sustaining the national debt. Critical readings of *A Rake's Progress* have emphasised that Tom's failings involved his belief in credit, his too-willing credulousness, as much as his willingness to become indebted. For David Bindman, for example, Tom is 'a gull, a person of infinite credulity and cupidity, who can act as foil or dupe of the voices of others'.[14] The dangerous connections between the fantasies that rule Bedlam and the financialised credit of paper money are made apparent not only in the 'alchemical experiments' depicted upon the walls of the debtor's prison but in 'A New Scheme for paying ye debt of ye Nation' proffered by one of Tom's cellmates, the reference clearly suggesting the financial crisis of 1720, so infamously allegorised by Hogarth's *The South Sea Scheme* (see also p. 133), in which the privatisation of money, the scheme established as a rival to the Bank of England of itself, led to a bubble that went so disastrously wrong.

For Hogarth, credit suggests an astronomically dangerous flight of fancy and debt suggests debasement, an absence (a lack of money) and an obligation (the need to repay the money). To be indebted is to lack moral rectitude, to be embarrassed by one's inability to cover one's needs, to be found wanting. The rakishness of Tom Rakewell is evident not in his indebtedness but in his willingness to accept money from the seamstress that he has already treated so badly. It is hardly surprising that the word debt corresponds to the word guilt (*schuld*) in the language of Freud, Marx and Nietzsche.

This sense of debt is clearly apparent in its most obvious of visual and linguistic metaphors. Hogarth's darkened sky and gloomy prison are commensurate with a visual language for debt as a dead-end, a place of physical entrapment and a curtailing of the future. These associations are long-standing. As Margaret Atwood noted in *Payback: Debt as Metaphor and the Shadow Side of Wealth*, we 'get "into" debt, as if into a prison, swamp or well, or possibly a bed; we get "out" of it, as if coming into the open air or climbing out of a hole. If we are "overwhelmed" by debt, the image is possibly that of a foundering ship, with the sea and the waves pouring in on top of us as we flail and choke'.[15] Debt is the end of our time as well as the end of our space. The figure of the moneylender, as Jacques Le Goff has made clear, has been figured since the Middle Ages as the 'thief of time'.[16] The association between debt and death is made apparent in the visual iconography of the bank whose symbolic presence in our lives, John Forrester has suggested, has now superseded the mausoleums in whose 'image they were built.'[17] It is hardly surprising, then, that individual debt should be personified as death itself, as it was depicted in cadaverous images from the early nineteenth century, such as Joseph Laurent Julien's *Le Riche du Jour ou le Préteur sur Gages* (*The rich of the day or the pawnbroker*) (Figure 2).

The representations of the national debt that emerged in the aftermath of the Financial Revolution made clear associations between these dangers and the political dangers of the credit money that it relied upon, dangers that were frequently identified with Government excess, especially in military spending. The scatological and suggestively Freudian images from the late 1790s, when William Pitt, both Prime Minister and Chancellor at the time, suspended the convertibility of paper money into gold (the Bank Restriction Act of 1797), include James Gillray's *Midas, transmuting all, into paper*, in which the gargantuan figure

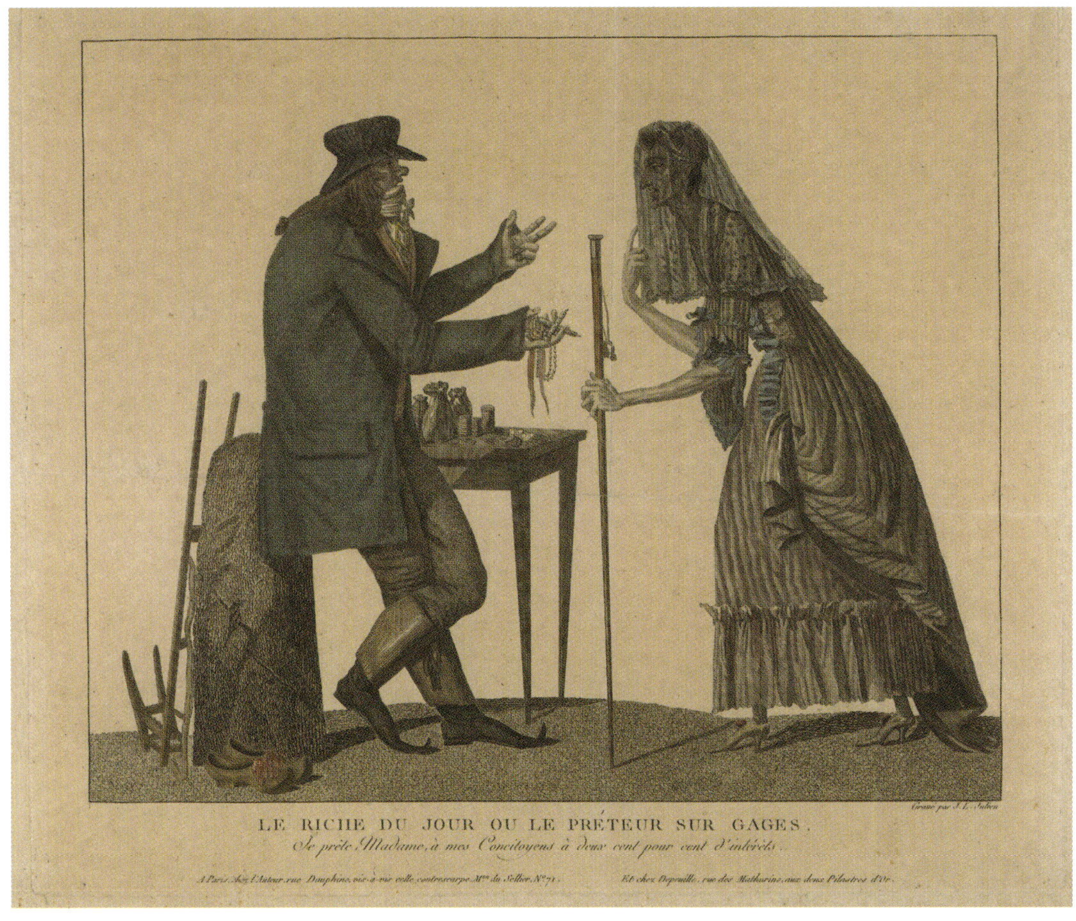

Figure 2

Joseph Laurent Julien, *Le Riche du Jour ou le Préteur sur Gages* (late eighteenth century). Hand-coloured engraving, Paris, chez l'auteur; et chez Depeuille.

Bleichroeder Print Collection, Kress Collection. Baker Library Historical Collections, Harvard Business School (olvwork308274).

of Pitt literally spews money from every orifice (Figure 3) and William Dent's *Public Credit or the State Idol* where a credit 'surplus' is represented as the bodily omissions of George Rose, the secretary to the Treasury (Figure 4). The images point to the fear that the 'Bank restriction act was an attempt by Government to co-opt the fragile credit of the Bank while hoarding the precious metals for its military adventures.'[18] The images thus express a clear anxiety about a credit economy that weakens the nation by placing it at the mercy of political expediency and they 'visualise', as Ian Haywood has suggested, 'tyranny, patronage and sycophancy by showing the powerful leader shitting or vomiting on hangers-on and suitors.'[19]

These grotesque images of the visceral dangers of public credit, the fear that paper money poisons the body politic that money's healthy circulation should otherwise serve, found a similar counterpart in American cartoons from the controversial 'free banking era' of Jacksonian America. This was the moment in which President Jackson dealt with the feared monopoly of the central Second Bank of the United States by removing its charter and allowing a range of smaller state banks to issue money instead. This was an act that

Figure 3

James Gillray, *Midas, transmuting all, into paper* (1797). Hand-coloured etching.

© Trustees of the British Museum.

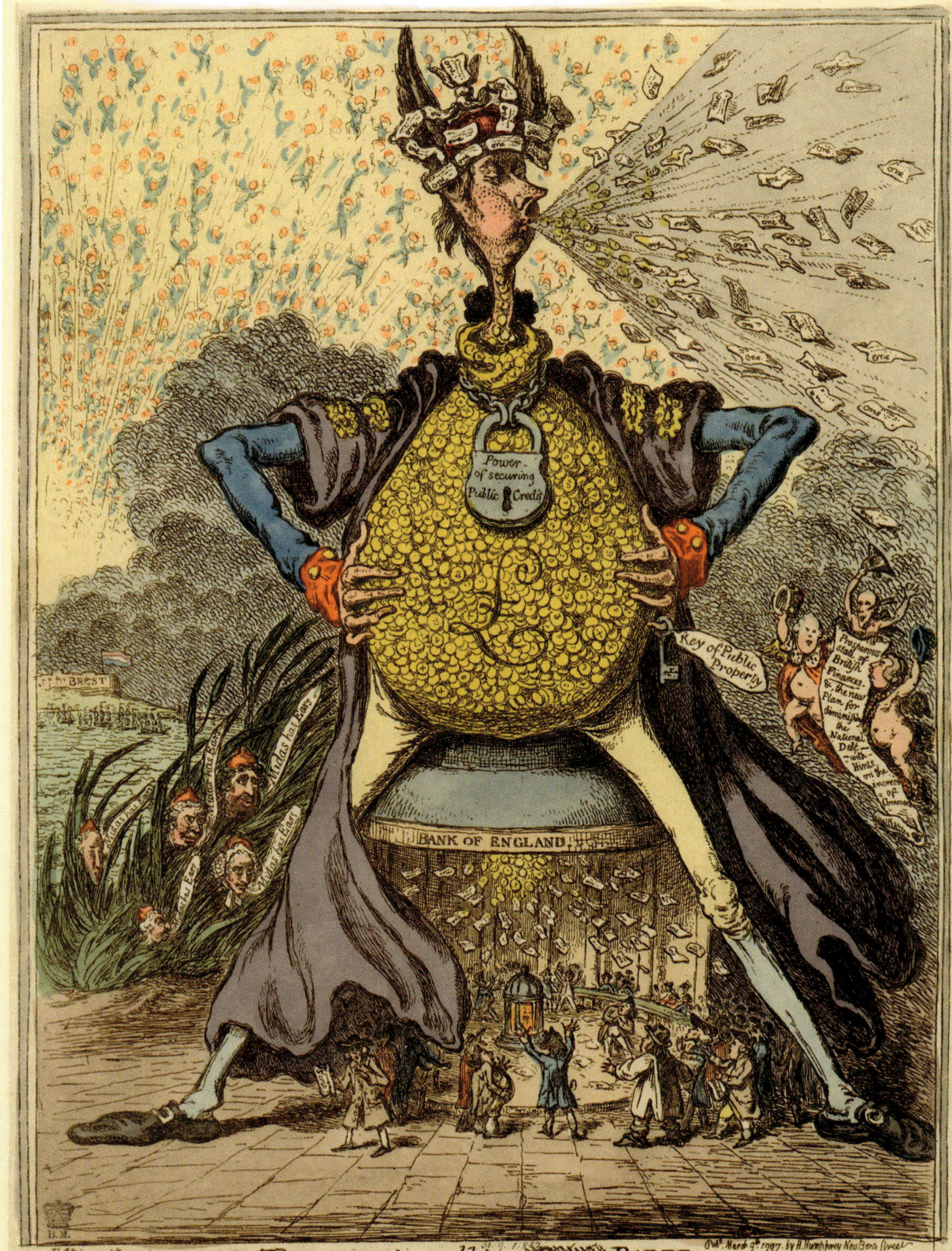

Power of securing Public Credit
Key of Public Property
BANK OF ENGLAND
BREST
J. Gy inv & f.
Pubd. March 9th 1797. by H. Humphrey New Bond Street
MIDAS, Transmuting all, into GOLD PAPER.
History of Midas, — The great Midas having dedicated himself to Bacchus, obtained from that Deity, the Power of changing all he Touched
Apollo fixed Asses Ears upon his head, for his Ignorance — & although he tried, to hide his disgrace with a Regal Cap, yet the very Sedges which g
from the Mud of the Pactolus, whisperd out his Infamy, whenever they were agitated by the Wind from the opposite Shore. —

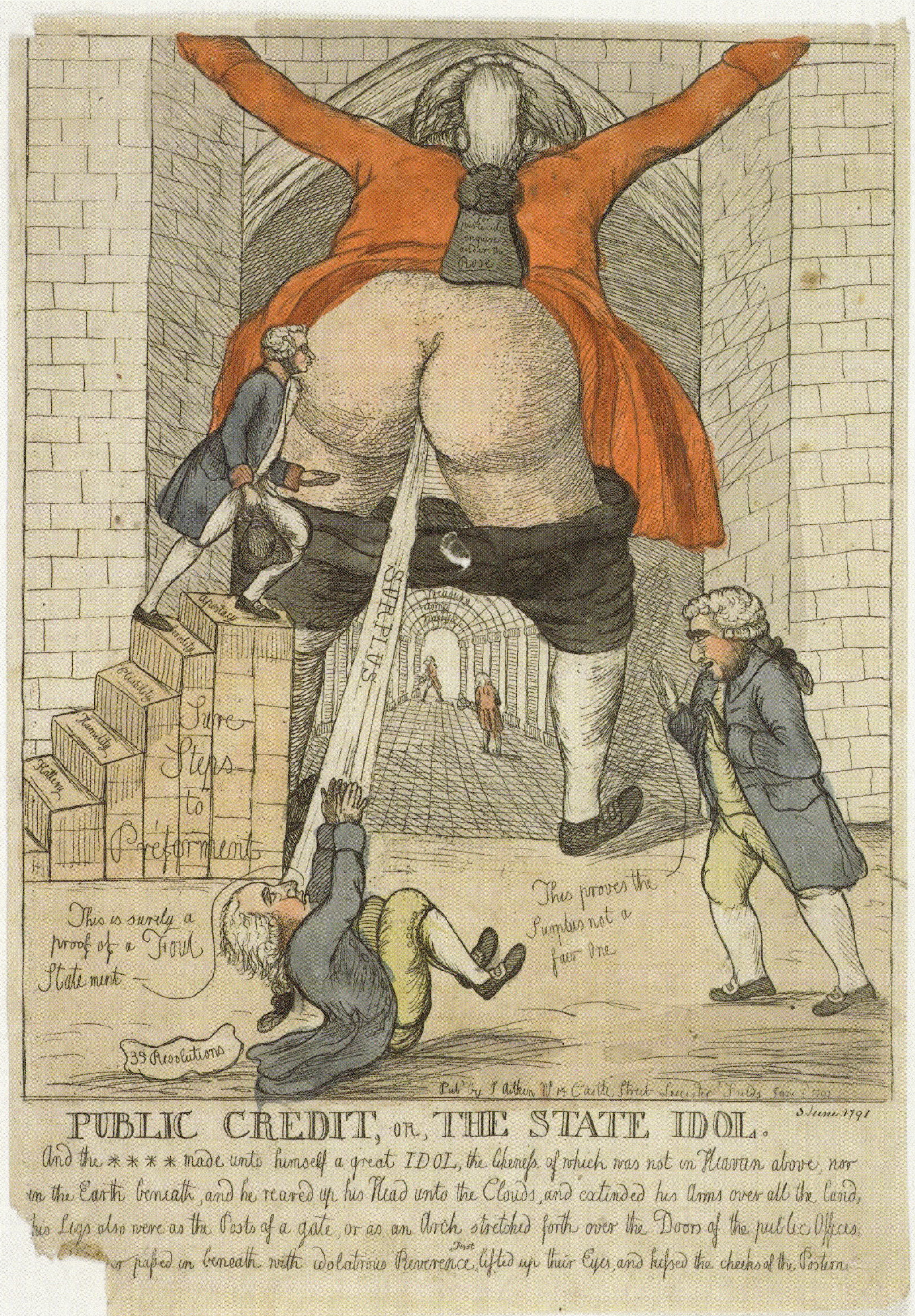

Figure 4

William Dent, *Public Credit or the State Idol* (1791).

had contradictory effects; as Jason Goodwin has noted, the 'Jacksonians promised hard money and gave easy credit instead. And easy credit, in the form of state banknotes, ruined the very kind of America Jacksonians revered'.[20] Such an irony is suggested in images such as the 1833 *The doctors puzzled, or, The desperate case of mother U.S. Bank* (Figure 5) or the 1834 *Uncle Sam in Danger* (Figure 6) where the creation of 'free' money, the transference of responsibility for money from a central bank to numerous smaller banks, is represented once more as an illness that leads to an abject draining of the symbolic body of the nation that threatens both its integrity and viability.

Other satirical prints from the end of the eighteenth century by Dent and Gillray make explicit the equivocal visual dyad between debt and credit, in which the former is seen as a heavy burden to be borne by the nation and the latter again a chimerically dangerous route to freedom. In an image by Dent from 1791, for example, *Bank Transfer, or, A new way*

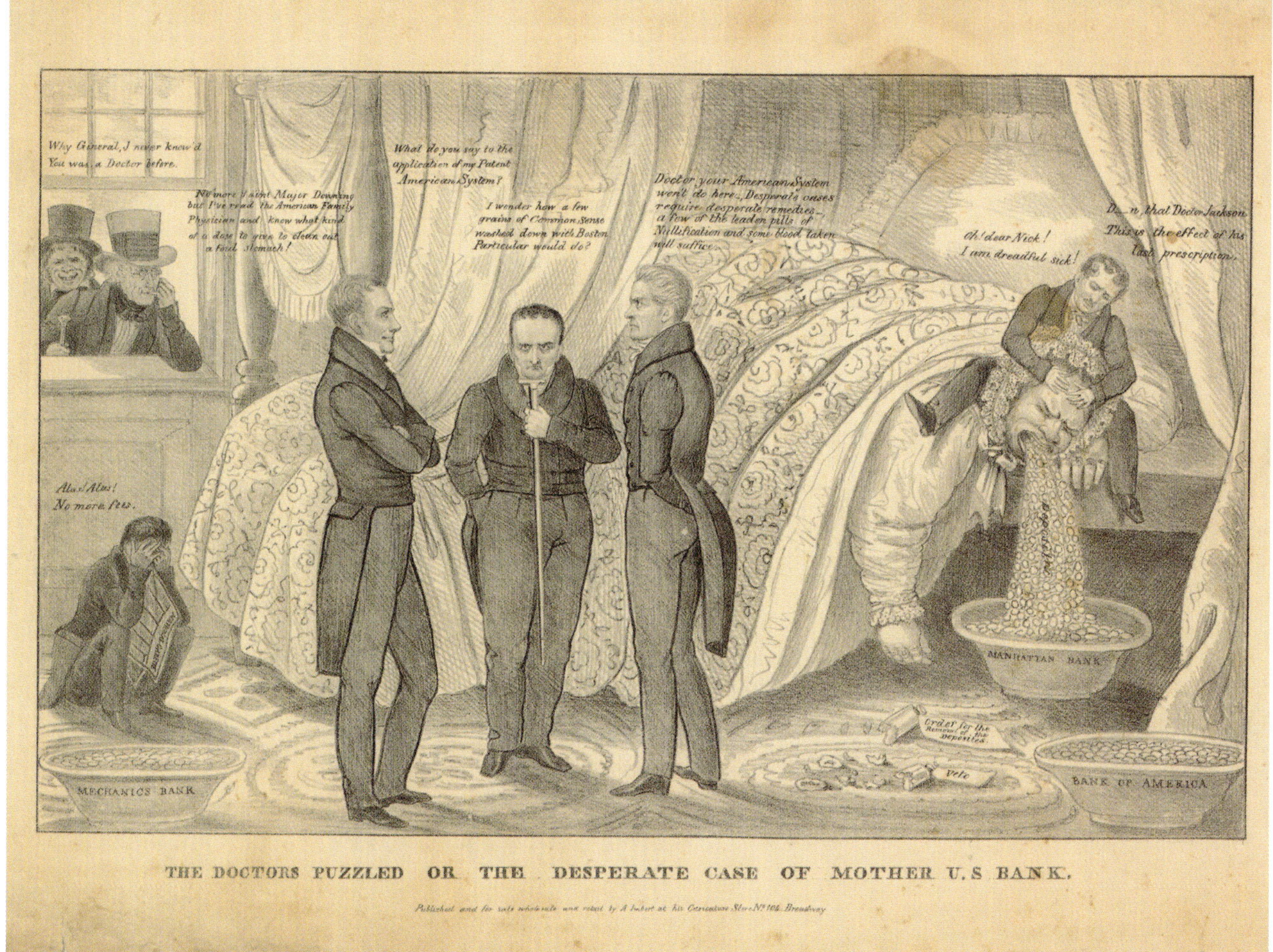

Figure 5

Antony Imbert, *The doctors puzzled, or, The desperate case of mother U.S. Bank* (1833).

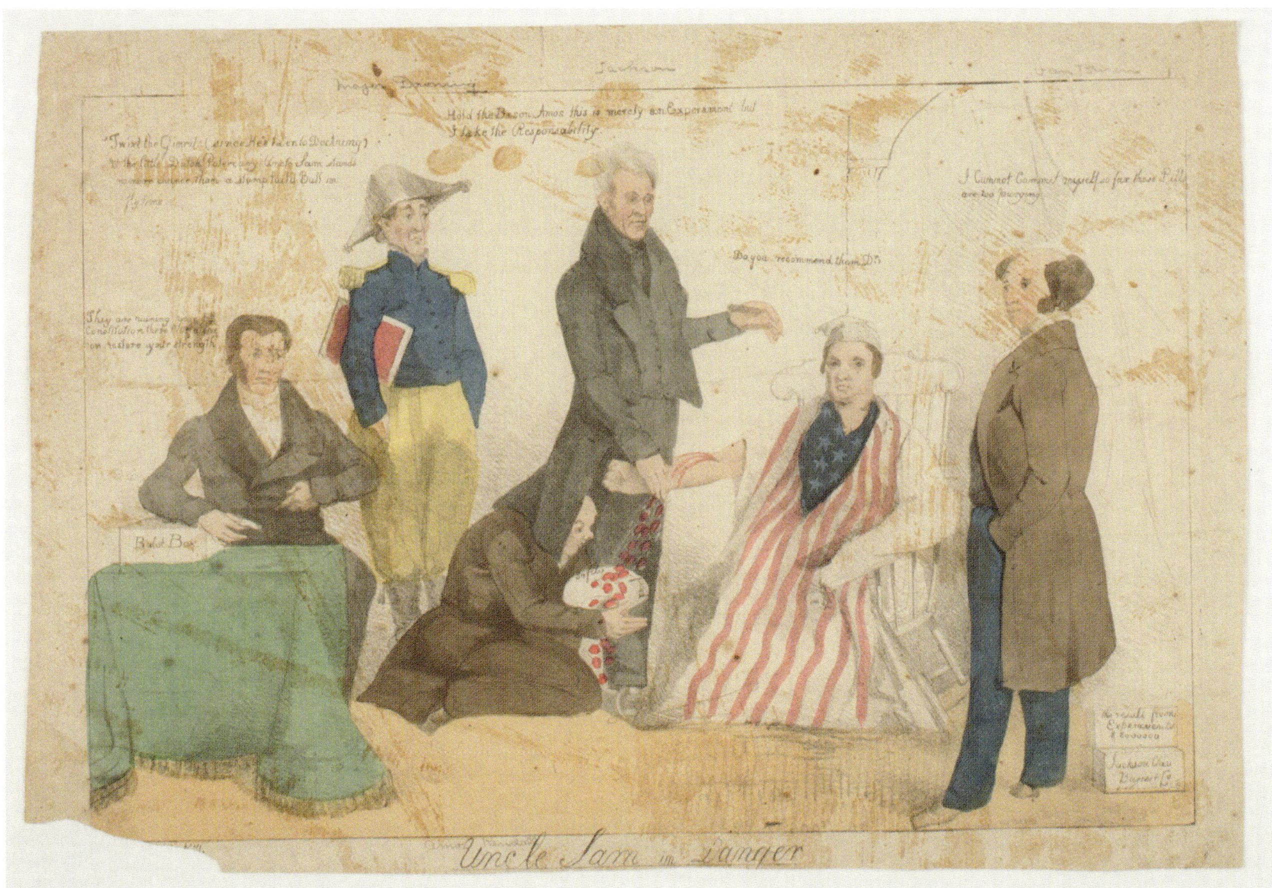

Figure 6

Thomas Whitley, *Uncle Sam in Danger* (1834).

of supporting public credit, we see Pitt physically shouldering the Bank of England as he tries to carry it into the narrow and high doors of the Exchequer (Figure 7). Underneath his feet are scraps of paper, representing 'public credit' and 'public faith' while above his head floats a balloon entitled 'Floating Balance'. A print by Gillray from 1802 carries a similar message (Figure 8). In *William Pitt ('The national parachute, – or – John Bull conducted to plenty and emancipation')* Pitt stands in a hot air balloon (an innovative mode of transport, then less than twenty years old) conducting John Bull to a land of freedom. The balloon represents 'the sinking fund' (the surplus from the Government budget set aside to pay off the debt) and its ironical source of elevation is the compound interest on the national debt that waves as a ragged red flag above both men.

The visual vocabulary which identifies credit as a form of transport, a fraught route of escape, was extended in the mid-nineteenth century in a series of images which associated paper money and public credit with the industrial inventions of modernity. Yet in these images the fear that public credit is subject to political expediency, especially in terms of military spending, is still apparent. Hence images such as *The Debt, or the British Juggernaut* (1833) and *The destruction of the good ship Public Credit, in the harbour of Independence, Uncle Sam, Commander* (1836) (both by anonymous artists) figure the threat that public credit poses to the nation through the iconography of the modern military rather than the tyrannical leader's body. In these images the physical momentum of the rapidly industrialising nations, represented by the British juggernaut or the American

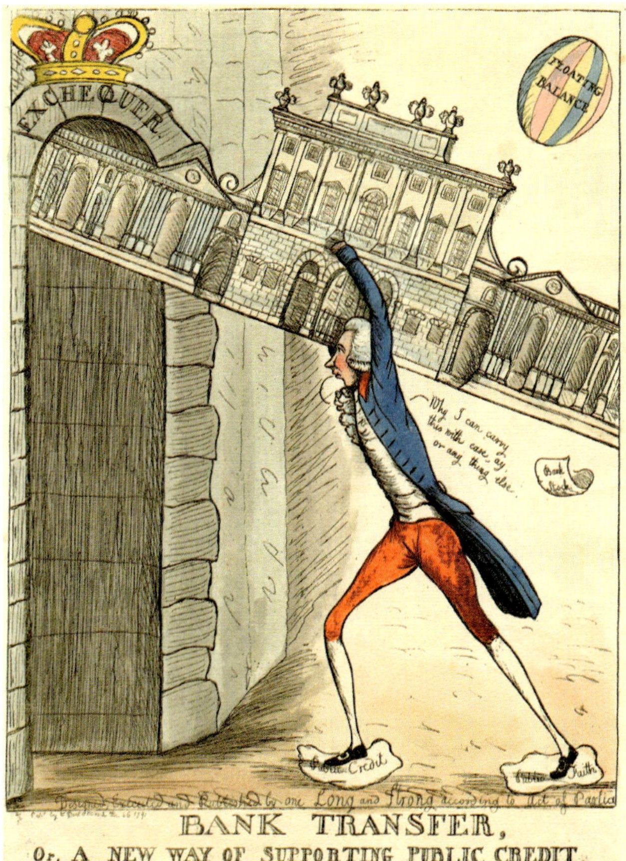

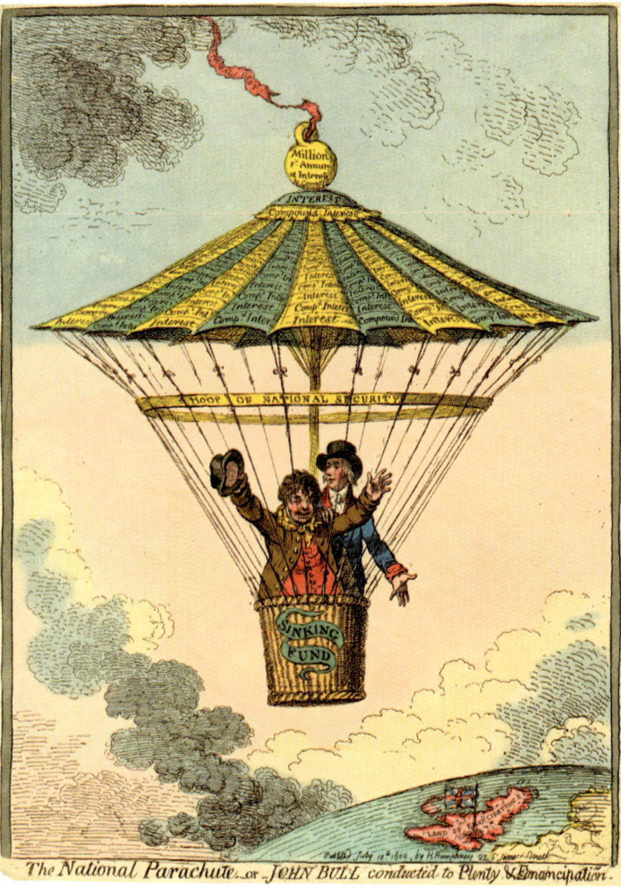

Figure 7

William Dent, *Bank Transfer, or, A new way of supporting public credit* (1791).

Figure 8

James Gillray, *William Pitt ('The national parachute, – or – John Bull conducted to plenty and emancipation')* (1802).

steam-ship, is associated with paper credit and both threaten to destroy the nations that they are also creating.

The rapid growth in *private* credit that began to occur half a century later, in the 1920s and 1930s, presented a different but equally complex account of the relationship between debt and credit. This was an installment-based credit boom that was led by women's domestic purchases (Lendol Calder has suggested that in 1914 'a banker who was an authority on credit estimated that at least 80% of personal credit was extended to women')[21] and this gendered vocabulary produced an interesting ambivalence. On the one hand, the associations with femininity rendered this domestic credit dangerous, able even to 'sap male strength', as men's control over the household economy was undermined.[22] Yet, on the other, critics such as Michael Tratner have argued that this explosion in consumer credit was facilitated by the superseding of Victorian values of thrift and restraint by a libidinised and Keynesian exhortation upon people to 'spend money' and 'indulge their desires'.[23] Certainly, the visual iconography that was used for credit, especially in advertising, can be read in these ways. A postcard by Fred Spurgin from 1925, *Money Simply Flies Now* (Figure 9), for example, captures the euphoria of an unleashed credit. In this image credit is once more associated with the escape provided by a new form of transportation but the association is rendered a more positive one, connected to other forms of social and sexual emancipation (most obviously, the daring of Amelia Earhart, just starting to gain notoriety). A similar impulse was apparent in the adverts that accompanied the early bank accounts for women. When the Trustee Savings Bank (TSB) first advertised such accounts in the 1950s they did so through a series of images attached to the strapline 'Keep a Good Balance' that showed women as exhilaratingly able and about to take flight, as smiling trapeze artists or water-skiers (Figure 10).

The visual associations between credit, escape and pleasure that these images suggest have now become familiar staples of the financial advertising vocabulary. Adverts for credit routinely promise an escape from the foreclosures of debt, replacing its downward trajectory with an effortless movement through both time and space. The 'bubble' of the credit-fuelled financial boom becomes serviceable in these images, as hot air balloons, airplanes, rockets, waterslides, empty beaches and blue seas dominate the visual lexicon of the credit card industry. It isn't only domestic credit that soars above the earth, however. The more obviously sober register of the financial industry promulgates a similar message, as an analysis of financial adverts written during the crash noted, financial institutions called upon the solid architecture of the City but were 'shown to exist above, outside, or across and beyond the cityscape' and that financial agents were subject to an '"architectural inflation" where the consulting partners are shown walking and talking casually on a platform or floor that towers above the towers'.[24]

It is not difficult to discern the dialectical tensions between credit and debt that this visual history reveals in the history of contemporary art practices. Art has long understood itself as a form of debt that is capable of engaging with the nuances of the social (with reciprocity, desire, exchange) and as a form of credit that marks their destructive financialisation (as it itself becomes the speculative object). Two years after

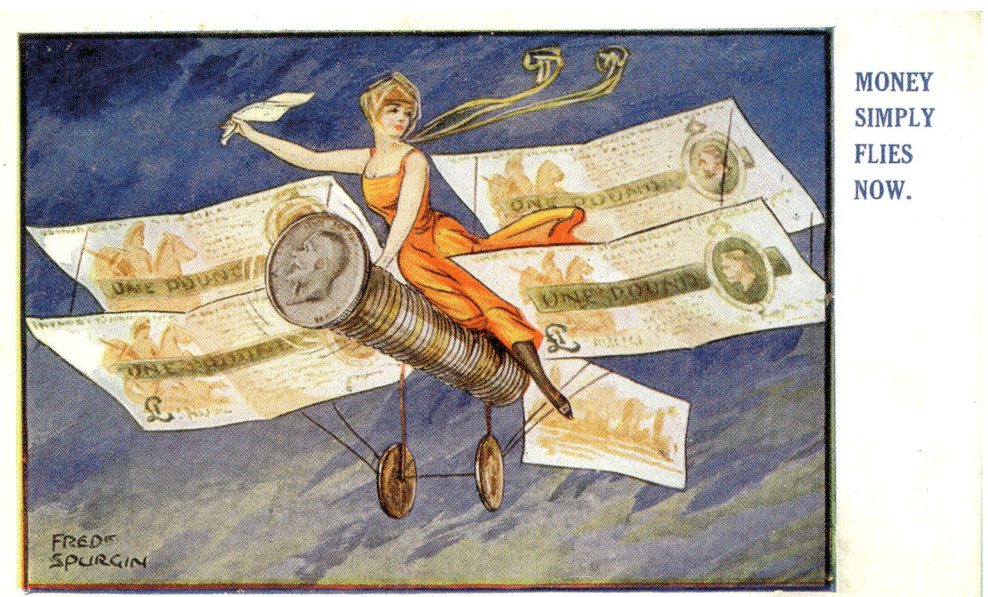

Figure 9

Fred Spurgin, *Money Simply Flies Now* (1925). Printed postcard.

© 2013 Amoret Tanner/ fotoLibra.

Figure 10

TSB, *Keep A Good Balance* (1950).

Courtesy of Lloyds Banking Group plc Archives.

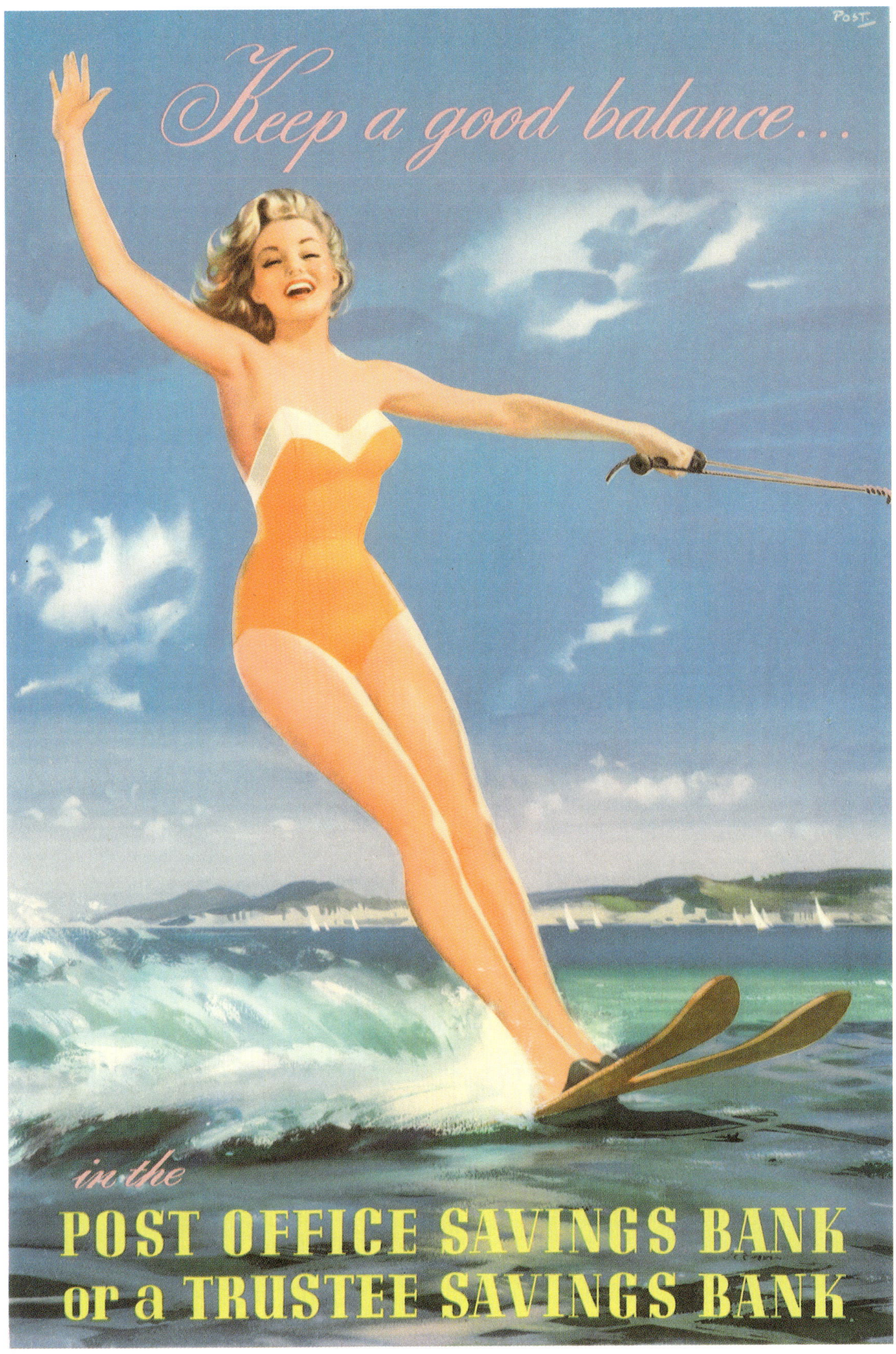
POST
Keep a good balance...
in the
POST OFFICE SAVINGS BANK
or a TRUSTEE SAVINGS BANK

placing his infamous *Fountain* into an art gallery, for example, Marcel Duchamp extended his ready-mades to include money itself, in the form of the 1919 *Tzanck Check*, a cheque 'drawn' from 'the Teeth's and Loan Trust' to pay his dentist (which he later bought back from the dentist, nervous of being imprisoned for forgery). The cheque, painstakingly and accurately detailed, was readily accepted by his dentist as payment and suggested a recognition of the reciprocity of the labour of the two men that was capable of excluding the need for a general equivalent. Yet, at the same time, such financial readymades also suggested a critique of the financialisation of art, taking Duchamp's 'general critique of value one step further by not only questioning the distinction between art and non-art, but also exposing the congruency between the art world and the economy. The financial documents made artworks equivalent to monetary tokens, conflating the categories of culture and finance in one object.'[25] The same ambivalence between art as debt (producing a gift-like reciprocity outside of the money economy) and art as credit (suggesting a critique of art as financial currency, something that defrauds both art and money) were central to the career of money artist J.S. Boggs. Boggs intervened in the way we understand both art and money as credits and debts. He called attention to the physical materiality of money and disrupted the hegemonic invisibility that its successful exchange relies upon. The perfection of Boggs's clearly handmade replicas of money produces something akin to the uncanny, a double-take on that which we already always knew to be a reproduction but that we used as if it were real, suggesting Slavoj Žižek's account of money, as not a 'mask' that hides 'the real state of things' but a form in which 'ideological distortion is written into its very essence.'[26] Yet Boggs's work also provides a commentary on the role of the debt and the commodity in the contemporary art world. For Boggs the work was not the replica note at all but the series of social exchanges that it facilitated: it was the object bought, the receipt and the forms of the change given, that he was at pains to record.[27]

Boggs's use of art as a currency that can be used to pay debts has expanded in the past ten years as debt has reached a crisis under the auspices of what Colin Crouch has dubbed neo-liberalism's 'privatized Keynesianism' in which debt pays for those things – health, education, housing, pensions – which were previously identified as the responsibility of the state.[28] The difficulty of understanding the dialectic between credit and debt, of separating out the social possibilities of debt from the financialisation of credit, has been central to the politicised representations of debt that have emerged since the financial crisis. Strike Debt! and the Rolling Debt Jubilee, for example, are movements that have emerged from the Occupy collectives and attempt to understand debt as a social obligation rather than as a process of financialisation, suggesting that 'debt is a tie that binds the 99% ... a major source of profit and power for Wall Street that works to keep us isolated, ashamed and afraid. ... We want an economy in which our debts are to our friends, families and communities'.[29]

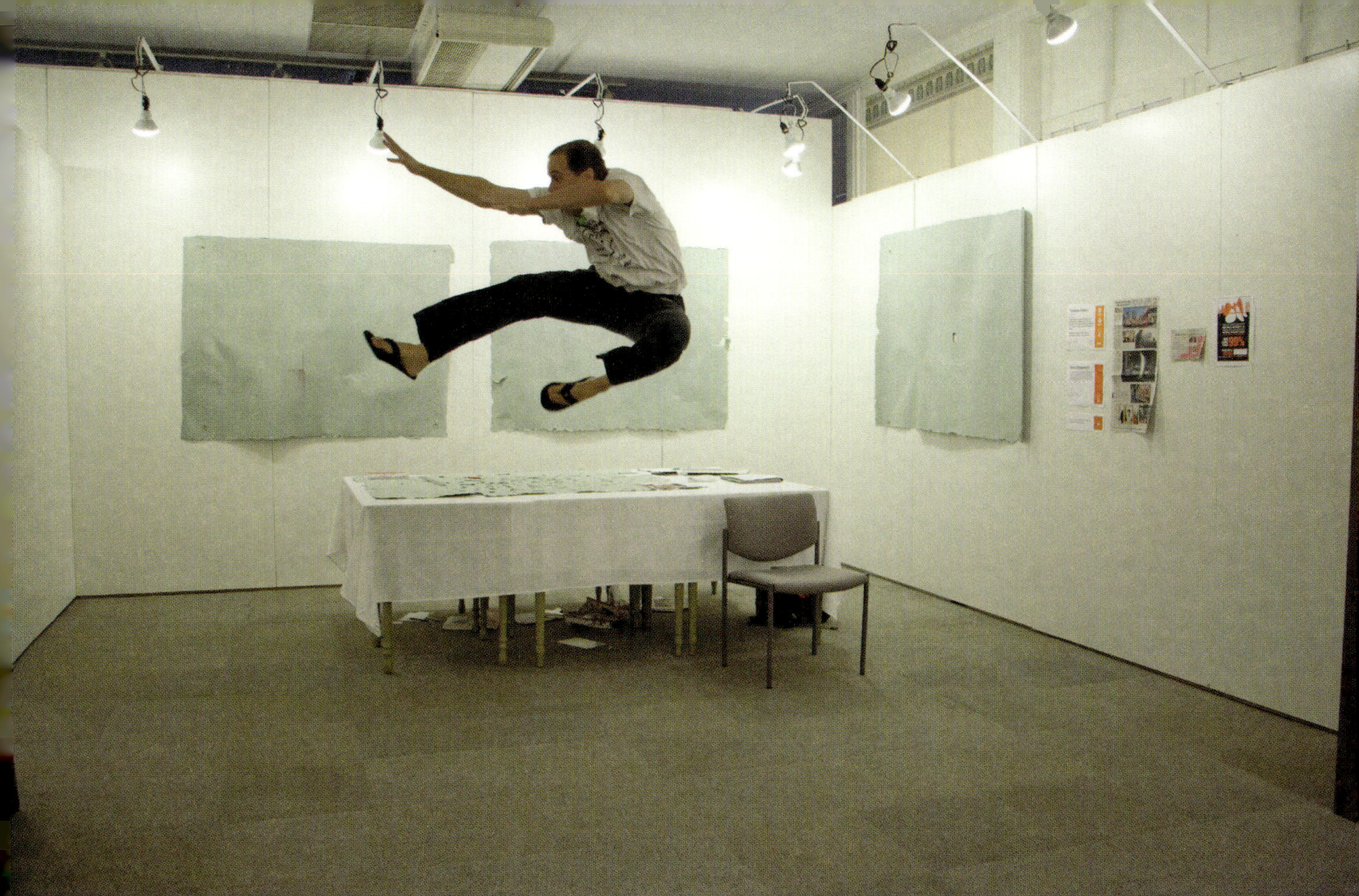

Figure 11

Thomas Gokey, *$49,983: Total Amount of Money Rendered in Exchange for a Masters of Fine Arts Degree to the School of the Art Institute of Chicago, Pulped into Four Sheets of Paper* (2012).

Courtesy of the artist. Photo credit Matt Gubancsik.

Artists have been active in many of these political movements that have emerged since the 2008 financial crisis and the connection between debt/credit and art has been made most sharply by those artists whose own practice is deeply enmeshed with their indebtedness. Artists have used art to counter debt: it has functioned as both a literal and pragmatic counter (artists exchanging their work for debt) and as an emotional and aesthetic counter (artists using their work to challenge the negative associations of debt). Thomas Gokey's piece *$49,983: Total Amount of Money Rendered in Exchange for a Masters of Fine Arts Degree to the School of the Art Institute of Chicago, Pulped into Four Sheets of Paper* (Figure 11) is, as the title implies, a literal re-representation of the cost of Gokey's education. Gokey, one of the creators of Rolling Jubilee, now sells this work for five dollars a square: the sizes of the square are calculated to correspond to the debt, so that once the entire work is sold then the debt is repaid.

What Gokey's work shares with that of other art activists is the attempt to explicitly recuperate debt, to resist the deathly entrapments it suggests, by realising it instead as a social process. Gokey photographs himself executing a flying karate jump in front of his pulped debt, literally and violently ascending the evisceration of the material that it represents. Cassie Thornton's project *Visualisations of Debt as a Thing or a Space* allows the indebted to 'approach their unconscious sense of economics'. The resulting testimonials share a register which consistently suggests the visual dialectic of credit

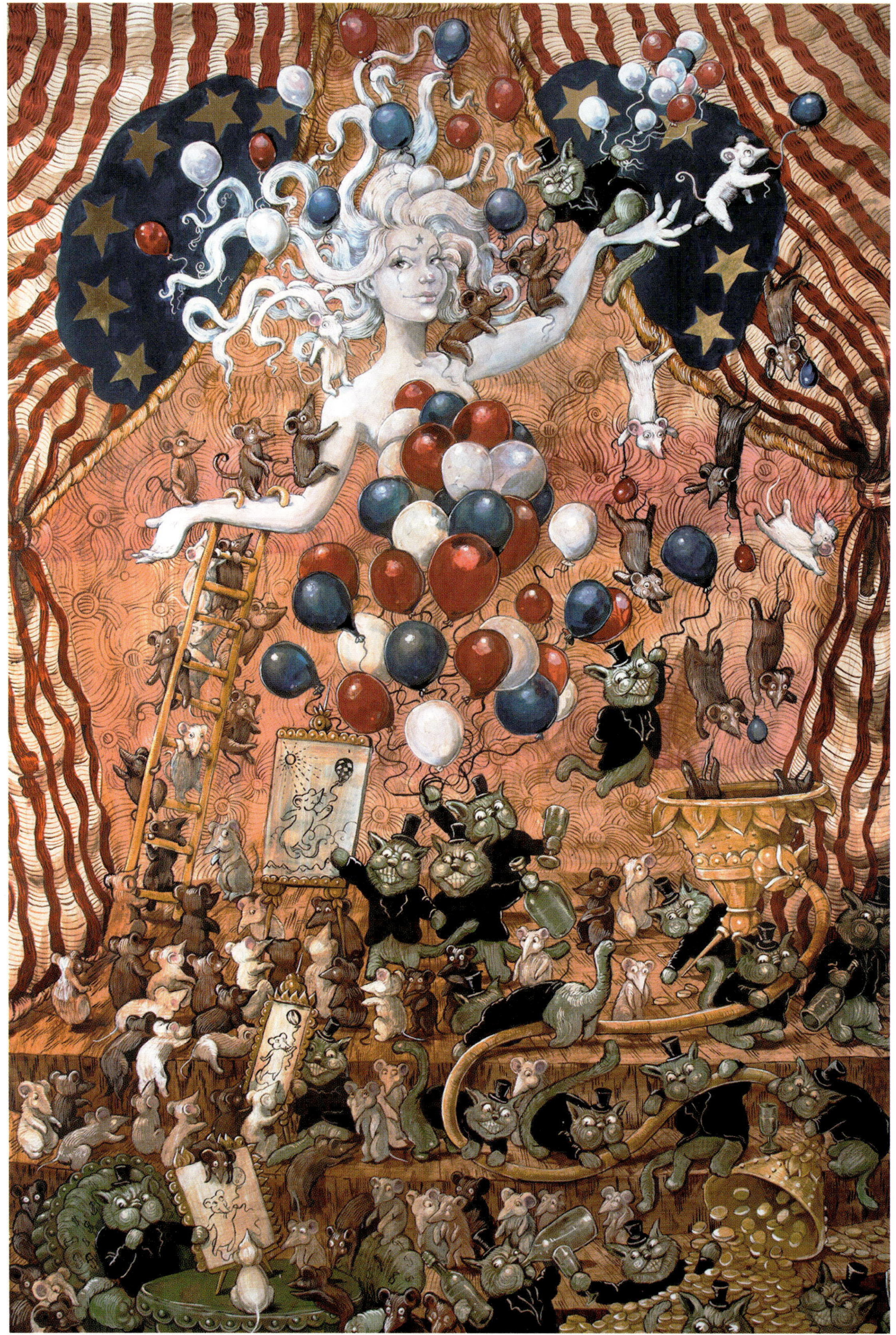

Figure 12

Molly Crabapple, *Debt and her Debtors* (2012).

Courtesy of Molly Crabapple.

and debt, both the enclosure of debt and the exposure of credit. The pieces evoke the work of Richard Dienst when he built upon David Harvey's memorable description of privatisation as an 'enclosure' of the social to suggest that credit produces an 'exposure' of those on 'the other side' which puts 'everybody at the risk of irreparable loss, whether the system functions or not'.[30] Most of the testimonials suggest the experience of being both outside and inside, experiencing both the freedom of credit and the containment of debt simultaneously in ways that undo the opposition between them. In many of the testimonials the opening references suggest the escape credit initially provides – 'flying on google street', 'the wind picks up', 'I'm floating, I don't feel my feet', but this sense of escape is quickly countered by the abject trap of debt – 'I keep slipping on the sidewalk … I'm back at my parents. A dirt path, dark and dusty', 'As I get closer it gets muddier, it's very sludgy, not like clay, like hard wet dirt, it slides out, it's kind of oily, it's hard not to look at the thing', 'If I step I'll be inside something large, claustrophobic, canopy on top, Not completely confined, a bubble.'[31]

Other art projects attempting to represent financial crisis have been concerned not with the private debt of individuals but with the debt of nations, the sovereign debt that has come to threaten the sovereignty that it once enabled. It seems entirely appropriate that Molly Crabapple's depictions of the national debt should return to Hogarth's allegorical mode. Crabapple has provided a lushly satirical visual documentation of the recent crisis, including *Discordia: Six Nights in Crisis Athens* and *Shell Games: A Crowd-Funded Show About the Financial Collapse*. Her illustrations lay the visual identifiers claimed by the Occupy movement (the masked face of Alan Moore's *V for Vendetta*, the banner proclaiming the rights of the '99%', the tear-gas bearing riot police) onto an older critical iconography for the financial market itself (the sprawling octopus, the fat cat, lady luck). The images offer a pointed critique of the language of credit. *Debt and her Debtors* (Figure 12), for example, figures American debt as a burlesque female torso floating above the fat cats on a cloud of red, white and blue balloons. It is only on second glance that one realies that she actually represents the tilted scales of debt and credit and that the mice who scrabble onto her balloons are captured on their way down by the cats who await them.[32]

Yet, of course, the history of sovereign debt extends much further. Artists such as Cildo Meireles and Oyvind Fahlstrom have been keen to explore the unequal power relations that sovereign debt creates and in this context American debt involves unequal international politics rather than the unequal class and race relations that the subprime mortgage crisis made momentarily apparent. Fahlstrom's *World Bank 1971* was an explicit attack on the macro debt-inducing policies of the Washington Consensus. The work was based 'entirely in historical and economic data and posited the gleaming solid architecture of the neatly arranged gold bars of the World Bank against small paper cut outs representing the economies of Southern American nations such as Brazil, Venezuela, and Chile'.[33] Fahlstrom's sensitivity to the inequality of international development, and to the ironies of debates about the emergence of the paper dollar and the nature of American credit, was also apparent in his '$108 bill' of 1973. One side of the bill is reminiscent of the satirical prints of the 1790s as it depicts an image of George Washington blowing out hot air. The reverse is very different, the image shows the international labour that literally sustains the value of Washington's dollar. This latter image, a pyramid formed from the bent backs of workers, is taken directly from *World Bank 1971* and makes clear the anachronistically exploitative social relations between North and South.

The Brazilian artist Cildo Meireles, emerging from and adapting both the European conceptual and the South American neo-Concrete artistic movements, has also been concerned with questions of exchange, value and circulation and their relationship to questions of debt and credit. In the single most oppressive year of the Brazilian military regime of the early 1970s, Meireles used the materiality of paper money, 'a psycho-phenomenology of embodiment', as a challenge to its abstract or symbolic values in ways that were overtly engaged with the political regime.[34] Meireles' *Insertions into Ideological Circuits* involved first Coke bottles and then money. Blunt political slogans, such as 'YANKEES GO HOME' and 'WHO KILLED VICTOR HERZOG?' (a socialist journalist who died in police custody) were printed on these objects which were then re-introduced into circulation (Figure 13). The project embedded political activism into the everyday while evading the active censorship of the Brazilian government. Yet the directness of Meireles' message (the project is now regarded as overly literal by some critics, including Meireles himself) contrasted against the subtleties of what it was suggesting about its medium.[35] The circulation of US dollar bills alongside Brazilian currency, itself a departure from a US post-war attitude to the national financial autonomy of Southern states, foregrounded the erosion of Brazilian territorial sovereignty under a regime claiming 'national security' as its primary self-justification.[36] The fact that these notes were beyond the reach of the government that they critiqued also allowed for a sardonic contrast of the brute literalism of a dictatorship with the capricious movement of international money.

The erosion of state sovereignty by the 'credit' money created by banks is also central to the work of the contemporary Swedish installation artists Goldin+Senneby. In the *Headless* project Goldin+Senneby address the ironies of the 'offshore', the realm created by the absence of state intervention which allows multinational corporations to avoid taxation and regulation and to benefit massively from the financialisation of their operations. The offshore is, as Angus Cameron and Ronen Palan have argued, 'a powerful metaphor providing a normative "space beyond", which states have no choice but to acknowledge and accommodate' the demands of finance, allowing it to 'rewrite, retroscriptively and proscriptively, the particular role of the state in is own narrative image'.[37] The ironies of this state-mandated suspension of power is at the centre of *Headless*, as it uses the corporate images of the real offshore company ironically named

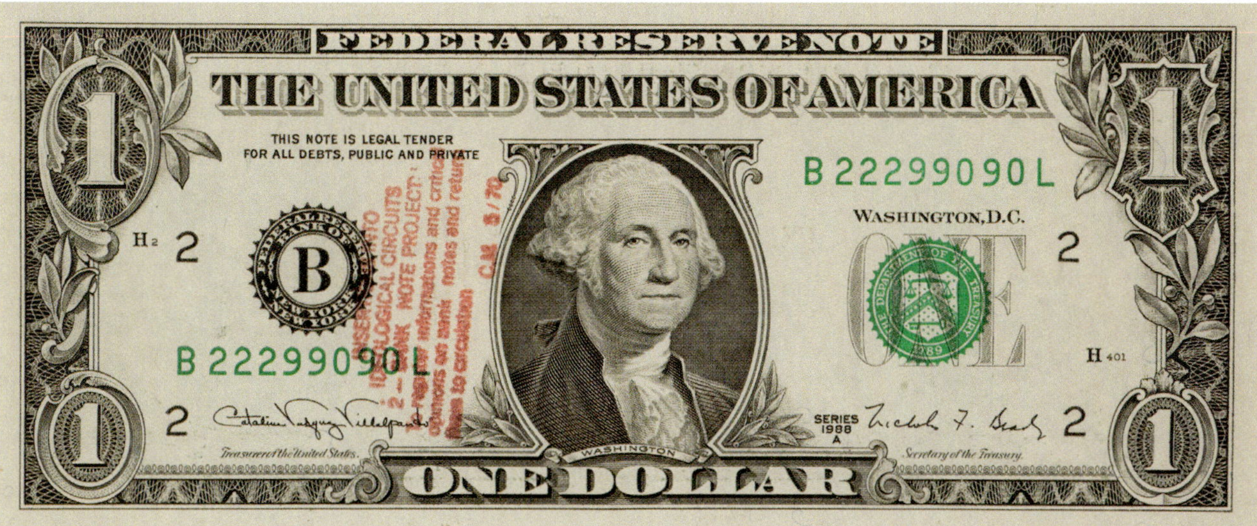

Figure 13

Cildo Meireles, Figure 2 *Insertions Into Ideological Circuits*. Rubber stamp on banknotes (1970).

© Cildo Meireles, image courtesy of the artist, Galerie Lelong New York and Tate.

'Sovereign' – impossible but familiar images of yellow beaches, blue seas and white sailing boats – to make knowing and mocking connections between the fantasies of credit and finance's evasion of state power. The glamorous bodies who populate the beaches and boats of Sovereign's promotional material are literally headless, their photographs cropped at the neck. Goldin+Senneby's re-presentation of the images dramatically alters the suggestion of client anonymity that Sovereign's use of the image suggests, replacing it with threatening symbols of decapitation. The ostensible purpose of *Headless* is the search for a specific offshore company named 'Headless' registered with Sovereign. It takes as its starting point the hypothesis that the company may be a contemporary incarnation of 'Acéphale', the secret society initiated by Georges Bataille in the 1930s and celebrated in his short lived-review of that name. Acéphale represents, as Benjamin Noys has suggested, a community that 'could exist which desired freedom rather than power ... to counter the fascination with power in politics Bataille used the model of the sorcerer's apprentice who releases energies that he cannot control and which rebound on him. Acéphale was an attempt to release these energies beyond the control of any head or leader.'[38] Goldin+Senneby's *Headless* is thus an artistic appropriation of the withdrawal and multiplication of authority that the offshore represents. The project describes itself as a complex 'web of confusion, concealment and fiction', as the artists function 'like CEOs, employing and enlisting various specialists – economists, authors, curators etc – to carry out aspects of their business'.[39] At the centre of its critique of the offshore is a critique of the Eurodollar, the credit of the offshore that exists beyond the regulation of the nation state. One of the exhibitions, at the Kadist Art Foundation in Paris in 2010, involved the recreation of the offices of the mid-century Russian Bank which first originated the offshore Eurodollar market in the early 1950s and the exhibition makes implicit connections between this event and the publication of Bataille's *The Accursed Share* in

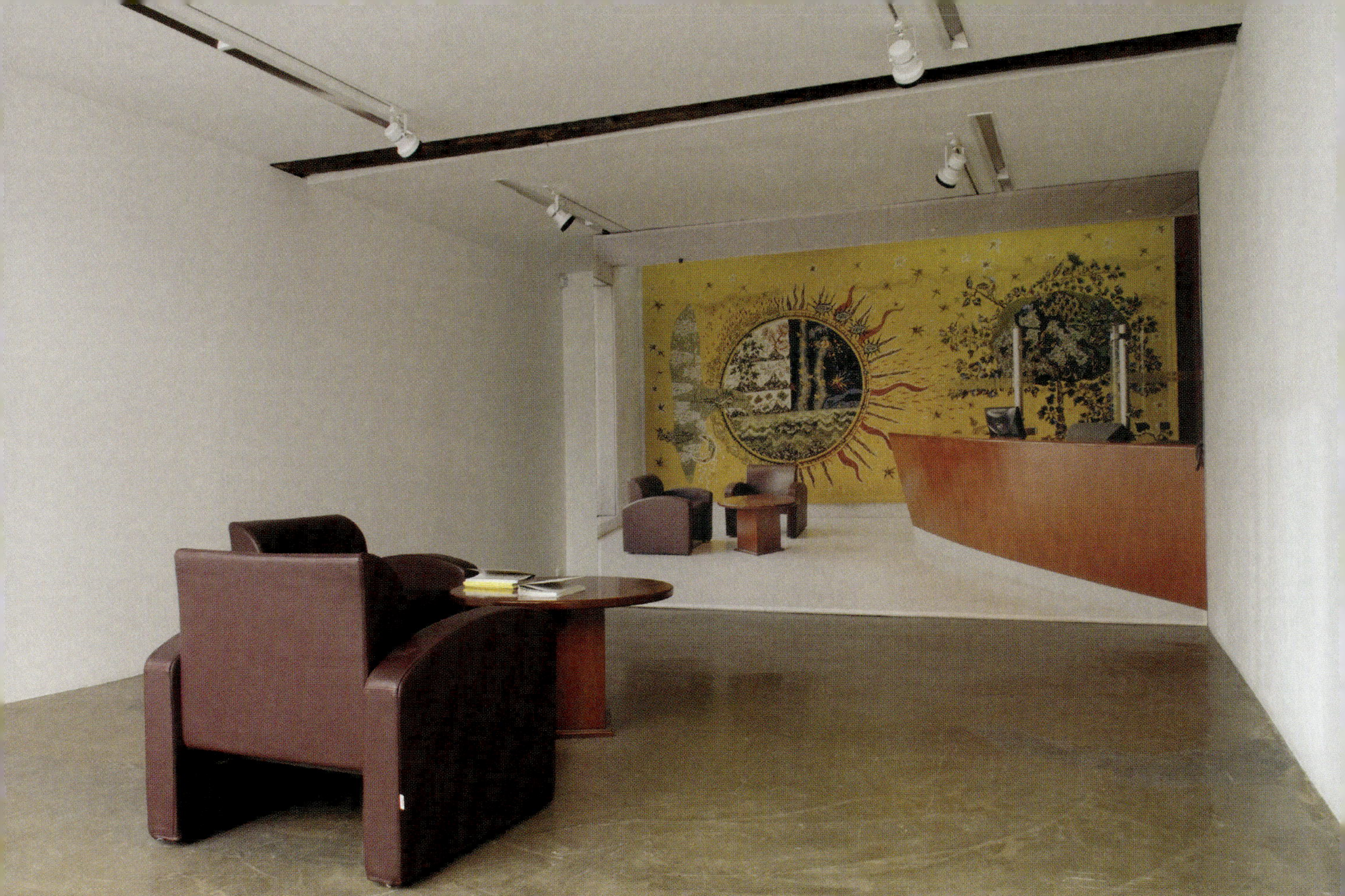

1949. (Figure 14). One of the project's central emissaries is Angus Cameron and his words are apparent in the self-description of this exhibition, when the 'Dollar escaped the US financial, territorial jurisdiction and the very nature of money changed from a symbolic value to a virtual one. Money entered a new space of exteriority, beyond the control of the sovereign state. Money was decapitated.'[40]

Figure 14

Goldin+Senneby, 'The Decapitation of Money', with Angus Cameron (economic geographer), K.D. (fictional author), Anna Heymowska (set designer), Johan Hjerpe (graphic designer), Kerwin Rolland (sound designer). Installation view: Kadist Art Foundation, Paris, 2010.

Photo: Aurélien Mole.

In evoking Bataille Goldin+Senneby also evoke a register that knowingly exceeds the fantasy of rational restraint that conventional economics appears to assume and opens up finance's own unconscious. In *The Accursed Share* Bataille replaced the 'restricted' economy of conventional economics with a 'general economy' capable of speaking to the 'excess energy', the 'effervescence of life' which 'animates the globe' and thus exceeds the instrumental restrictions of the Weberian bourgeois order.[41] The destructive and libidinal drives that Bataille calls upon, as they encompass both the wanton violence of war and the potlatch or gift, are actually deeply embedded in the languages of the financial industry, as cultural and literary critics have recently demonstrated.[42] These languages are useful for both revealing the limits of financial rationality, the nature of its erotic and phantasmagoric investments, as well as opening the opportunity that art offers for delivering alternatives to them.

Contemporary art has focused upon the ways in which it can be posited as a 'gift' economy that functions as an alternative to, rather than only a parallel with, the financial world.

Neil Cummings and Marysia Lewandowska's 2001 piece *Capital (Bank of England Monetary Analysis)*, for example, presents a series of encounters between the Tate Modern Gallery in London and the Bank of England that highlights the differences and similarities between the two institutions in relation to the history of debt and credit from the Financial Revolution onwards. The premise of the project is that the Bank of England 'regulates the financial economy by managing the availability and price of debt' and that the Tate is 'the principle institution in a parallel symbolic economy', responsible for the 'integrity and value of the artworks and images it distributes'.[43] The parallels between the two institutions are apparent, the project asserts, in both their origins and endpoints. The Tate was founded upon a gift and the Bank of England upon a debt and both institutions possess the authority for producing, measuring and regulating the exchange of other gifts and debts: the Bank of England guarantees the validity of money and the Tate guarantees the provenance and cultural importance of the art object. Cummings and Lewandowska intervene in this parallel by theorising and literally offering their art as a gift, bestowing limited edition prints upon randomly selected gallery-goers and taking from Aristotle in their description of this practice, suggesting that 'giving correctly – not to one's family or immediate friends, but towards the public good – ensures that one's gifts are seen as virtuous acts' and their intention is to 'initiate an engagement with some sense of the social imagination'.[44]

This act of giving as an alternative to speculating with art, the desire to open up the 'social imagination', was also central to the practice of Felix Gonzalez-Torres. In an era in which 'market driven sensibilities generated an economic frenzy', Nancy Spector has noted, the Cuban-American artist 'made a gift of his work, and thereby shifted the focus from artist to audience'. His work took two principal forms; it was comprised of neatly stacked rectangles of paper and of edible 'spills' of sweets, both of which are offered to the viewer and 'conceived of as infinitely replenishible'. Spector reads the 'gift' that Gonzalez-Torres makes of his work, an art that cannot be exhausted or completed by its own commodification, as offering a social critique of the art market, reading the work against Bataille's 'description of eroticism as the transgression of corporeal boundaries, the breakdown of physical limitations imposed by human beings, who are customarily "discontinuous"'.[45]

The most obvious and compelling context for reading Gonzalez-Torres' work was that of the HIV/AIDS crisis of the late 1980s and his work can thus be read through the 'queering' of economic language as a mode of resistance that the feminist economist J. K. Gibson-Graham has advocated.[46] Gonzalez-Torres lost his partner, Ross Laycock, to the disease in 1991 and many of his 'candy spills' are works of private and political mourning, suggesting both elegy and anger. The weight of pretty pale-blue sweets that constitute *'Untitled' Loverboys*, for example, corresponds to the combined weight of Gonzalez-Torres and his lover and the piece memorialises 'the expenditure at the heart of eroticism... each act of consumption registers, metaphorically, a momentary fusion of bodies' while 'its excessive generosity – its willingness to give itself away to any admiring beholder' also renders the sculpture uniquely vulnerable, 'risking the 'danger of total dissipation.'[47] These private works went alongside explicit public works. In 1989 Gonzalez-Torres placed a billboard at Sheridan Square commemorating the '20th anniversary of the Stonewall Rebellion' and was it hoped that the 'public will stop for an instance to reflect on the real and abstract relationships of the different dates'.[48]

Gonzalez-Torres was also explicit about the connections between the failure of American political culture to respond to this crisis and the onslaught of neo-liberal financialisation. His piece *'Untitled' (A Portrait 1991)*, for example, an installation featuring twenty-five television screens, with single phrases appearing on each, made explicit the connections between his private mourning, encroaching illness and a public crisis in the United States. Alongside 'a view to remember' and 'a new lesion' the televisions bore the headlines 'a merciless cardinal', 'an environmental disaster', and a 'stock market crash'.[49] The piece produces a critique of the connections between an emerging neo-liberalism's successful seizing of the public space and the financialisation of the role of the state. Elsewhere Gonzalez-Torres damned the 'brilliance' of the Republican move to publish their 'Contract with America' in a TV guide[50] and also rued the fact that 'we're no longer a welfare state, because in America every dollar we spend on welfare, we spend six dollars to bail out the savings and loans'.[51] The result, he suggested, in a phrase that predicts the enclosures and exposures that have been produced by the current financial crisis, was 'a virtual state of containment'.[52]

The libidinous evocations of the gift at the centre of Gonzalez-Torres' work offered a particularly effective response to this 'containment' as it re-appropriated the vocabulary of infection, Fredric Jameson's 'epidemic of epidemics', that was used to suggest the auto-generative and yet perverse properties of finance capital.[53] Gonzalez-Torres qualified the resistance to commodification that the instant expenditure of his art work insisted upon by implicitly acknowledging the power of his institutional presence: he was well aware of his necessarily co-opted status and embraced it as a site of possibility. Gonzalez-Torres cast himself as a 'virus that belongs to the institution. All the ideological apparatuses are, in other words, replicating themselves, because that's the way that culture works. So if I function as a virus, an imposter, an infiltrator, I will always replicate myself along with those institutions.'[54] For him the gift enables the art piece to exist outside of the practices of the financial marketplace while remaining importantly inside the languages of cultural power and it offers a bracing corrective to the temptation to see the two as entirely entwined.

Debt and credit are, then, both the same thing and yet entirely different. Credit has been represented since the Financial Revolution as a flighty escape from the deathly entrapments of debt but the complex visual history of the relationship between the two also suggests that this is a flight that is knowingly hubristic in its representations:

bubbles will always pop; paper money can cause a sickness in the body politic; hot air balloons, planes, boats and trains can as easily be weapons of destruction as vehicles of freedom. Art and visual culture have played important roles in making this ambivalence apparent, and in tracing the different intellectual and political contours that private and public forms of the debt/credit dyad involves.

Contemporary art has also been important in suggesting an entirely different conceptual, social and aesthetic tradition for debt: one that critiques the financialised language of credit and replaces it with a language of sociality, imagination, pleasure and loyalty. These latter aspirations, that can be found in the wittily subversive credit notes circulated by Duchamp, Meireles and Boggs, in Gokey and Thornton's angry manifestation of their own debt, as well as in Gonzalez-Torres and Cummings and Lewandowska's gifting of art, all suggest ways in which art can exceed the divisive financial relations of credit in order to give debt a different meaning. In all of these works debt is figured not as a debased ending but rather as an opportunity. They each, albeit in very different ways, make the social relations that the artwork depends upon, relations of reciprocity, obligation, circulation and community, integral to their meaning. Yet the social relationships that these works insist upon do not exist entirely outside of the financial relations against which they establish themselves. These pieces depend upon the market for the realisation of their meaning – the total price of Gokey's work is equivalent to his debt, the notes of Meireles, Boggs and Duchamp all need to function *as* notes – while also disrupting the financialised circuits of the credit industry. Meireles, for example, has been clear that the *Insertions* series have no price and cannot be sold, Gonzalez-Torres' 'candy spills' have negligible cash value and are realised and disposed of in the same moment. Hence these works function within the marketplace of the artwork in order to make apparent its practices and assumptions because, as Gonzalez-Torres indicated, there is little point in being 'outside of the structure of power. I do not want to be the opposition, the alternative. Alternative to what? To power? No. I want to have power. It's effective in terms of change.'[55]

Notes

1 Carl Wennerlind, *Casualties of Credit: The English Financial Revolution*, 1620–1720 (Cambridge, MA: Harvard University Press, 2011).

2 Patrick Brantlinger, *Fictions of State: Culture and Credit in Britain 1694–1994* (Ithaca, NY: Cornell University Press, 1996), p. 3.

3 Graeber describes not only the human relations of reciprocity and exchange promised by the market economy but also debt's anthropological antecedents, which he calls communism and hierarchy, and from which he draws entirely different ways of reading debt as a social relation. David Graeber, *Debt: The First 5,000 Years* (London: Melville House Publishing, 2011).

4 Richard Dienst, *The Bonds of Debt* (London: Verso, 2011), p. 148.

5 Fred Harney and Stefano Moten, 'Debt and Study', *e-flux* 14:3 (2010), http://www.e-flux.com/journal/debt-and-study/, accessed 28 January 2014.

6 Maurizio Lazzarato, *The Making of Indebted Man* (London: Semiotexte, 2011).

7 Jenny Uglow, *Hogarth: A Life and a World* (London: Faber and Faber, 1997), p. 254.

8 Ibid., p. 244.

9 Ronald Paulson, *Hogarth's Graphic Works: First Complete Edition* (New Haven, CT: Yale University Press, 1965), p. 161.

10 Walter Benn Michaels, *The Gold Standard and the Logic of Naturalism* (Chicago: University of Chicago Press, 1987), p. 144.

11 Ronald Paulson, *Hogarth: The 'Modern Moral Subject', 1697–1732* (Cambridge: Lutterworth Press, 1991), p. 17.

12 Ibid., p. 9.

13 John Trusler, *The Works of William Hogarth* (London: Simpkin, Marshall, Hamilton, Kent and Co.).

14 David Bindman, *Hogarth* (London: Thames and Hudson, 1981), p. 44.

15 Margaret Atwood, *Payback: Debt as Metaphor and the Shadow Side of Wealth* (London: Bloomsbury Publishing, 2009), p. 82.

16 Jacques Le Goff, *Your Money or Your Life: Economy and Religion in the Middle Ages*, trans. Patricia Ranum (New York: Zone Books, 1998).

17 John Forrester, *Truth Games: Lies, Money and Psychoanalysis* (Cambridge, MA: Harvard University Press), 1997.

18 Alexander Dick, *Romanticism and the Gold Standard: Money, Literature, and Economic Debate in Britain 1790–1830* (London: Palgrave, 2013), p. 46.

19 Ian Haywood, *Romanticism and Caricature* (Cambridge: Cambridge University Press, 2013), p. 52.

20 Jason Goodwin, *Greenback: The Almighty Dollar and the Invention of America* (London: Picador, 2004), p. 204.

21 Lendol Calder, *Financing the American Dream: A Cultural History of Consumer Credit* (Princeton, NJ: Princeton University Press, 1999), p. 218.

22 Louis Hyman, *Debtor Nation: The History of America in Red Ink* (Princeton, NJ: Princeton University Press, 2012), p. 41.

23 Michael Tratner, *Deficits and Desires: Economics and Sexuality in Twentieth-Century Literature* (Stanford, CA: Stanford University Press, 2001), p. 3.

24 Christian De Cock, James A. Fitchett and Christina Volkmann, '"Myths of a near Past: Envisioning Finance Capitalism Anno 2007"', *ephemera: theory & politics in organization* 9:1 (2009): 8–25.

25 Olav Velthuis, 'Duchamp's financial documents: Exchange as a source of value', *tout-fait: The Marcel Duchamp Studies Online Journal* 1:2 (May 2000).

26 Slavoj Žižek, *The Sublime Object of Ideology* (London: Verso, 1989).

27 Lawrence Weschler, Boggs: *A Comedy of Values* (Chicago: University of Chicago Press, 1999).

28 Colin Crouch, *The Strange Nondeath of Neo Liberalism* (London: Polity Press, 2011).

29 http//strikedebt.org, accessed 28 January 2014.

30 Dienst, *The Bonds of Debt*, p. 63.

31 http://debt-visualizations.tumblr.com/, accessed 28 January 2014.

32 http://mollycrabapple.com/, accessed 28 January 2014.

33 Mike Kelley and Jane Livingston, *Oyvind Fahlstrom: The Installation* (Cantz and Bremen: Gesellschaft fur Aktuelle Kunst, 1995), p. 75.

34 Stephen Horne, 'Cildo Meireles: The Gold Thread', *Third Text: Critical Perspectives on Contemporary Art and Culture* 52 (2000), 31–44.

35 Guy Brett, 'Corners and crossroads', *Frieze* 117 (2008), http://www.frieze.com/issue/article/corners_and_crossroads/, accessed 28 January 2014.

36 In the post-war period, Eric Helliner notes, the US 'encouraged Southern governments to eliminate the use of foreign currencies within their territory wherever that practice was still widespread. It was very difficult, US Officials argued, for a central Bank to develop a strong and independent monetary policy devoted to national development unless the currency it issued held a monopoly position inside the country' but this stance was gradually abandoned after the ending of the Bretton Woods agreement in the early 1970s. Eric Helleiner, *The Making of National Money: Territorial Currencies in Historical Perspective* (Ithaca, NY: Cornell University Press, 2003), p. 191.

37 Angus Cameron and Ronen Palan, *The Imagined Economies of Globalisation* (London: Sage, 2004), pp. 107–8.

38 Benjamin Noys, *Bataille: A Critical Introduction* (London: Pluto Press, 2000), p. 9.

39 The project includes a large cast of real and fictitious characters who have participated and produced an almost bewildering range of exhibitions, events and texts. These include numerous art installations, a travel blog, a series of site-specific presentations (a walk around the City of London, a talk given in a Parisian wood), a documentary and a growing number of academic lectures, critical essays and conferences. For more details on these events, see www.goldinsenneby.com/gs/, accessed 28 January 2014.

40 http://www.kadist.org/index2.php?lang=en, accessed 28 January 2014.

41 George Bataille, *The Accursed Share: Volume I*, trans. Robert Hurley (New York: Zone Books, 1991), p. 10.

42 Paul Crosthwaite, 'Blood on the trading floor: Waste, sacrifice, and death in financial crises', *Angelaki: Journal of the Theoretical Humanities* 15:2 (2010), 3–18 and Nicky Marsh, 'Desire and disease in the speculative economy: a critique of the language of crisis', *Journal of Cultural Economy* 4:3, 301–15.

43 Frances Morris, 'Gift, economy, trust', in *Capital: A Project by Neil Cummings and Marysia Lewandowska* (London: Tate Publishing, 2001), p. 11.

44 Neil Cummings and Marysia Lewandoska, 'It's the thought that counts', in *Capital: A Project*, p. 31.

45 Nancy Spector, *Felix Gonzalez Torres* (New York: Guggenheim Museum, 1995), p.vii.

46 J.K Gibson-Graham, *The End of Capitalism (as we knew it)* (Cambridge: Blackwell, 1996), p. 135.

47 Spector, *Felix Gonzalez Torres*, p.vii.

48 Felix Gonzalez-Torres, 'Statement of Sheridan Square billboard', in Julie Ault (ed.), *Felix Gonzalez-Torres* (New York and Gottingen: Steidl, 2006), p. 198.

49 Felix Gonzalez-Torres, 'Practices: The problem of divisions of cultural labour', in Ault (ed.), *Felix Gonzalez-Torres*, p. 147.

50 Robert Storr, 'Interview with Felix Gonzalez-Torres Part Ii 13 December 1994', in Christiane Meyer-Stoll and Sammlung Goetz (eds), *Felix Gonzalez-Torres and Roni Horn* (New York: Guggenheim, 1995), p. 31.

51 Felix Gonzalez-Torres and Joseph Kosuth, 'A Conversation', in Ault (ed.), *Felix Gonzalez-Torres*, p. 349.

52 Felix Gonzalez-Torres, '1990: LA: "The Gold Field"', in Ault (ed.), *Felix Gonzalez-Torres*, p. 147.

53 Fredric Jameson, 'Culture and finance capital', *Critical Inquiry* 24 (Autumn 1997): 246–65.

54 Robert Storr, 'Felix Gonzalez-Torres: Etre Un Espion', in Ault (ed.), *Felix Gonzalez-Torres*, p. 238.

55 Ibid.

What do you think about when you think about a market?

Andy Haldane

At the heart of the City of London, behind a towering colonnaded facade, sits the Bank of England. The heart metaphor is an apt one. For over three hundred years, the Bank has pumped oxygen to the City of London's vital organs – its financial firms and financial markets. Today, with its balance sheet larger than at any time in its history, the Bank's heart has never galloped faster.

Inside the Bank, just outside its Court room where traditionally the Bank's Board of Directors (the 'Court') would meet, is a painting by Bill Jacklin (Figure 1). Unlike much of the Bank's artwork, it is a modern piece dating from 1988. It depicts traders on London's International Financial Futures Exchange, just a stone's throw away from the front of the Bank in another towering colonnaded building, the Royal Exchange.

The image is a kaleidoscope of colour, movement and noise. The traders are dressed in garishly coloured jackets. They are seen frantically darting between counterparties, ducking and diving both physically and financially. Adding to the mêlée, traders shout out prices in a method known as Open Outcry. The description is appropriate. This is a cacophony of capitalism.

It is a portrait that captures the essence of markets at work. The image is at the same time both ancient and modern. Modern because of the sophisticated nature of the transactions. But also because, if you squint your eyes, the scene would not be out of place in market squares in towns the length and breadth of the country and in almost every country in the world.

The colours are now fruit and vegetables rather than jackets and ties. The bobbing and weaving is between pensioners and pushchairs rather than buyers and sellers. The Open Outcry is of the politically incorrect market trader variety – 'Come on ladies ...' These, too, are markets at work, capitalism in cacophony.

That scene is as ancient as civilisation. For as long as people have bartered, they have attracted customers with the colours of their wares, the sounds of their voices, the movements of their hands and arms. For many, this is the very definition of a market economy. For 300 years, the London Stock Exchange operated much like a town-square fruit market. Its origins in the seventeenth century were a coffee shop called Jonathan's up a small street at the back of the Bank of England, called Exchange Alley. It was a small step from here, physically and financially, to the stock exchange trading floors of the 1980s, where brokers and jobbers jostled for business.

That trading floor has now largely been lost (if not forgotten), a bygone era. The London International Futures Exchange still exists, but its trading floor is long gone. The Royal Exchange instead houses high-end retail outlets – Tiffany's, Rolex and Paul Smith. The traders are now tourists. The atmosphere is more cathedral than cacophony. The Royal Exchange no longer trades futures; it sells presents.

These scenes are replicated throughout the financial world. The coffee houses and the trading floors have been replaced by machine and fibre-optic cable. Today, trading is remote and

Figure 1

Bill Jacklin, *Futures Market, Royal Exchange, London* (1988). Oil on canvas.

anonymised. The market square has been moved to the clouds. Traders, like the Martini-drinkers of the 1970s, can execute any time, any place, anywhere. They are as likely to be wearing pyjamas as pinstripes. Trading was once done on a nod and a wink. Today, it takes place faster than you can blink.

Technology has made this virtual trading world possible. And where finance has led, other industries have followed. New or old, global or local, virtually everything these days can – and increasingly is – purchased or traded virtually. Any time, any place, anywhere. Sometimes by people in pinstripes; more often by people in pyjamas.

Increasingly, that includes trading in money and loans. For more than 800 years, depositing and lending were the preserve of high street banks. Yet we may be about to enter an era where banking, too, becomes virtual. A world where payments are electronic and contactless, where lending is anonymous and digitised. The high street banks might, in time, feel the same pinch that is today felt by the high street shops.

And, yet, I wonder. Markets are much more than convenient meeting points for exchange by colourless, inert, noiseless automata. The reason is simple. Trade relies on repeat business, on reputation, on trust. Trust is earned by individuals – colourful, active, noisy individuals – not automata. Trust is built not on transactions but relationships. Even eBay, the world's largest online marketplace, is held together by one thing and one thing only – reputational glue.

Finance is not the exception, but the exemplar of this rule. The world of finance is no more than a trade in promises. But promises need to be kept if trade is to be maintained. In other words, finance (like eBay) is a market whose glue is trust. That is why the word 'credit' originates from the Latin 'credo', meaning 'I believe'. And it is why many financial institutions globally retain to this day the word trust in their title.

The financial crisis illustrates, on a global scale, the consequences of a collapse in trust. Once financial trust is lost, people queue in the streets for cash, businesses take to the hills with their money, banks hunker down and hoard rather than lend. That is the very definition of a financial crisis, a crisis of confidence in promises, a seizing-up of the credit arteries. Only the pumping heart of a central bank can then keep blood coursing through the veins of the economy. And that is why the Bank of England's heart continues to gallop. Five years into this crisis, surveys reveal that banks remain at the very bottom of the trust league table. Trust is hard-earned and easily lost. Regaining that trust is far from simple. Doing so may require more than a financial make-over, a bonus-tuck here, a liquidity-lift there. It may require us to rethink – or remember – what a market really is. Not an anonymised transaction, but a personalised relationship. Rebuilding banking means restoring its social glue.

Perhaps banking is beginning to heed this lesson. The fastest growing bank in the UK today is a Swedish bank called Handelsbanken. Its business model is simple: Handelsbanken is a high street bank with a physical presence and a personal face. It lends to those within sight of the town church spire, within walking distance of the market square. It is a short journey from the Handelsbanken model of banking and the markets (for loans and for lemons) of the past.

For thousands of years markets have been meeting places with colour, movement and noise, like a Bill Jacklin painting. Until recently, financial markets were no different. When financial change came it whitewashed the colour, boxed in the movement, soundproofed against the noise. That sowed the seeds of the biggest financial crisis, perhaps not just in our lifetime but perhaps in any lifetime.

Avoiding that mistake in future calls for a rethink not just of how markets work, but why they exist. It calls for strengthening, not weakening, the social glue that holds them in place. If markets are to add value, they must first have values.

Framing finance 2

Paul Crosthwaite

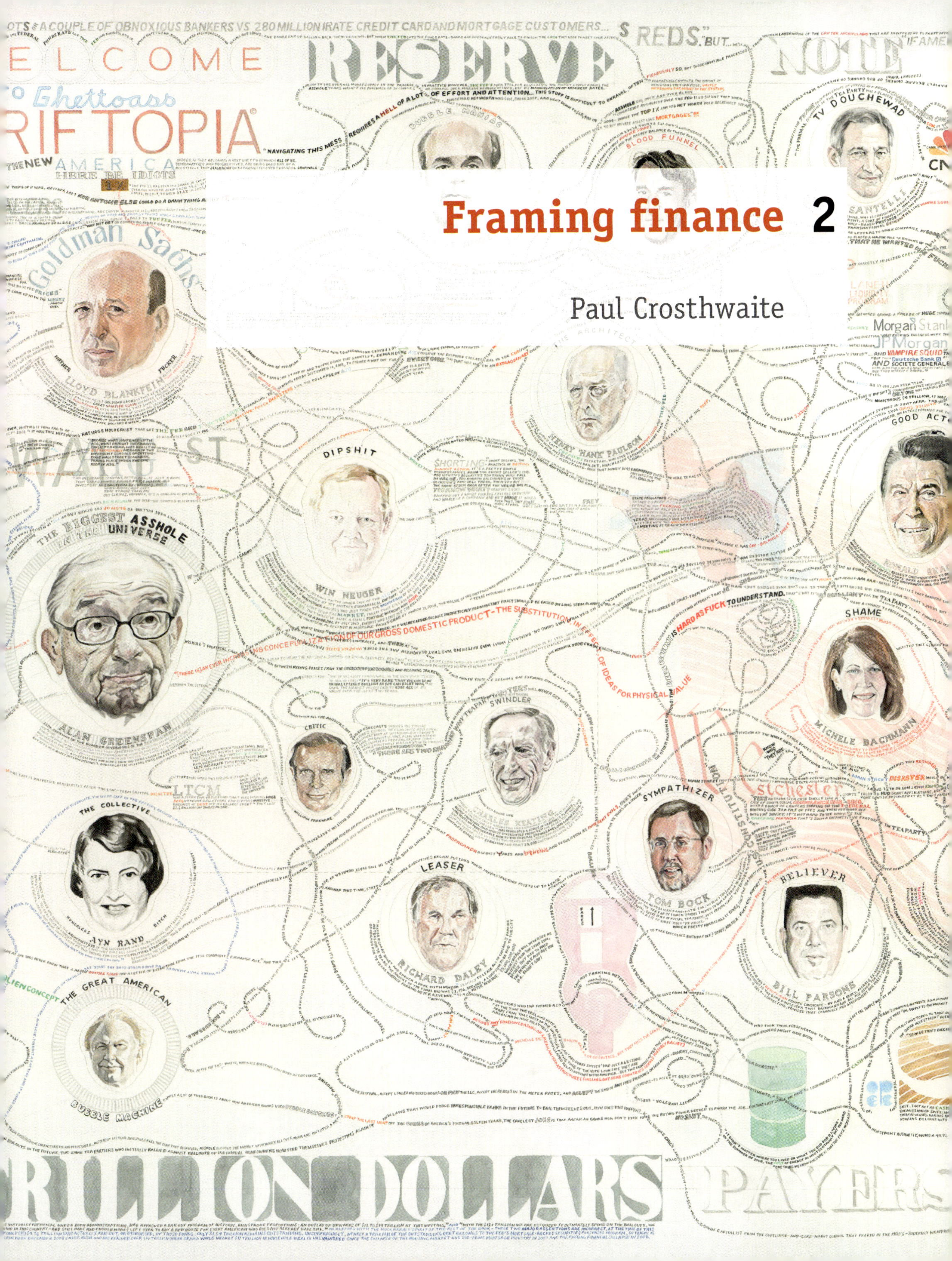

Framing finance

Paul Crosthwaite

'The image of finance' presupposes a frame, a set of boundaries within which the image is contained. But how do you construct a frame capacious enough to contain something as sprawling and diffuse as 'finance' or 'the market'? And how do you ensure that what is most essential to financial activity – the exchange of intangible instruments – is made visibly present within the frame and not left in the obscurity beyond it? Illustrators and artists have been contending with these questions since at least as long ago as the eighteenth century. As the scale and complexity of finance have grown over the last three centuries or more, so the image of finance has been captured from a progressively more remote, panoramic vantage point, in an attempt to enframe as much content as possible; in the process, figuration – the direct or literal representation of people or things – has given way to mounting abstraction. But abstraction – of finance and of its image – was there from the start, in the rapid financialisation of early modern Europe. At the same time, even as finance has become increasingly placeless and disorientating, its visualisers have pursued the dream of an image that would also do justice, within the same frame, to the grounded particularities from which such vast complexity emerges. Similarly, in an effort to register those aspects of finance that are most intangible and ineffable, image-makers have repeatedly incorporated elements of allegory, caricature, fantasy or folklore into their works as supplements to more rigorously objective and rational, but often less revealing, modes of visualisation.

A notable sub-genre of financial imagery in the early modern period consisted of etchings of the financial and commodity exchanges then springing up in major European cities, first Antwerp, whose 'Bourse' opened in 1532, and later Amsterdam, Hamburg, Frankfurt, London, Copenhagen, St. Petersburg and other centres.[1] Perhaps the most striking example of this style of illustration is a hand-coloured engraving of the Royal Exchange in London produced around 1750 after an etching by Thomas Bowles (Figure 1). The original Royal Exchange was opened in 1571 by Queen Elizabeth I as a dedicated site for the mercantile business that had for generations been transacted in impromptu huddles on nearby Lombard Street and in its surrounding network of lanes and alleyways. Bowles's interior elevation of the second Royal Exchange (the first was destroyed in the Great Fire of 1666) depicts the animated but orderly negotiations of smartly dressed merchants, underwriters and investors who are comfortably accommodated within the expansive courtyard of Edward Jarman's magnificent baroque building. With its masterful deployment of linear perspective and adoption of a centralised vantage point, Bowles's image trains a panoptic, Enlightenment gaze on a rigidly demarcated, circumscribed and rationalised spatial field. The perimeters of the etching echo the monumental walls of the Exchange, which themselves enframe the mercantile activity within, emphasising the boundedness of the market, its amenability to a single, encompassing viewpoint. As the sociologist Alex Preda insists in his book *Framing Finance: The Boundaries of Markets and Modern Capitalism*, 'control of space' was a crucial element of the 'boundary work' performed by financial markets in the eighteenth century.[2]

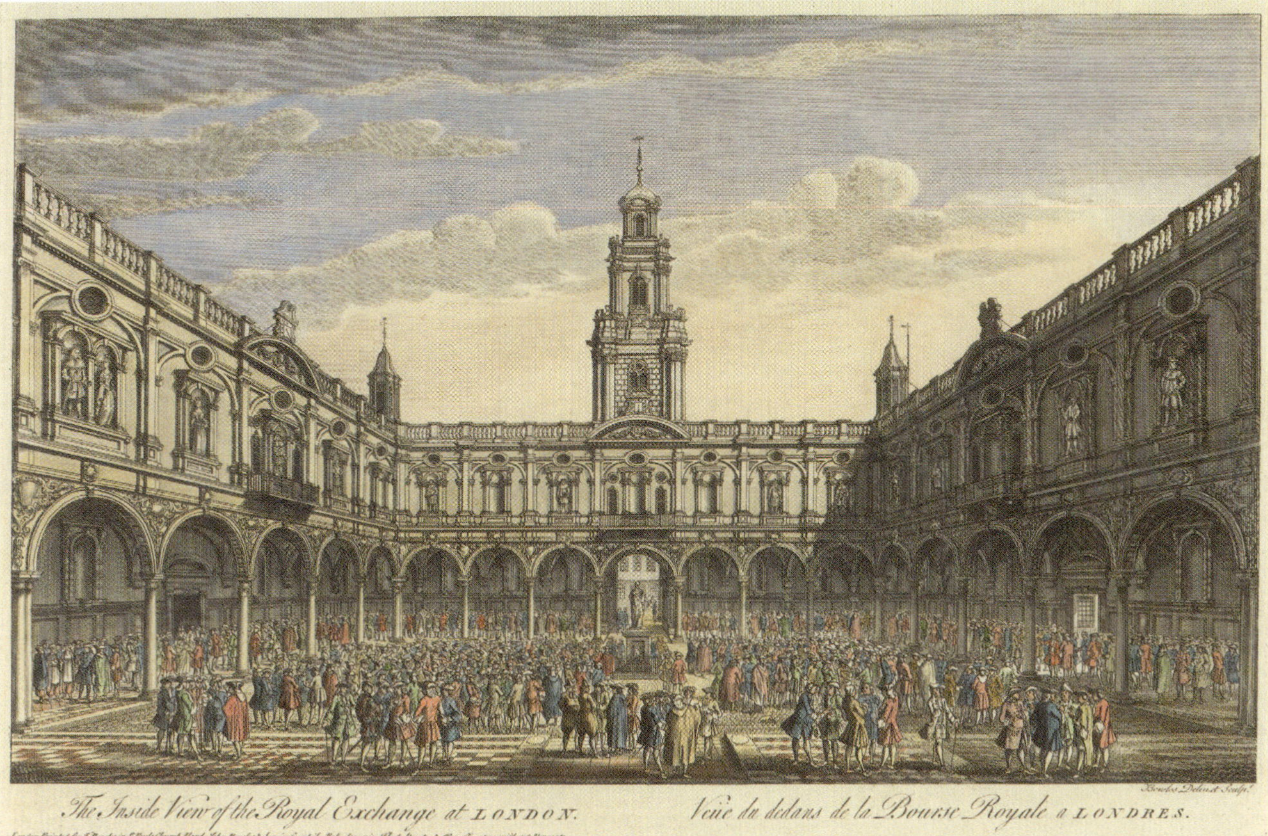

Figure 1

Thomas Bowles, *The Inside View of the Royal Exchange at London* (c. 1750). Hand-coloured engraving.

Yale Center for British Art, Paul Mellon Collection.

One group with no place within the frame of Bowles's image – or of the Exchange itself by this time – is the contingent of stock dealers who had been expelled in 1698 for rowdy behaviour. Dealers no longer welcome at the Exchange gravitated towards the less formal surroundings of the neighbouring streets and coffee houses. The prime location was Jonathan's Coffee House on Exchange (or Change) Alley, which runs between Lombard Street, traditional home of dealers and traders, and Cornhill, site of the Exchange itself. Jonathan's is the subject of a famous 1763 print, *Jonathan's Coffee House or an Analysis of Change Alley* (Figure 2). Where Bowles's view of the Royal Exchange exemplifies one branch of Enlightenment visual culture – the principles of order, symmetry and proportion associated with neoclassicism – this print embodies another, the virulent strain of satirical caricature that aimed at subverting the authority of the wealthy and powerful.[3] *Jonathan's Coffee House* resembles *The Inside View of the Royal Exchange* in surveying a bustling scene of financial transaction, but, produced in response to the continent-wide panic that accompanied the end of the Seven Years' War in 1763, it is, fittingly, a considerably more mordant vision. The plate purports to feature 'a Group of Characters from the Life', as its subtitle has it, 'some of whom may have been identifiable by contemporaries'.[4] However, following the lead of illustrators like George Townshend and Arthur Pond, who had imported Italian traditions of caricature into Britain earlier in the eighteenth century, the image exaggerates and distorts the physiognomies of those under view into grotesque parodies, the better to convey the venality and corruption of their financial activities.[5]

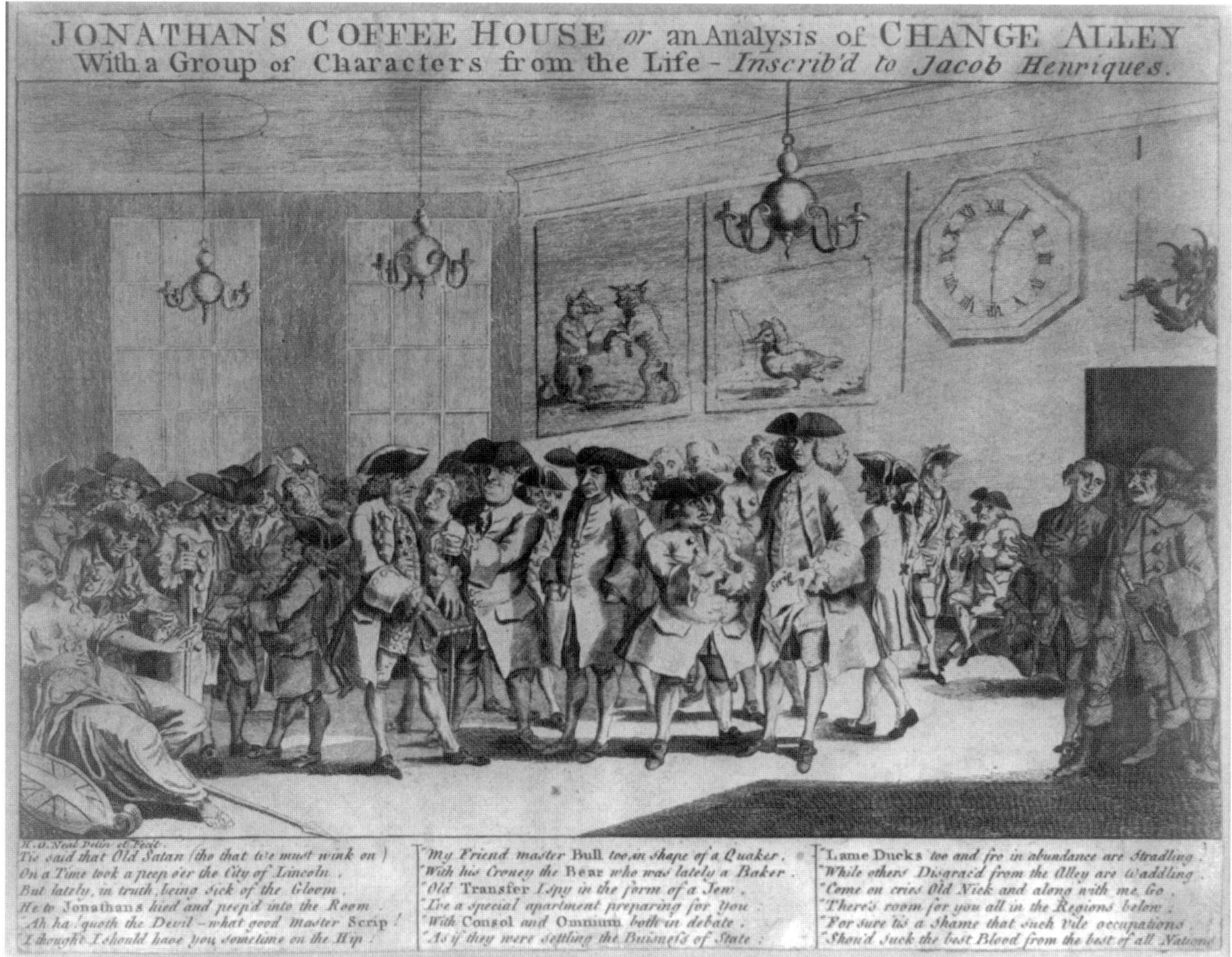

Caricature is accompanied in this image by emblematic and allegorical elements. On the wall are a bull and bear (totems of those who gamble, respectively, on rising and falling markets) and a bewigged 'lame duck' or ruined investor. In the bottom left hand corner, meanwhile, a swooning Britannia, exsanguinated by three snakes, personifies the lament in the print's inscription panel: ''tis a Shame that such Vile occupations Shou'd Suck the best Blood from the best of all Nations'. This visual and verbal rhetoric draws on a well-established tradition of sanguineous financial imagery. Notable earlier examples include Thomas Hobbes's claim that 'Mony [is] the Bloud of a Commonwealth' that 'passeth from Man to Man … Nourishing … every part', and the likening of the South Sea Company's directors, at the time of the Bubble, to vampires draining the nation's blood.[6] The other key symbolic presence in *Jonathan's Coffee House* is the devil, whose leering visage intrudes into the upper right portion of the scene, and whose plan to carry off the frequenters of the dealing room to 'the Regions below' is elaborated in the inscription. This figure recalls the similarly triumphant diabolical onlooker in William Hogarth's *The South Sea Scheme* (1721) (see Chapter 5) and has something in common with the *Diable d'Argent* or 'Money Devil' who appears in illustrations dating back to the sixteenth century

Figure 2

Jonathan's Coffee House or An Analysis of Change Alley With a Group of Characters from the Life (1763). Engraving.

British Cartoon Prints Collection, Prints and Photographs Division, Library of Congress, LC-USZ62-22422.

and was the subject of a popular series of prints that began to appear in France in the early eighteenth century.[7]

The portrayal of 'Old Nick' with a telescope is a distinctive and suggestive detail, which lends particular significance to the use of caricature in this picture, implying that what we are seeing is not a bird's-eye view of the market, as is common in the genre of architectural stock exchange etchings to which Bowles's depiction of the Royal Exchange belongs, but a 'devil's-eye view', in which inner spiritual perdition becomes visible in the distorted outer forms of the dealers and speculators. At the same time, the devil and the monstrous human figures and other mythic and symbolic elements of the image seem to suggest the desire for a visual language to evoke that for which Bowles's etching, for all its precision and command, has no analogue: namely, the intangible, in many ways imaginary, assets, rights and obligations being bought and sold in these sites of financial exchange, units of value that for many eighteenth-century commentators – including Daniel Defoe, Jonathan Swift and Alexander Pope – occupied the realm of fantasy, magic and make believe. Looking back on the South Sea Bubble in his *Epistle to Bathurst* (1733), for example, Pope described a 'tempter' or 'demon' who pours 'stocks and subscriptions ... on every side' until he 'possesses' the speculator-protagonist 'whole'.[8] In such visual or verbal rhetoric (further examples of which we will encounter later in this chapter) there is always a danger of mystification, of intensifying the strangeness and obscurity of finance in ways that are complicit with the notional object of critique. Yet the rich history of supernatural depictions of finance has always retained substantial critical power, not only because of its stinging moral force (the equation, for example, of speculation with devilry), but also, and more importantly, because of its philosophical capacity to highlight the imaginary and ungrounded aspects of financial systems, and hence the potential to re-imagine those systems along alternate lines.

In the mid-eighteenth century, according to the cultural historian Mary Poovey, squibs on financial themes like the verse inscription printed with *Jonathan's Coffee House*, as well as longer satirical treatments like Pope's, were in the process of differentiating themselves from, but were not yet fully independent of, other kinds of financial writing that to our eyes look like entirely distinct genres.[9] One such form consisted of lists of market prices designed to keep merchants up to date with the patterns of trade at the exchanges. Lists of this sort originated in Antwerp and Venice in the sixteenth century,[10] but the best known was launched in 1697 by the Huguenot broker John Castaing from 'his Office at Jonathans Coffee-house' (an earlier incarnation, which burned down in 1748). Collating stock prices, commodities prices and exchange rates, *The Course of the Exchange, and other things* (Figure 3) quickly established itself as London's leading source of financial information, and continued to appear for almost a century. While it might have been distantly affiliated to more imaginative forms of financial representation, *The Course of the Exchange* was a far cry from illustrations of the hustle and bustle of traders at work,

(1)

The Courſe of the *Exchange*, and other things.

London, Tueſday *4th January*, 1698.

Amſterdam	35	9a10
Rotterdam	35	11a36
Antwerp	35	9a10
Hamburgh	35	2a3
Paris	47	$\frac{1}{4}$
Lyons	47	$\frac{1}{4}$
Cadiz	51	$\frac{1}{4}$a51
Madrid	51	$\frac{1}{4}$
Leghorn	52	$\frac{1}{4}$
Genoua	51	$\frac{1}{4}$
Venice	49	$\frac{1}{2}$
Lisbon	5	7$\frac{3}{4}$
Porto	5	6$\frac{3}{4}$
Dublin	16	$\frac{1}{2}$

Gold	4 *l.* 00 *s.* 6 *d.*
Ditto Ducats	4 · 5 6
Silver Sta.	5 *s.* 1 *d.* $\frac{1}{2}$ a 2 *d.*
Foreign Bars	5 3 $\frac{1}{2}$
Pieces of Eight	5 3 $\frac{1}{2}$

	Saturd	*Monday*	*Tueſd.*
Bank *Stock*	86$\frac{1}{2}$ a $\frac{3}{4}$	86$\frac{1}{2}$ a $\frac{3}{4}$	86 $\frac{3}{4}$
India	53 $\frac{3}{4}$	53 $\frac{3}{4}$	53 $\frac{3}{4}$
African	11 $\frac{3}{4}$	11 $\frac{3}{4}$	11 $\frac{3}{4}$
Hudſon Bay	110	110	110
Orphans Chamb.	53	53	53
Blank Tick.M.L.	6 15	6 15	6 15

No Transfer of the Bank *till* January 7.

In the Exchequer *Advanced.*		*Paid off.*
1ſt 4 Shill.Aid	1896874	1814575
3d 4 Shill. Aid	1800000	1392377
4th 4 Shill. Aid	1800000	886492
$\frac{3}{4}$ Cuſtom	967985	764328
New Cuſtom	1250000	655200
Tobacco, *&c.*	1500000	119400
$\frac{3}{4}$ Exciſe	999815	864260
Poll-Tax	569293	479328
Paper, *&c.*	324114	65512
Salt Act	1904519	73772
Low Wines, *&c.*	69959	11100
Coal Act&Leath.	564700	17162
Births and Marr.	650000	2000
3 Shill. Aid	1500000	601555
Malt Act	2000000	163746
Exchequer Notes, ſunk		585000*l.*

Coyn'd in the *Tower*, laſt Week, 0000*l.*

By* John Caſtaing, *Broker, at his Office at* Jonathans *Coffee-houſe.

Figure 3

The Course of the Exchange, and other things, Tuesday 4 January 1698.

Image courtesy Lordprice Collection.

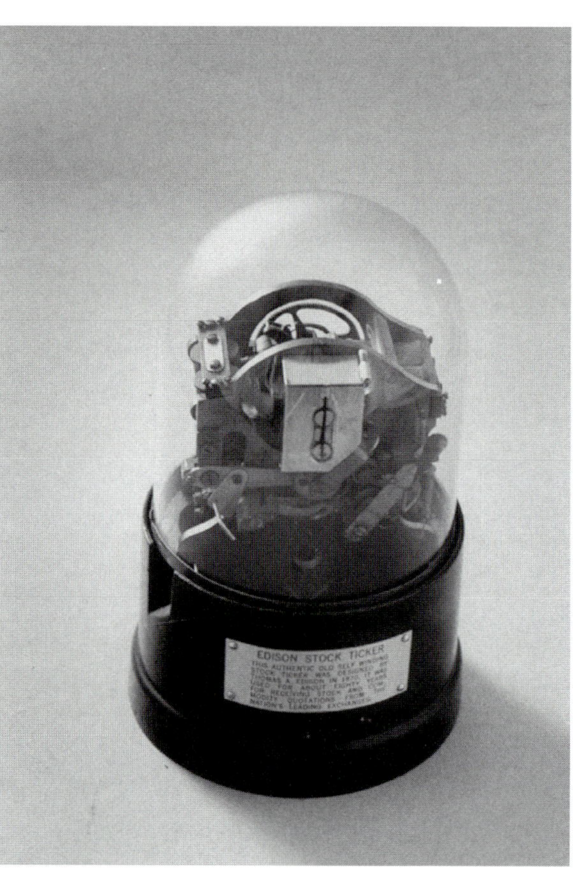

Figure 4

Self-winding stock ticker designed by Thomas A. Edison. Photo by Charles H. Phillips.

Time & Life Pictures/Getty Images.

or poetic lampoonings of speculators' folly and greed. Here, columns of facts and figures stood in for the heat and drama of the living, breathing market.

As such, *The Course of the Exchange* was a rudimentary but important forerunner of perhaps the most historically significant mediator of financial information: the stock ticker. In the latter part of the eighteenth century and throughout the nineteenth, improvements in communications infrastructure (initially, faster and more reliable postal services and, later, the telegraph) meant that it was less and less necessary for those who wished to participate in financial markets to be physically present in sites of exchange. In order to 'play the market' remotely, however, one required ready access to up-to-date and accurate price information. Circulars like *The Course of the Exchange* and the price listings later widely published in newspapers were prone to manipulation and inevitably obsolete before they even appeared. Consequently, brokers and speculators continued to congregate in throngs in and around the stock and commodity exchanges, not because they intended to trade in person, but simply in order to observe the moment-by-moment fluctuations of prices. Invented by Edward A. Calahan in 1867, and refined in the 1870s by Thomas Edison and Henry van Hoveberg, the stock ticker was intended to disperse these crowds and permit the geographical expansion of market activity to continue unchecked.[11]

A compact telegraphic device, whose basic components were a battery, a reel of paper tape and two wheels, one for printing abbreviated names of companies and the other for typing out prices and trading volumes (see Figure 4), the stock ticker had a huge economic and cultural impact in the United States, where it was first introduced, and later around the world. Recent histories have stressed the complex ways in which the ticker altered visualisations of finance. As Alex Preda writes:

> The new visual experience of the market was ... radically different from that of the eighteenth-century marketplace. Not only did one not need to be present anymore in places like the Exchange Alley or the Tontine Coffee House [on Wall Street] in order to 'see' the market, but this latter became something very different from the noise and the conglomerate of colorful figures associated with those places ... . The observer of the market was now the observer of abstract variations, not of picturesque and more or less morally dubious characters, a shift which dislocated transactions from their local embedding ....[12]

The advent of the ticker was understood as radically expanding the 'frame' of finance: the 'boundaries of the stock exchange were torn down' and the market now 'existed everywhere'.[13] What ticker-fixated speculators lost in vividness and particularity they stood to gain in comprehensiveness, for the new device promised 'a bird's eye perspective on the sublime vastness of the financial market and the whole economy'.[14] The ticker was widely hailed as a minutely sensitive recorder or 'seismograph', which encoded every flicker in economic conditions and investor sentiment, yet for dedicated 'tape readers' the significance of the streaming letters and numbers lay not in what they represented or reflected, but simply in their own autonomous rhythms and regularities.[15] In a further contradiction, 'while acting as an instrument that rationalised stock trading', the ticker was also viewed as an 'apparatus that hypnotised the speculating subject – and thus deprived the speculator of rationality'.[16] Indeed, according to the master tape readers, it was only by entering into such a trance-like state that the speculator could glimpse those uncanny instants when 'the market momentarily indicates its own immediate future'.[17]

The stock ticker was a notable presence in the melodramatic tales of finance that were popular features of mainstream American magazines around the turn of the twentieth century and played important roles in shaping public understandings of speculation and investment. Though such stories relentlessly personalised financial upheavals, rendering them as matters of individual greed and hubris, and tying them to the protagonists' wider emotional and romantic entanglements, their recurrent interruptions by the mechanical chatter of the stock ticker were reminders of the facelessness and placelessness of the market at large. Tickers also featured prominently in many of the illustrations that accompanied narratives in this genre; indeed, they were often the focal points of such images. A drawing printed alongside Charles Dudley Warner's tale of Wall Street folly *The Golden House* in an 1894 issue of *Harper's* magazine is especially symptomatic in this regard (Figure 5). The stock ticker is spatially and symbolically central to William Thomas Smedley's illustration, the element towards which the eye of the viewer is drawn as surely as is the attention of the two male figures, who study the device's emissions with rapt fascination. The grey watercolour wash that forms the background of the image is darkest in the vicinity of the ticker and gradually fades out as it approaches the extremities, suggesting a radiating (and perhaps malign) force emanating from the machine. The two human figures, meanwhile, are rendered thoroughly anonymous, not only by their positioning with their backs to the viewer, but also by their generic attire, which reduces them to the status of stock 'types': the traditional nineteenth-century 'man of business', with his frock coat and top hat, on the left, and his emerging 'modern' counterpart, clad in checked 'sack suit' and bowler hat, on the right. The men are mere ciphers, passively subservient to the ticker, the dynamic agent at the centre of the image.

The vast quantities of price data that became readily available on a mass scale after the introduction of the stock ticker were quickly combined to form new ways of conceptualising and visualising financial markets. One was the dollar average of twelve leading stocks launched by Charles Dow in 1896 to provide an at-a-glance picture of American finance. Today, the single figure that is the Dow Jones Industrial Average serves, like other leading stock indices such as the S&P 500, the FTSE, the Nikkei and the Hang Seng, as a succinct distillation of that amorphous thing known as 'the market'. A similar representational role is played by the jagged charts on which the performances of single stocks, or whole indices, are plotted over timescales ranging from hours to decades. While such charts aggregate the individual price fluctuations displayed on the ticker at

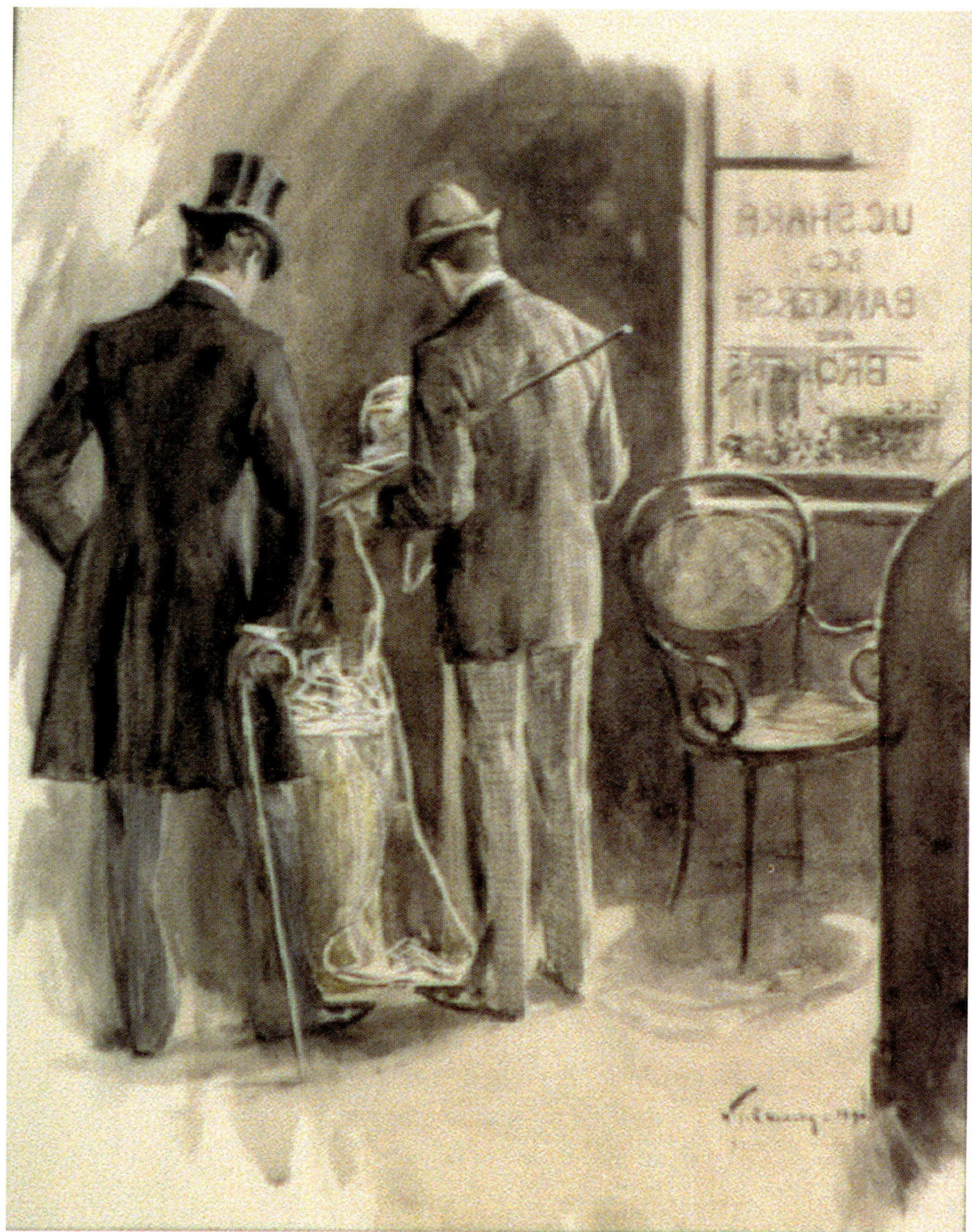

Figure 5

William Thomas Smedley, 'Men looking at ticker tape in broker's office', *Harper's* magazine, September 1894. Drawing; wash.

Cabinet of American illustration, Prints and Photographs Division, Library of Congress, CAI – Smedley, no. 43 [B size] [P&P].

a higher level of abstraction, they possess a visual expressiveness that pure streams of letters and numbers (whether on paper strips or, now, digital displays) notably lack. The peaks and valleys of stock charts give price movements a readily intelligible form; in their resemblance to features of the physical landscape, moreover, they seem to correlate the abstractions of finance with a recognisable material world, even as they evoke notions of the sublime – a paradoxical effect literalised in a project by the new media artists David Cornford and Matthew Cross, *The Lost Horizon*, which maps the undulations of the FTSE onto towering mountain ranges (see Chapter 5).

The charting of financial data was pioneered in the early twentieth century by Roger Ward Babson, whose 'Babsonchart' (Figure 6) was first issued in 1907. Just as the ticker

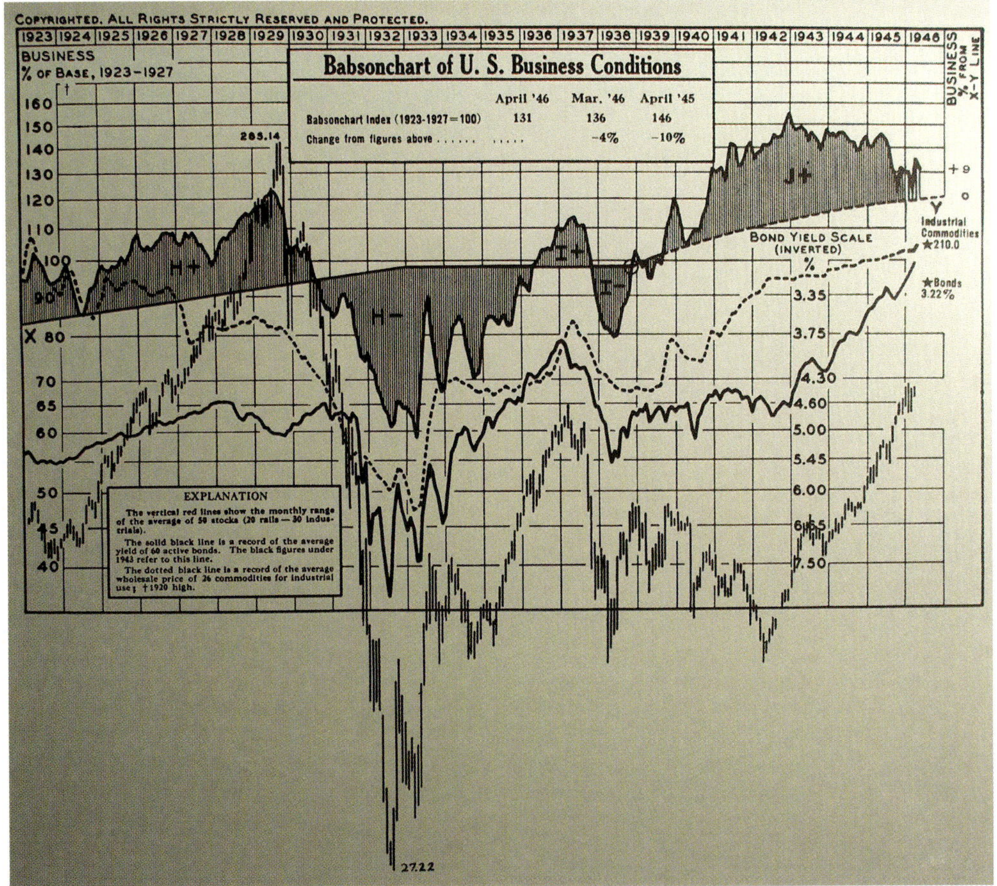

Figure 6

Babsonchart of U.S. Business Conditions (1946).

Reproduced courtesy of the Babson College Archives.

tape spawned legions of 'tape readers', convinced that it was possible to foresee imminent price movements in the passing flow of numbers, so financial charts brought into being a community of 'chartists' (or 'technical analysts'), who sought patterns and periodicities in charts of historical data as routes to divining future trends. Indeed, charts were designed from the start as predictive technologies. According to Babson's theory, analysts could tell that the market was about to enter a prolonged boom phase, for example, when an 'area of depression' (H- and I- on the chart here) was equal to the preceding 'area of overexpansion' (H+, I+, J+). The most striking feature of the Babsonchart reproduced in this volume, which covers the period 1923 to 1946, is the precipitous decline in stock, bond and commodities prices triggered by the Wall Street Crash of October 1929. Particularly arresting is the extent to which the vertical lines (showing the monthly range of the average of 50 stocks) exceed the horizontal axis – literally going 'off the chart' – as if the crash surpassed all conventional frames of reference, and perhaps even threatened the boundaries of representation themselves. Though his chart might later have barely been able to accommodate it, Babson – drawing on his chartist studies – was one of the most prominent figures to sound the alarm ahead of the crash. In a speech on 5 September 1929, he announced, 'Sooner or later a crash is coming, and it may be terrific'. Later that day, the market slumped by 3 per cent, a fall known as the 'Babson Break'. If Babson was right about the coming collapse, however, it was – in the words of John Kenneth Galbraith in his classic study *The Great Crash 1929* – 'for the wrong reasons'. Mainstream economists have long associated chartism with astrology and other pseudosciences, and the work of Babson is no exception. In Galbraith's words: 'Babson was not a man who inspired confidence as a prophet … . The methods by which he reached his conclusions were a problem. They involved a hocus pocus of lines and areas on a chart. Intuition and even mysticism played a part.'[18]

Despite such sceptical voices, the idea that on the chart or ticker tape one may observe not only the past or present of the market but also its future remains irresistibly compelling for many financial professionals and amateur investors. Perhaps we should not be surprised that so many participants in financial markets have been drawn to the esoteric lore of chartism or tape reading (or even the outright occultism of astrology, numerology, clairvoyance and shamanism),[19] for, as we have already seen, the very instruments in which such individuals deal amount to little more than figments of the imagination. It may be that the 'shadow of coming events'[20] that one investment guru of the 1920s claimed to be able to discern in patterns of price data is simply a latter-day equivalent of the devil and the other monstrous and mythical beings commonly depicted in eighteenth-century prints on financial themes: a partial but revealing figurative proxy for the deeper mystery that is financial accumulation itself in its capacity to make 'something (money, capital) out of nothing (… ideas, concepts, fictions and consensual hallucinations)'.[21]

The forms of financial mediation and representation prevalent around the turn of the twentieth century – tickers, charts, indices – all utilised the resources of abstraction in order to provide more commanding perspectives on the market for brokers, speculators and other perpetuators of the logic of financial capitalism. In the same period, however, abstract modes of visualisation were also employed by parties opposed to the power of a plutocratic financial class. The most significant campaign of this kind was led by Arsène Pujo, a Democratic Representative from Louisiana. In 1912–13, Pujo chaired a congressional subcommittee tasked with investigating the so-called 'money trust'. The Pujo Committee, as it became known, concluded that substantial portions of American industry, transport, telecommunications and finance were under the sway of a cabal of Wall Street bankers and financiers that exercised its power via an opaque system of interlocking directorships. A team of clerks methodically tabulated these intersecting interests and produced two schematic diagrams that highlighted the extent of the cartel's influence. One of these diagrams, Exhibit 243 (Figure 7), shows the lines of command radiating out from J.P. Morgan and Company. Morgan, perhaps the greatest financial titan of the age, had been hailed as a hero in 1907 when he had orchestrated interventions by the leading Wall Street houses to head off a series of bank runs and a crash on the New York Stock Exchange. Morgan's prominent role in stemming the Panic of 1907 drew public attention to his byzantine business interests, however, and by 1912 the 'Napoleon of Finance' was an object of widespread popular suspicion and resentment. One of the strengths of Exhibit 243 is its ability to capture some of the negative associations that

FOLLOWING SPREAD

Figure 7

Exhibit 243, Pujo Committee Report (1913).

Courtesy FRASER (Federal Reserve Archival System for Economic Research, Federal Reserve Bank of St. Louis).

Exhibit No. 243–
Feb. 25, 1913.

[D]iagram Showing Affiliations Of J. P. Morgan & Co., National City Bank, First National Bank, Guaranty Trust Co. And Bankers Trust Co. Of New York City With Large Corporations Of The United States.

Affiliations of J. P. Morgan & Co. are shown in Black
Affiliations of {1st National Bank, Guaranty Trust Co., Bankers Trust Co.} are shown in Red
Affiliations of National City Bank are shown in Green
The Various Forms of Affiliation are shown as follows
——— = One Director in Indicated Corporation
∿∿∿ = One Voting Trustee " "
- - - - = One Director in Subsidiary Company
IIIIIII = Ownership of Large Stock Interest
—·—·— = Affiliation through Underwriting or Purchase of Large Blocks of Securities

United States Steel Corporation $1,390,000,000
Cambria Steel Co. $41,600,000
Lackawanna Steel Co. $54,000,000
Penna. Steel Co. $45,500,000
Pullman Company $194,000,000
Baldwin Locomotive Works $45,000,000
International Harvester Co. $178,000,000
Safety Car Heating & Lighting $11,000,000
[illegible]
J. I. Case Threshing Mach. Co. [illegible]
Miscellaneous
Farm Machinery
Manufacturing
Iron & Steel
R. R. Equip.
Elec. Mach.
Other Metals
American Can Co. $80,000,000
U.S. Motor Co. $10,000,000
W. T. Stamp & Enam. $6,000,000
General Electric Co. $268,000,000
Westinghouse Elec. & Mfg. $65,000,000
Phelps Dodge & Co. $96,800,000
Amalgamated Copper Co. $181,900,000
Inspiration Consol. Copper $19,000,000
Copper
Brass
Nickel
Amer. Brass [illegible]
International Nickel Co. $42,900,000

Chicago Rock Island & Pacific and Rock Island Co. $345,000,000
El Paso & So. West. $49,000,000
Chicago, Milwaukee & St. Paul $659,000,000
Toledo St. Louis & West. $88,000,000
Union Pacific $603,000,000
Chicago & Northwestern $455,000,000
Gt. Nor. & Nor. Pac. Jointly Control C. B. & Q.
Northern Pacific $490,000,000
Chicago Burlington & Quincy $495,000,000
Great N[orthern] $430,000,000
Atchison, Topeka & Santa Fe $640,000,000
Southern Pacific $867,000,000
New York, New Haven & Hartford $849,000,000
Hocking Vy. $48,000,000
Chesapeake & Ohio $199,000,000
Erie R.R. $342,000,000
Dela., Lackawanna & Western $289,000,000
Delaware & Hudson $17,500,000
Norfolk & Western $265,000,000
Cincinnati Hamilton & Dayton $64,000,000
B & O to purchase 51% under agreement
N.Y. Cent. System owns $30,000,000 Reading Stock
Reading Co.
Central R.R. of N.J. $181,600,000
$379,600,000
B & O owns $30,000,000 Reading Stk.
Baltimore & Ohio $515,000,000
New York Central Lines $1,446,000,000
Penna. System owns $47,000,000 N. & W. Stock
Pennsylvania System $1,193,000,000
Penna. System owns $40,000,000 B & O Stock
Illinois [Central] $373,000,000

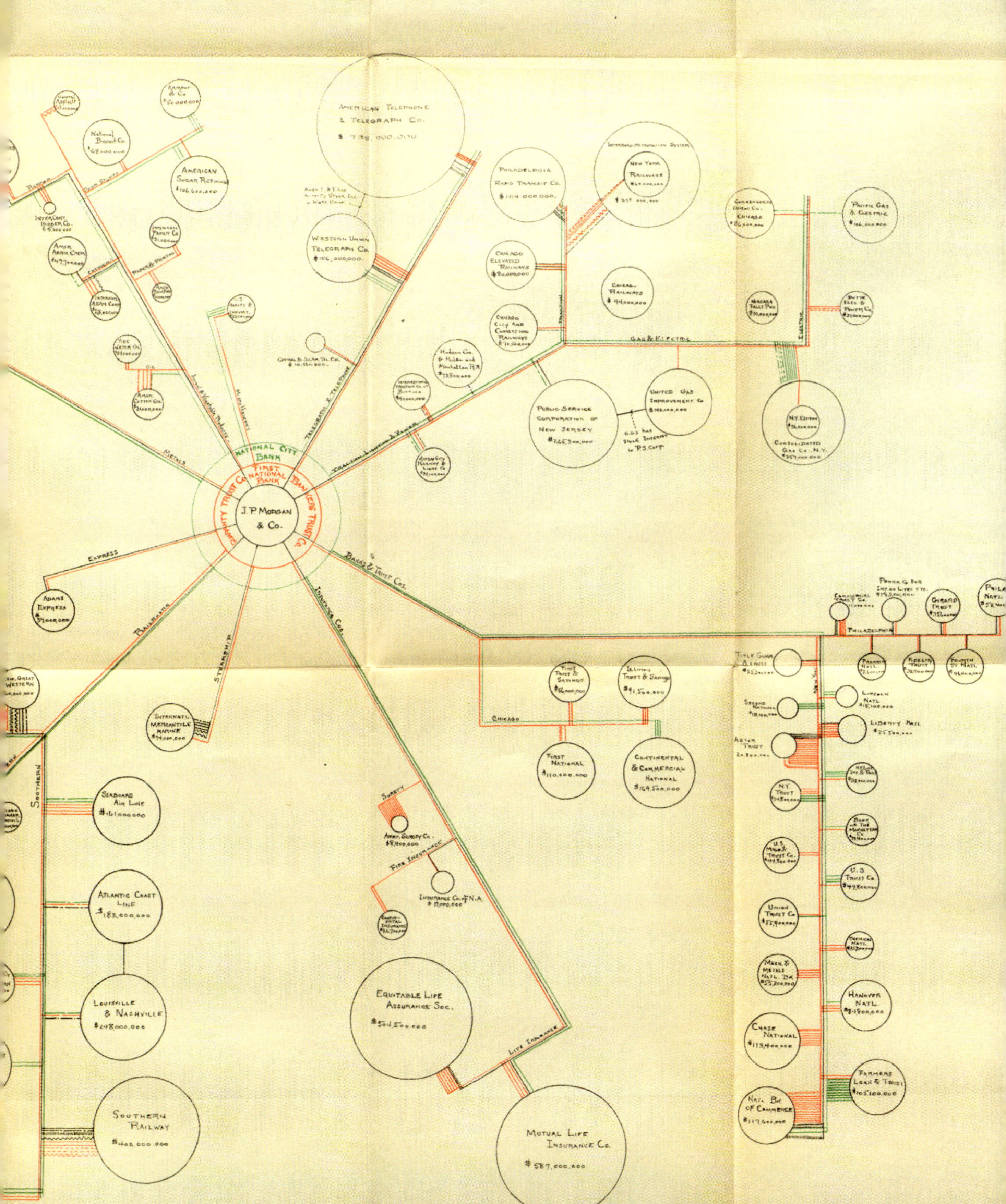
J. P. Morgan & Co.
National City Bank
First National Bank
Guaranty Trust Co.
Bankers' Trust Co.
American Telephone & Telegraph Co. $ 735,000,000
Amer. T. & T. Co. has minority stock int. in West. Union
Western Union Telegraph Co. $156,000,000
Telegraph & Telephone
Philadelphia Rapid Transit Co. $164,000,000
Interboro-Metropolitan System
New York Railways
Chicago Elevated Railways $80,000,000
Chicago Railways $94,000,000
Chicago City and Connecting Railways $70,500,000
Hudson Co. & Hudson and Manhattan R.R. $73,800,000
Traction
Traction, Lighting & Power
Gas & Electric
Electric
Commonwealth Edison Co. Chicago $86,000,000
Pacific Gas & Electric $106,000,000
Niagara Falls Pwr.
United Gas Improvement Co.
U.G.I. has stock interest in P.S. Corp.
Public Service Corporation of New Jersey $265,300,000
N.Y. Edison
Consolidated Gas Co. N.Y. $257,000,000
American Sugar Refining $106,600,000
National Biscuit Co. $68,000,000
Armour & Co.
General Asphalt
Inter-Cont. Rubber Co. $5,000,000
Rubber
Food Stuffs
Amer. Agric. Chem.
Chemical
Internat'l. Paper Co.
Paper & Printing
Tide Water Oil
Oil
Amer. Cotton Oil
Animal & Vegetable Products
Miscellaneous
Metals
Express
Adams Express
Railroads
Steamship
Internat'l. Mercantile Marine
Southern
Seaboard Air Line $161,000,000
Atlantic Coast Line $182,000,000
Louisville & Nashville $248,000,000
Southern Railway $402,000,000
Chicago Great Western
Insurance Cos.
Surety
Amer. Surety Co. $8,400,000
Fire Insurance
Insurance Co. of N.A.
Life Insurance
Equitable Life Assurance Soc. $504,500,000
Mutual Life Insurance Co. $587,000,000
Banks & Trust Cos.
Chicago
First National $110,000,000
Continental & Commercial National $169,500,000
Illinois Trust & Savings $91,500,000
First Trust & Savings
Philadelphia
Commercial Trust Co.
Penna. Co. for Ins. on Lives etc. $19,200,000
Girard Trust
Fidelity Trust
Fourth St. Natl.
Phila. Natl.
New York
Title Guar. & Trust
Second National
Lincoln Natl. $15,100,000
Liberty Natl. $25,500,000
Astor Trust
N.Y. Trust
Bank of the Manhattan Co.
U.S. Mtge. & Trust Co.
U.S. Trust Co.
Union Trust Co.
Chemical Natl.
Mech. & Metals Natl. Bk. $55,200,000
Hanover Natl.
Chase National $113,400,000
Farmers Loan & Trust $105,100,000
Natl. Bk. of Commerce $117,600,000

surrounded Morgan and his company, even as it functions as a meticulously logical abstract schema. Like a stock chart, this diagram possesses a residual figurative dimension – the ghost of a resemblance to real-world objects or scenes. In this case, the layout calls to mind a spider's web (with the Morgan Company as the malignant arachnid at the centre) or a monstrous octopus – both common images in satirical cartoons depicting the robber barons of the Gilded Age. At the same time, the diagram also shares with a stock chart the capacity to collate, rationalise and schematise a wide array of disparate information so as to form a coherent and intelligible whole. Abstract forms of representation are often thought of as obscuring how things 'really are' or how the world 'really works', but if the challenge posed by a collusive network like the money trust is precisely the difficulty of seeing its shape from a perspective 'on the ground', amidst local events and conditions, then it falls to an abstract plan like this one to indicate where each discrete node fits into a much larger grid, thereby revealing the structural realities of financial and economic power.

If the Pujo Committee's diagram suggests a way of resolving the tension between proximity and distance that is integral to attempts to visualise or 'frame' finance, the peculiar strength of the work of the late twentieth-century American neo-conceptual artist Mark Lombardi is precisely the way in which it stages this tension, and highlights it as the political and aesthetic problem it is. From the early 1990s until his death in 2000, Lombardi used a carefully archived file of news reports (eventually running to some 12,000 entries) to produce meticulous pencil-on-paper diagrams of financial and political scandals ranging from Whitewater and Iran-Contra to the savings and loan and Vatican Bank affairs. *Banca Nazionale del Lavoro, Reagan, Bush, Thatcher, and the Arming of Iraq, c. 1979–1990* (1998) (Figure 8) charts the role of the Atlanta, Georgia branch of the Italian government-owned Banca Nazionale del Lavoro within a 'dispersed, semi-coordinated network of conduits through which money and technology made their way into Iraq up until the invasion of Kuwait'[22] – a network that, as the title suggests, had links to major Western leaders. A comparison with the Pujo Committee's exhibit is instructive. The physical dimensions of Exhibit 243 (which took the form of a foldout in the Committee's official report) are such that, perusing the document laid out on a table, the viewer can make out, from a single position, both the details of individual enterprises and the links between them. Considerably larger (at around four feet by ten feet), and designed to be displayed on a gallery wall, *Banca Nazionale del Lavoro*, in contrast, presents the viewer with an either/or proposition: *either*, with nose pressed up against the paper, a clear view of the identities of particular parties involved in the network, *or*, stepping back to survey the diagram as a whole, a sight of the interweaving relationships between them – but not both at the same time. Lombardi's drawing is at once too crammed with signifying elements and too abstract: what looks from one perspective like an obsessive catalogue of facts appears from another as an exercise in pure formalism. And this conflicted effect is the great achievement of Lombardi's work, staging, as it does, the difficulty (interventions

Figure 8

Mark Lombardi, *Banca Nazionale del Lavoro, Reagan, Bush, Thatcher, and the Arming of Iraq, c. 1979–1990* (4th version) (1998). New York, Museum of Modern Art (MoMA). Coloured pencil and pencil on paper, 127 x 304.8 cm. Gift of Shirley and Donald Lombardi. Acc. n.: 2638.2001.

Figure 9

William Powhida, *Griftopia* (2011). Graphite, watercolour, acrylic ink and coloured pencil on paper, 152 x 305 cm.

Image courtesy William Powhida.

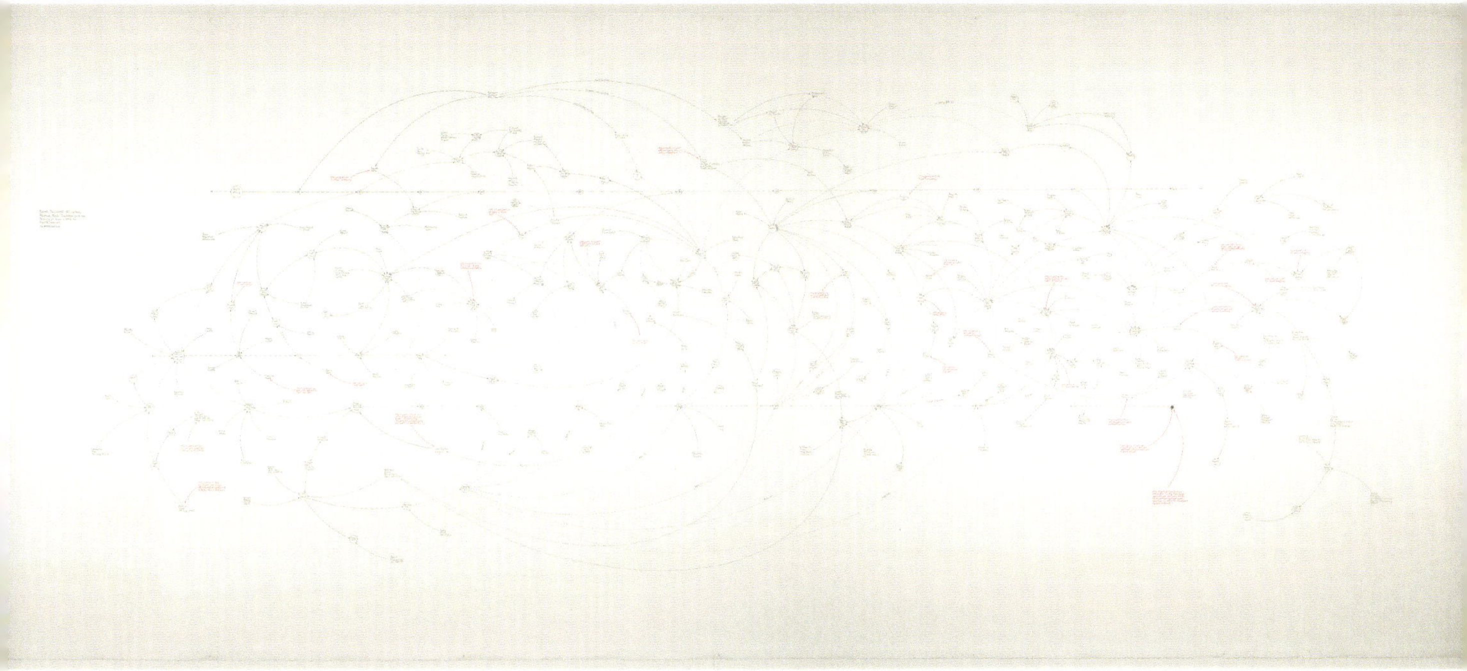

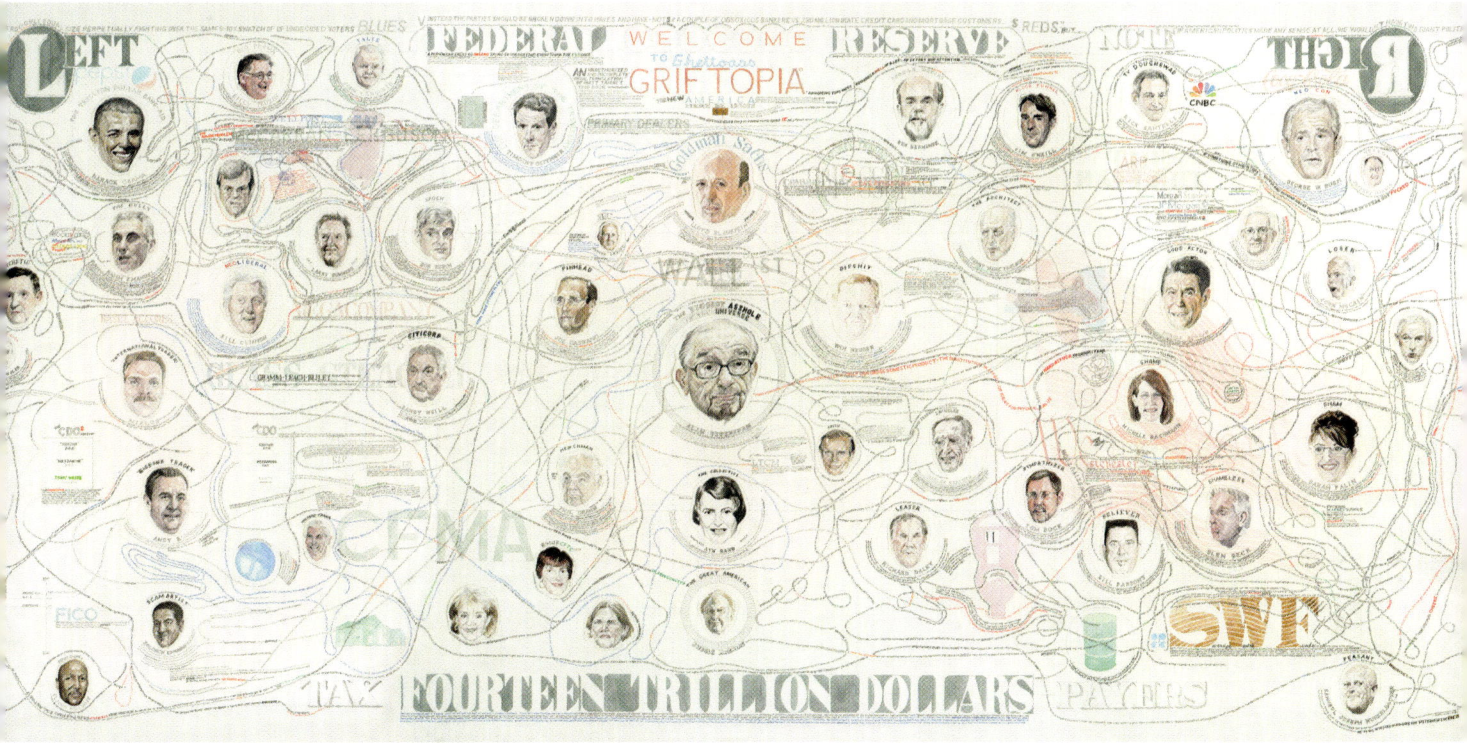

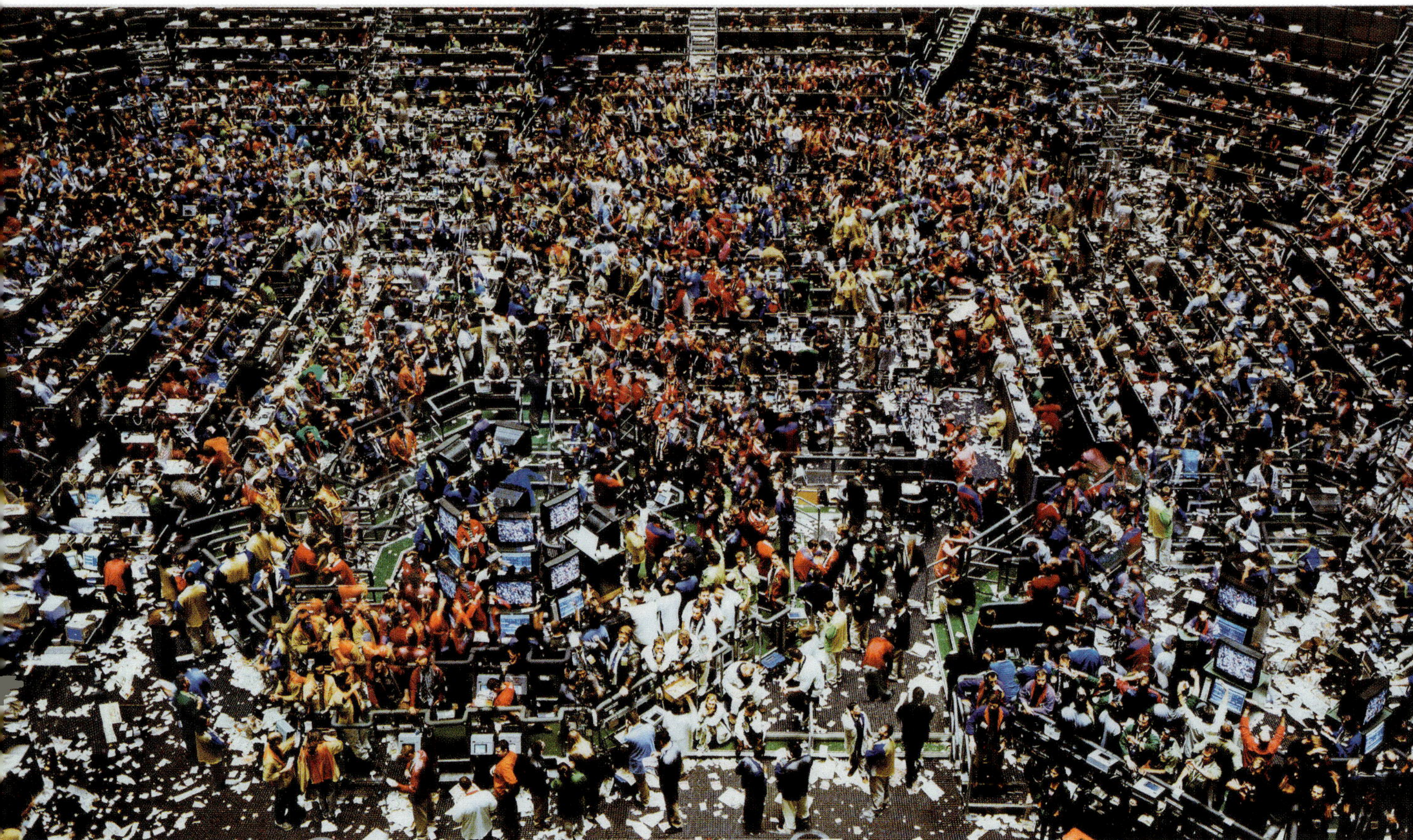

like the Pujo Committee's notwithstanding) of holding whole and part in focus as we contemplate the vast financial and economic networks in which we are enmeshed.

Figure 10

Andreas Gursky, *Chicago Board of Trade II* (1999). Chromogenic print on paper.

Lombardi's sombre, austere compositions have a zany counterpart in William Powhida's similarly huge (five by ten feet) satirical illustration *Griftopia* (2011)(Figure 9), an etch-a-sketch jumble of lines linking many of the architects of the neoliberal ascendancy, whose capture of economic policy in the United States resulted in the disasters of credit crunch and bailout. Taking its title and much of its content from a work of latter-day muckraking by *Rolling Stone* journalist Matt Taibbi, *Griftopia* implicates bankers, regulators, broadcasters, libertarian ideologues and successive presidents and secretaries of the Treasury in a concerted effort to install free market doctrine in Washington and beyond. At the centre resides Alan Greenspan, the former Chairman of the Federal Reserve whose celebrated maintenance of the 'Great Moderation' turned out merely to be preparing the way for the Great Recession. Criss-crossed by meandering lines of text so densely packed as to be virtually illegible, *Griftopia* (much like Lombardi's work) is, as Powhida acknowledges, less about conveying information than about triggering in viewers a recognition of just 'how confusing' the financial world really is.[23]

The minutely detailed quality of Lombardi's and Powhida's works testifies to the challenge of tracing occulted networks of connivance that cross multiple national, legal and institutional boundaries. According to the cultural critic Fredric Jameson, however, the process of tracking conspiracies, even if they do in fact exist, is little more than a compensatory effort in the face of a prospect 'even more difficult for our minds and imaginations to grasp': namely, that political and economic conspiracies, far from being the underlying shapers of history, merely amount to small clusters of organisation, authority and control within an otherwise decentred and anonymous system that is animated by its own impersonal, self-perpetuating logic. The task of 'cognitively mapping' this 'whole new decentred global network' of contemporary capitalism is, Jameson argues, the primary aesthetic and political imperative for artists and thinkers today.[24]

A 1999 work by the German photographer Andreas Gursky, *Chicago Board of Trade II* (Figure 10), gives some hints as to what such a project of 'cognitive mapping' might look like. On the face of it, it must be said, Gursky's image is not the most obvious candidate to fulfil such an urgently contemporary function, even amongst his own oeuvre. While some of the other shots of financial trading floors taken by Gursky since the early 1990s – such as *Hong Kong Stock Exchange, Diptych* (1994) – depict futuristic expanses of desks and computer terminals, here he captures a scene of traditional face-to-face 'open outcry' trading that, with its shouts, hand gestures and scraps of paper, appears in many ways as an archaic holdover from an earlier century. Indeed, at first glance, Gursky's late twentieth-century image of the pit at the Chicago Board of Trade resembles nothing so much as Thomas Bowles's mid-eighteenth-century depiction of the courtyard of the Royal Exchange in London (Figure 1). The vibrant coats, cloaks and breeches of the men in the coloured engraving of Bowles's etching have present-day counterparts in the garish jackets worn by the derivatives traders in Gursky's photograph. Both images, too, seem to dramatise the spontaneous emergence of order from the background hubbub – though in Gursky's photograph the conditions for this emergence bear a distinctly closer resemblance to chaos. The two images also invite similar styles of viewing, ones which parallel those prompted by Lombardi's and Powhida's works. Performing close-up examinations of Bowles's crisp, if spare and economically rendered, figures and Gursky's human subjects, the viewer can make out the details of individuals' poses and expressions. More remote views of the two scenes as wholes, though, find these individuals anonymised, aggregated. This effect is intensified by Gursky's intentional blurring of his high-definition image (he customarily superimposes several exposures over one another), a technique that both captures the rapid movements of the traders and tends to render the image 'reminiscent of an Abstract Expressionist painting'.[25] The drift that the two images undergo from the figurative portrayal of people and things towards something, in Gursky's case at least, approaching the pure, geometric arrangement of colour, form and pattern associated with abstraction reminds us that, though the depersonalisation of financial exchange may have intensified since the eighteenth century, such exchange has always entailed a complex interplay between the myriad bodily, affective and relational interactions that constitute the market and the anonymity and abstraction of the market as a totality.

It is with respect to this question of totality that Bowles's and Gursky's works most sharply diverge. As we have seen, there was some truth in the impression, conveyed by Bowles's image, that the physical plot of the Royal Exchange in the mid-eighteenth century was coterminous with the market for the assets and commodities exchanged there. By the late nineteenth century, however, following the introduction of the stock ticker, there was a stark disparity between the scope of the market and the tightly confined space of the trading floor, a disparity rendered all the more glaring by the global economic integration and the numerous communications innovations of the twentieth century. Fittingly, then, whereas the Royal Exchange is neatly contained within the borders of Bowles's etching, the Chicago trading floor overspills the edges of Gursky's photograph, as if it extended endlessly in every direction. This boundlessness, combined with the high angle at which Gursky positions his camera, as well as the large depth of field, which renders details in the background almost as sharp as those in the foreground, lend the image a 'flat, all-over quality' that 'makes the architecture of the room hard to read'.[26]

In Gursky's depiction, the contemporary trading floor is a 'hyperspace' in which a 'suppression of depth' challenges the 'capacities of the individual human body to locate itself, to organize its immediate surroundings perceptually, and cognitively to map its position in a mappable external world'.[27] This challenge itself stands as a 'symbol and analogon of that even sharper dilemma which is the incapacity of our minds ... to map the great global multinational and decentred communicational network in which we find ourselves caught as individual subjects'.[28] If Gursky's image enacts the difficulties of 'cognitively mapping' this system, however, it also, as I have suggested, makes an attempt to offer at least a 'representational shorthand' for that same system.[29] It does so, in particular, through what Jameson refers to as a contemporary 'technological sublime'.[30] Though the camera is not trained here on one of the scenes of desk-bound, computerised exchange that are now the standard trading environments in financial centres across the world, there is nonetheless (in another signal of Gursky's contemporaneity and distance from Bowles) a massive technological presence in this image: technologies of recording, representation, calculation and transmission – descendants of the ticker that already, in the late nineteenth century, endowed the functioning of the market with an impersonal, placeless air. The trading floor itself, moreover, bears a striking resemblance to a vast microchip or circuit board – or, as Jameson puts it, 'some immense communicational and computer network'. This network in turn, though, would again be 'but a distorted figuration of something even deeper, namely the whole world system of present-day multinational capitalism'.[31]

In its resemblance to a labyrinthine computer system, Gursky's richly suggestive image also anticipates the fate not only of the particular financial site it depicts, but of global finance more generally. Since this iconic picture was captured, the Chicago Board of Trade has followed other major exchanges in migrating its operations away from the trading pit

Figure 11

Beate Geissler and Oliver Sann, *High-Frequency Trading Work Space 9, Willis Tower, Chicago* (2010). Inkjet print, 100 x 145 cm.

Image courtesy the artists and Taubert Contemporary, Berlin.

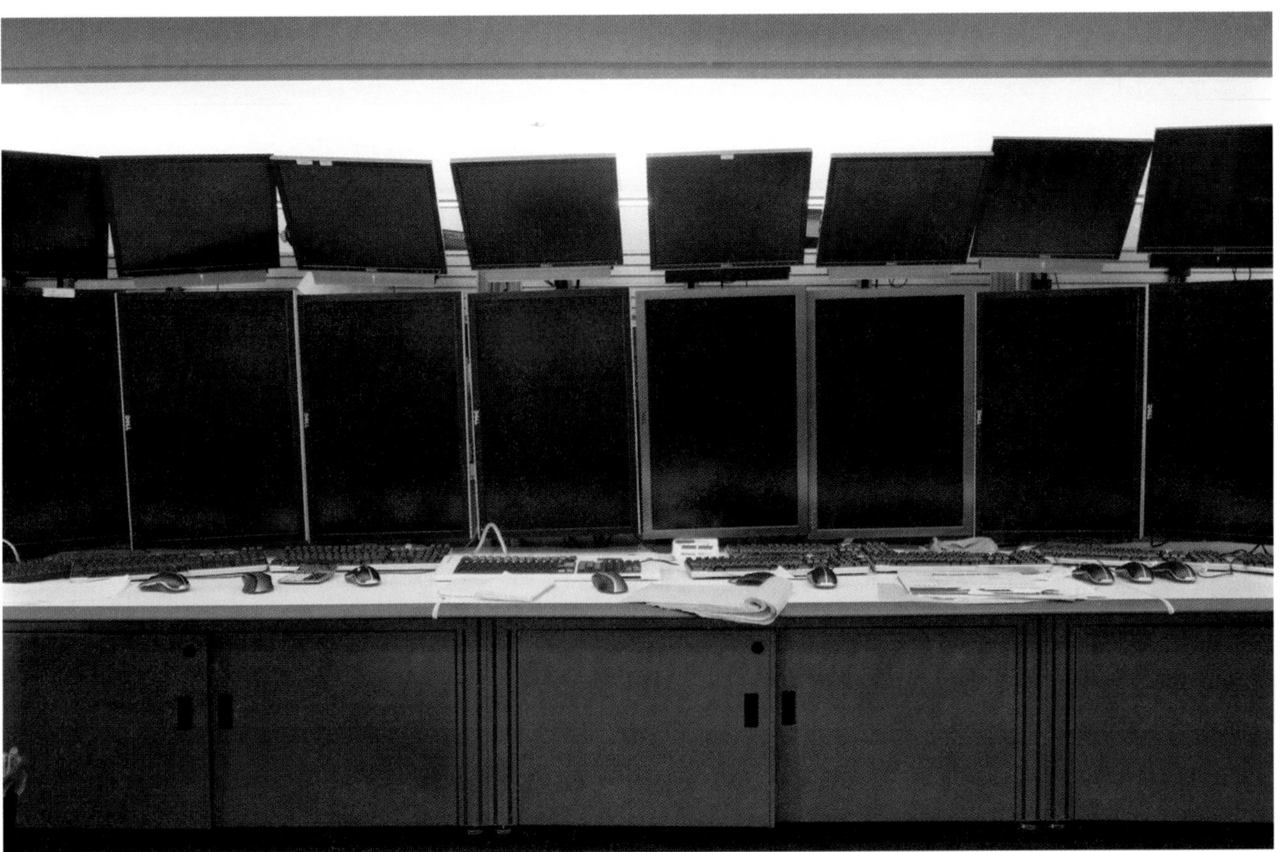

and towards offices arrayed with desks and work stations.[32] In recent years, a great deal of trade in Chicago and elsewhere has been conducted not only remotely and electronically, but also automatically, by computers running trading algorithms programmed to initiate orders in split-second response to shifting market conditions. Such 'high frequency trading' accounted for somewhere between 50 and 70 per cent of all stock trades in the United States between 2008 and 2012. It was the inspiration for a recent project by two German-born, Chicago-based photographers, Beate Geissler and Oliver Sann. Their *Volatile Smile* (2010) series (including Figure 11), shot in the office of a high frequency trading outfit in the Willis (formerly Sears) Tower, offers a very different vision of Chicago's financial district to that found in their compatriot Gursky's view of the Board of Trade. Save for the occasional soda can, sheaf of paper or box of tissues, Geissler and Sann's images of trading desks are devoid of traces of human presence. If Gursky's *Chicago Board of Trade II* calls to mind the energy and expressiveness of a Jackson Pollock drip painting, then, as Frank Wagner suggests, the multiple darkened computer screens that dominate the frames of *Volatile Smile* echo the austere, depersonalised brand of abstraction brought to a peak of perfection by Kasimir Malevich's *Black Square* (1915).[33] Algorithmic trading, of which high frequency trading is the major variant, is often dubbed 'black box trading' because the inner workings of the programme remain invisible to the user as they churn away at near light speed. *Volatile Smile* literalises this conceit by presenting financial exchange as the province of dark, impenetrable and inscrutable devices, which offer no humanly intelligible sign of their operations. The humble human sensorium, Geissler and Sann imply, is not equipped to catch even a glimpse of the robot-world that contemporary finance has become.[34] The political implications of such a depiction are ambiguous: if, on one view, *Volatile Smile* presents a sharp critique of the automation of much contemporary financial exchange, then, from another perspective, it risks appearing complicit with those same processes in its heightening of the aura of opacity and inscrutability that surrounds them.

Volatile Smile takes its name from the language of 'quants' or quantitative analysts – the (sometimes actual) 'rocket scientists' who turned finance into an essentially mathematical (and computerised) business from the 1970s onwards. Specifically, the title refers to the 'volatility smile', an anomaly in the pricing of US options contracts – that is, derivative contracts granting the option to buy or sell an asset at a given price (the strike price) in a set timeframe. As the sociologist Donald MacKenzie describes, prior to the 'Black Monday' crash of October 1987, which hit options markets in Chicago particularly hard, the relationship between the strike price and the implied volatility (or extent of price fluctuation) of options on the same underlying asset with the same time to expiration date formed a flat line on a graph, as the famous Black-Scholes-Merton model of options pricing dictated. After Black Monday, however, 'the flat-line relationship ... disappeared, and was replaced by a distinct "skew"' or 'smile', which still persists. On that day, investors learned that 'stock markets could suddenly fall by previously unthinkable amounts', threatening 'the very existence of derivative markets'. It is this 'collective trauma', MacKenzie postulates, that sustains the skew or smile – an 'incorporation into option prices of the possibility of a catastrophic but low-probability event'. Prices, in other words, 'have incorporated the *fear* that the 1987 crash would be repeated'.[35] Perhaps somewhere around the blank and impassive screens pictured in Geissler and Sann's photographs, then, hovers a Cheshire Cat grin, a wry smile at the faith (and capital) that humans have invested in their equations, and the machines that perform them.

The Black-Scholes-Merton options pricing model invoked by *Volatile Smile* earned Myron Scholes and Robert C. Merton a Nobel Prize in 1997 (the other originator of the model, Fischer Black, had died in 1995). The model's reputation has been severely tarnished, however, by its heavy implication in no fewer than three major financial crises (Black Monday in 1987; the collapse of Scholes and Merton's own hedge fund, Long-Term Capital Management, in 1998; and the global credit crunch in 2008).[36] This iconic but infamous equation provides the title for another important artwork that engages with the real-time digital technologies of contemporary finance: Lise Autogena and Joshua Portway's *Black Shoals Stock Market Planetarium* (Figure 12).

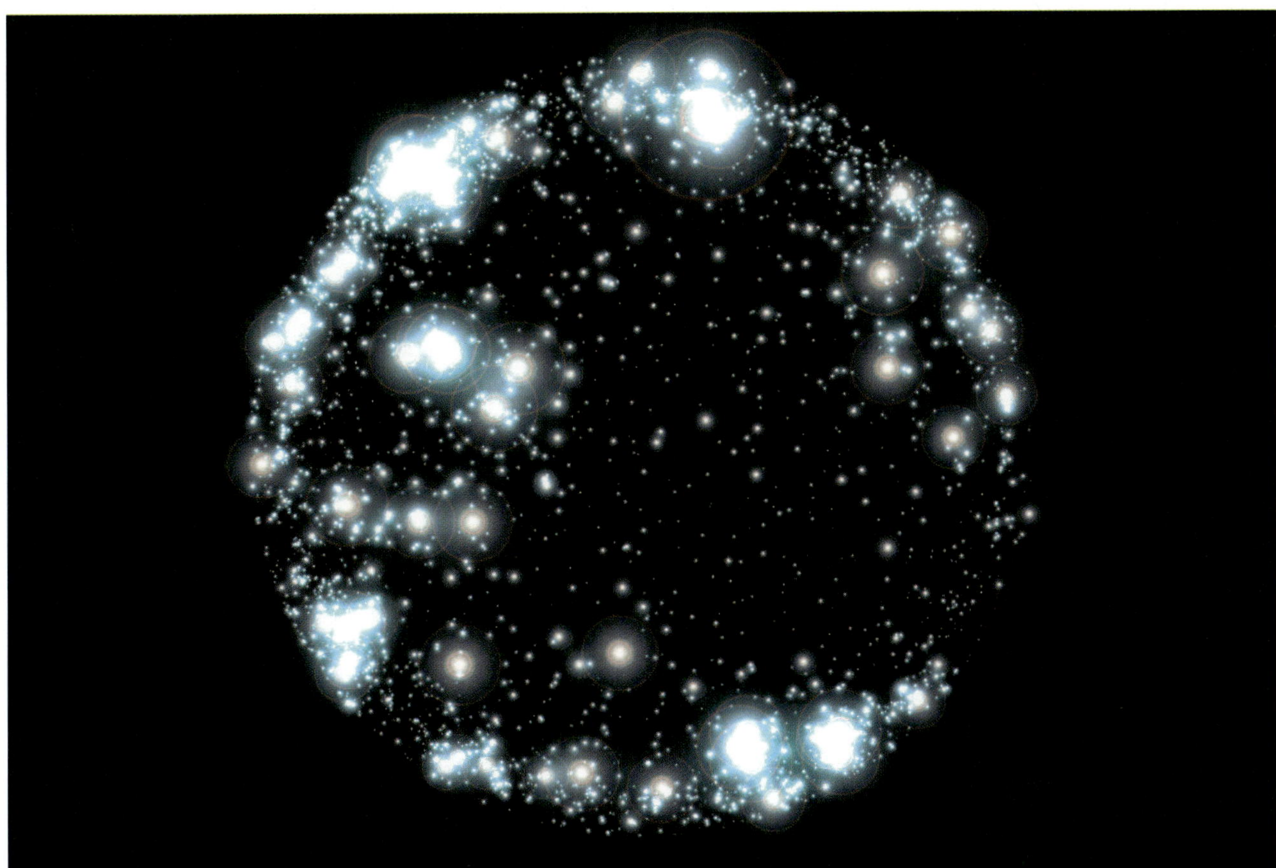

Figure 12

Lise Autogena and Joshua Portway, *Black Shoals Stock Market Planetarium* (2001, 2004).

Image courtesy Lise Autogena.

Viewers of Autogena and Portway's installation – at Tate Britain in 2001 and at the Nikolaj Contemporary Art Centre in Copenhagen in 2004 – entered a darkened room to gaze up at a computerised night sky projected onto a domed ceiling above their heads. Each star in this artificial firmament represented a single stock, which glowed whenever a live Reuters data feed relayed news of trading activity anywhere in the world. Over time, correlations in trading on stocks in the same sector caused individual stars to gravitate together to form galaxies and nebulae. The other key elements of Autogena and Portway's digital cosmos were 'shoals' of artificial organisms that 'fed' on the light emitted by the stars, their numbers waxing and waning with the rhythms of trading. As the programmer of these electronic beings, Cefn Hoile, observes, 'The creatures' relationship with their artificial world of stars is a mirror image of our relationship with the financial markets – they strive to survive, competing with each other in a world whose complexity they are too simple to fathom'.[37] To contemplate the Black Shoals universe is to see the markets as vast, remote, radiant and unknowable (an effect heightened in the work's initial installation when Reuters refused to allow the stars to be tagged with the names of their corresponding companies, rendering the dome a wholly abstract expanse of pulsing light and impenetrable darkness). On this reading, *Black Shoals* is at once an open book, which, like Exhibit 243, *Banca Nazionale del Lavoro*, *Griftopia* and *Chicago Board of Trade II*, promises to shows us everything, and a closed box, which, in a manner akin to *Volatile Smile*, permits us to know and understand nothing. Thinking about Autogena and Portway's installation differently, however, it is possible to argue that the very

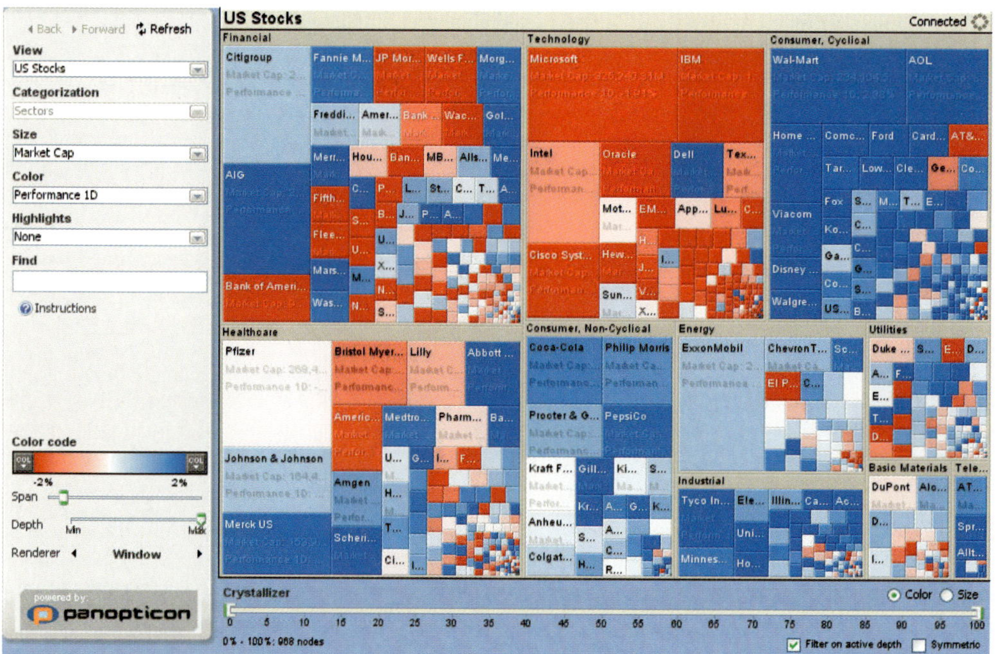

Figure 13

Panopticon 'Tree Map' showing US stocks grouped by sector. The size of each box indicates the market capitalisation for the stock. The colour indicates the price change during the past day.

perfection with which *Black Shoals* distils a view of financial markets as natural, eternal and serenely indifferent to everyday human existence performs a satirical and didactic function, making visible to us not the reality of financial capitalism as such, but rather its own idealised self-image. As Autogena and Portway themselves state, '*Black Shoals* was designed as a kind of parody of the trading desk of the übermensch – the Mount Olympus from which they would survey their creation'.[38] Perhaps what we really see projected in the darkened confines of the Black Shoals planetarium are the flickering dreamscapes of these financial 'masters of the universe'.

Fantasies of total surveillance pervade the contemporary financial imagination, from espousals of the efficient market hypothesis, with its central claim that current prices reflect all available information, to plans to use futures trading to identify terrorist threats (part of the US military's 'total information awareness' initiative),[39] to market visualisation software platforms like the aptly named Map of the Market and Panopticon (Figure 13), which aim to give traders a commanding view of market movements as they unfold. It was this aspiration – to have the most comprehensive and telling array of financial information laid out before one's eyes – which inspired the production of publications like *The Course of the Exchange* in the seventeenth and eighteenth centuries. And its imperatives can be detected today, alongside those sites just mentioned, in the most direct descendants of those early circulars: the stock listings pages that are fixtures of the financial sections of major newspapers, resources that, though long since surpassed for professional purposes by more dynamic forms of visualisation, remain amongst the most familiar instantiations of 'the markets' for the layperson. As we have seen, however, such technical, numerical records of market activity tell only half the story, their abstractions of cold, hard data from the seething mass of buying and selling conveying an impression of order, rationality and objectivity, and eliding the strange, uncanny and chaotic elements of the financial system.

Figure 14

Gordon Cheung, *Revelations X (Apocalypse)* (2009). Laser pyrographic etching, vaporised stock listings on plywood.

Image courtesy Gordon Cheung.

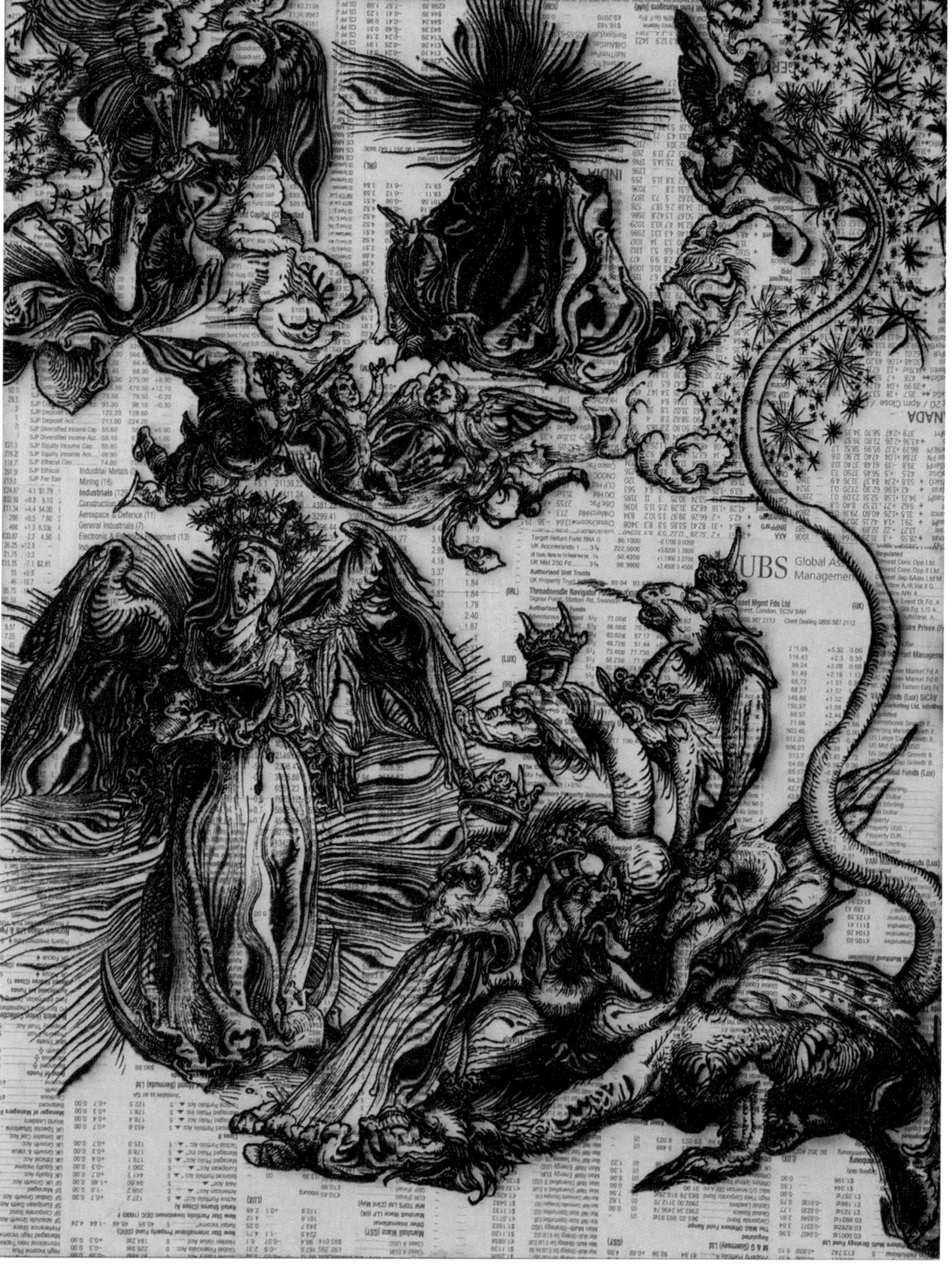

One contemporary artist who aims to bring this shadowy underside of finance to the surface is the British-born Chinese painter and collagist Gordon Cheung. Since the late 1990s, the basic raw materials of Cheung's works have remained consistent: the stock listings pages of the *Financial Times* (*FT*). Cheung's signature method begins with him combining the *FT*'s distinctive pink sheets into a background. He then overlays computer-generated images of chimerical creatures, desolate landscapes and other weird scenes, which lend a surreal, phantasmagoric air to the blank, neutral financial data dimly visible beneath. As he says: 'I'm interested in hallucinatory spaces. The stock market is this place people are chasing after. Like the pot of gold at the end of a rainbow. So I want this "delirious" aspect to the work.'[40] A sense of delirium is especially palpable in a series of prints produced by Cheung in response to the global financial crisis of 2008. In the *Revelations* series (2009), pages of the *FT* are superimposed with digitally distorted versions of Albrecht Dürer's late fifteenth-century woodcut illustrations of scenes from the Book of Revelation. A connoisseur of apocalyptic artistic traditions (earlier works include a series created in response to the lurid apocalyptic visions of the nineteenth-century British painter John Martin), Cheung finds in Dürer's woodcuts 'a classic idea of the end' that at the same time 'capture[s] the global financial crisis in 2008 when some news headlines read "End of Capitalism"'.[41] In the tenth print of the series (Figure 14) a dragon rampages across the densely packed field of stock prices with which Cheung has replaced Dürer's natural backdrop, one of its seven heads (symbolising the seven deadly sins) seemingly tagged 'UBS'. The other prints teem with saints, angels, devils, sea monsters, horned beasts, Babylonian whores and apocalyptic horsemen, their often grotesque forms warped still further by Cheung's digital manipulations.

In adapting religious imagery of sin and judgement to a financial subject, Cheung's series recalls images such as *Jonathan's Coffee House* or Hogarth's *Emblematical Print of the South Sea*, as well as writings by the likes of Defoe, Swift and Pope. Like these eighteenth-century predecessors, Cheung imagines financial markets as environments swept by tumultuous, otherworldly forces that defy rational understanding and leave devastation in their wake. And, as in the eighteenth century, his work signals the amenability to such figurative purposes of an allegorical mode that is also *phantasmagorical*. According to the German critic Walter Benjamin, writing in the 1930s, one of the effects of the rise of capitalism was that emblematic images that once stood for divine or diabolical forces – like the figures in Dürer's woodcuts – came to allegorise the secular enchantments of capitalism itself. Such is Benjamin's interpretation of the 'phantasmagoria', the magic lantern spectacle that rose to popularity in Europe at the end of the eighteenth century. For Benjamin, the procession of ghosts, skeletons and devils projected by the phantasmagoria figured not the archaic beliefs of a premodern, precapitalist past, but rather the strange, fleeting, insubstantial qualities of an emergent capitalist modernity.[42] Suggestively, the etymological roots of 'phantasmagoria' (like those of 'allegory') have been traced to the Greek word *agora*, meaning public place or marketplace. As Margaret Cohen writes: 'one plausible etymology for the *phantasma agoreuein* [is] the ghosts of the public place or marketplace .... The supernatural ... at issue in phantasmagoria is ... the specter *of* the market place in the senses of both firmly located there and generated by it'.[43] It is fitting, then, that in Cheung's work, as elsewhere, supernatural or 'phantasmagoric' imagery provides a figurative vocabulary with which to meet the challenge of making visible the host of unseen entities that populates the financial markets.

This challenge, to put it in different terms, is the one posed by the mounting abstraction and dematerialisation of financial exchange. As we have seen, the prevailing reaction to the abstraction of finance has been a corresponding abstraction of its image. I hope, though, that this chapter has given the lie to a simplistic story in which, once upon a time, in some more innocent age, the image of finance was consistently figurative, transparent, realistic or representational, and only later underwent an alienating abstraction, as trade moved from exchanges, alleyways and coffee houses to brokerages and bucket shops to office blocks and day traders' living rooms, and as the assets traded grew ever more complex and ethereal. On the contrary, an element of abstraction has always been integral to the image of finance – just as abstraction is a constitutive feature of finance itself. By the same token, this abstraction of the image has been accompanied, all along, by a desire to retain traces of the particular, the local, the tangible and the material. And yet: the self-evident fact remains that, to put it very crudely, *Chicago Board of Trade II* is more abstract than *The Inside View of the Royal Exchange*, *Griftopia* more abstract than *Jonathan's Coffee House*, the Panopticon 'Tree Map' more abstract than *The Course of the Exchange*. Abstraction has always been with us, that is, but it has indeed undergone a progressive intensification. The economist Giovanni Arrighi has argued that the last 250 years – a *longue dureé*, inaugurated amidst the speculative clamour of eighteenth-century London – is marked by phases in which financial exchange predominates over the materialities of commodity production and consumption. Each periodic resurgence, however, finds the forms of financial accumulation raised to a higher power: yet more expansive, more pervasive, more abstract.[44] As with finance, so with its image.

Notes

1 A selection of such images is available on the web site of the Harvard Business School's Baker Library: www.library.hbs.edu/hc/cc/stockexchanges.html.

2 Alex Preda, *Framing Finance: The Boundaries of Markets and Modern Capitalism* (Chicago: University of Chicago Press, 2009), p. 66.

3 Attribution of the work is uncertain: the British Museum notes that 'the lettering [in the lower inscription panel] recording that [Jefferyes Hamett] O'Neale etched this plate is probably an error' (see www.britishmuseum.org/research/collection_online/collection_object_details.aspx?objectId=3078490&partId=1&school=13279&page=2227, accessed 28 January 2014).

4 British Museum description, ibid.

5 William Hogarth (whose work features in Chapters 1 and 5) stands as another formative influence on later eighteenth-century satirical printmakers, though Hogarth himself insisted on distinguishing his own rendering of 'character' ('the physical expression of a vice or virtue') from caricature (see Stephen J. Bury, 'British visual satire, 18th–20th centuries', *Benezit Dictionary of Artists*, Oxford Art Online, www.oxfordartonline.com/public/page/benz/themes/BritishSatire, accessed 28 January 2014).

6 Thomas Hobbes, *Leviathan*, ed. Richard Tuck (Cambridge: Cambridge University Press, 1996), p. 174. The attack on the directors appeared in the journal the *Craftsman* (cited in Patrick Brantlinger, *Fictions of State: Culture and Credit in Britain, 1694–1994* (Ithaca: Cornell University Press, 1996), p. 60).

7 For examples, see www.library.hbs.edu/hc/cc/moneydevil.html.

8 Alexander Pope, *An Epistle to Allen Lord Bathurst*, in Pat Rogers (ed.), *Alexander Pope: Selected Poetry* (Oxford: Oxford University Press, 1996), p. 87, lines 369–74.

9 Mary Poovey, *Genres of the Credit Economy: Mediating Value in Eighteenth- and Nineteenth-Century Britain* (Chicago: University of Chicago Press, 2008), pp. 125–6.

10 Ibid., p. 31.

11 See Urs Stäheli, *Spectacular Speculation: Thrills, the Economy and Popular Discourse*, trans. Eric Savoth (2007; Stanford: Stanford University Press, 2013), pp. 197–8.

12 Preda, *Framing Finance*, pp. 142–3.

13 Stäheli, *Spectacular Speculation*, p. 211.

14 Peter Knight, 'Reading the ticker tape in the late nineteenth-century American market', *Journal of Cultural Economy* 6:1 (2013), 45–62, p. 52.

15 See Stäheli, *Spectacular Speculation*, pp. 208, 224, 227–8; Knight, 'Reading the ticker tape', p. 50.

16 Stäheli, *Spectacular Speculation*, p. 218.

17 Richard Wyckoff (Rollo Tape, pseudo.), *Studies in Tape Reading* (New York: Ticker Publishing, 1910), p. 5; quoted in Stäheli, *Spectacular Speculation*, p. 222.

18 John Kenneth Galbraith, *The Great Crash 1929* (1954; London: Penguin, 2009), p. 85.

19 On the contemporary prevalence of chartism and its links to supernatural belief systems (some actively propounded by those in the field), see Paul Crosthwaite, 'Phantasmagoric finance: Crisis and the supernatural in contemporary finance culture', in Paul Crosthwaite (ed.), *Criticism, Crisis and Contemporary Narrative: Textual Horizons in an Age of Global Risk* (London: Routledge, 2011), pp. 178–200, esp. pp. 184–6.

20 H. J. Wolf, *Studies in Stock Speculation* (1924; Burlington, VT: Fraser, 1966), p. 96; quoted in Stäheli, Spectacular Speculation, p. 229.

21 Mark C. Taylor, *Confidence Games: Money and Markets in a World Without Redemption* (Chicago: University of Chicago Press, 2004), p. 163.

22 Y. Yeadon, 'Occasional notes on Mark Lombardi's *Banca Nazionale del Lavoro, Reagan, Bush, Thatcher and the Arming of Iraq, c. 1979–1990, 3rd Version*', *Rethinking Marxism* 15:3 (2003): 343–9, pp. 344–5.

23 'The art of Griftopia' (William Powhida in conversation with Felix Salmon and Blake Gopnik), *Reuters*, 2 December 2011, http://blogs.reuters.com/felix-salmon/2011/12/02/the-art-of-griftopia/, accessed 28 January 2014.

24 Fredric Jameson, *Postmodernism, or, The Cultural Logic of Late Capitalism* (London: Verso, 1991), p. 38.

25 Rachel Taylor, '*Chicago Board of Trade II*', Tate Online, 2004, par. 3, www.tate.org.uk/servlet/ViewWork?workid=27067&tabview=text, accessed 28 January 2014.

26 Ibid., par. 3.

27 Jameson, *Postmodernism*, pp. 43, 44.

28 Ibid., p. 44.

29 Ibid., p. 38.

30 Ibid., p. 37.

31 Ibid.

32 The gradual thinning out of the pit at the Chicago Board of Trade in favour of electronic trading platforms is charted in Caitlin Zaloom, *Out of the Pits: Traders and Technology from Chicago to London* (Chicago: University of Chicago Press, 2006). The process has continued apace over more recent years.

33 Frank Wagner, exhibition catalogue for *Volatile Smile*, Neue Gesellschaft für Bildende Kunst (New Society for Visual Arts), Berlin, 2011, http://culturehall.com/artwork.html;jsessionid=24704531119640FFC6D48772BAA76EDD?page=19241.

34 See Paul Crosthwaite, 'Is a financial crisis a trauma?', *Cultural Critique* 82 (2012), 34–67.

35 Donald MacKenzie, *An Engine, Not a Camera: How Financial Models Shape Markets* (Cambridge, MA: MIT Press, 2006), pp. 202, 206, 205, emphasis in original.

36 On the role of Black-Scholes-Merton in 1987 and 1998, see MacKenzie, *An Engine, Not a Camera*, Chapters 7 and 8. On 2008, see Ian Stewart, 'The mathematical equation that caused the banks to crash', *Observer*, 12 February 2012, www.theguardian.com/science/2012/feb/12/black-scholes-equation-credit-crunch, accessed 28 January 2014.

37 Quoted in Rita Raley, *Tactical Media* (Minneapolis, MN: University of Minnesota Press, 2009), p. 148.

38 Lise Autogena and Joshua Portway, 'Thoughts behind the project', www.blackshoals.net/Thoughts.html, accessed 28 January 2014.

39 On this plan for a so-called 'Policy Analysis Market', see Geoff Lightfoot and Simon Lilley, 'The glass beads of global war: Dealing, death and the Policy Analysis Market', *Critical Perspectives on International Business* 3:1 (2007), 83–100.

40 Quoted in Tim Birch, 'Breathing space: Regarding Gordon Cheung, Artist in Residence at the Chinese Arts Centre', *City Life*, May 2004, www.gordoncheung.com/PAGES/archive/Arc_Press_Reviews/Rev_CityLife_May04.html, accessed 28 January 2014.

41 Artist's statement at www.facebook.com/media/set/?set=a.10151669665573315.1073741828.46697908314&type=1, accessed 28 January 2014.

42 Walter Benjamin, 'Paris, capital of the nineteenth century: Exposé of 1939', in *The Arcades Project*, trans. Howard Eiland and Kevin McLaughlin (Cambridge, MA: Belknap Press of Harvard University Press, 1999), pp. 14–26, p. 26.

43 Margaret Cohen, 'Benjamin's phantasmagoria: *The Arcades Project*', in David S. Ferris (ed.), *The Cambridge Companion to Walter Benjamin* (Cambridge: Cambridge University Press), p. 209, emphasis in original.

44 See Giovanni Arrighi, *The Long Twentieth Century: Money, Power and the Origins of Our Times*, 2nd edn (London: Verso, 2009). See also the fascinating use made of Arrighi's ideas in Fredric Jameson, 'Culture and finance capital', *Critical Inquiry* 24:1 (1997), 246–65, and Ian Baucom, *Specters of the Atlantic: Finance Capital, Slavery and the Philosophy of History* (Durham, NC: Duke University Press, 2005).

Channels and codes, rails and freight: can you hear me now?

Bill Maurer

When you care about transmission, the question of value recedes—that is, the question of what value is, where it comes from. All you care about, if you care about transmission, is how it gets from A to B to C without degrading, evaporating, how it endures over time and space. This is a very particular kind of problem. Guided by payments industry professionals, as well as by social scientists and theorists concerned to elucidate the material infrastructures of the economy, this is how I have begun to see the market. I see channels and codes, rails and freight carried over those rails. This is what I see when I see money: a series of interlocking infrastructures for the acceptance and transmission of value.

Nota bene: the question of infrastructure does not enter into the realm of representation, that old saw that has occupied commentators, philosophers and artists of money forever and ever. When the focus is on how money gets moved around, then how money 'represents' value is irrelevant. Infrastructure is about pipes and tubes, 'rails', in the words of my interlocutors in payments, how they are built, the switches that connect them, the portals into them. And the noisiness, the cacophony, of the freight train.

The modal payment rails since the 1950s have been the interbank card networks (those associations that grew into Visa and MasterCard) as well as the publicly mandated infrastructures that sit alongside them (in the United States, the Automated Clearing House, majority-owned by the US Federal Reserve). But there are new rails being built as we speak. For one thing, entire swathes of large continents – central Africa! – not yet connected into the global electronic network facilitating payments, are seeing a new race to build, to own and to toll the channels that would carry money. The race is on. Will it be Citi? Visa? A public entity? China's UnionPay? Payments rails are not merely metaphorically associated with trains: their wires often follow the tracks. If China is building a road network through central Africa, will it lay the payment rails alongside?

For another thing, entirely new kinds of rails are being built, with professionals and regulators alike having to pause and ask, 'Wait. Is *this* a new payments rail? Is *that*?' Here is an example: mobile phone airtime. Imagine one box consisting of the servers, fibre optic and copper cables, software and database architecture that keep track of electronic credits, and retail shops that accept paper currency in exchange for paper cards with numeric codes on them. Those codes activate credits usable for voice and data communication. These connect to another box, the mobile network communications towers that transmit information between their servers and that take in these electronic credits in exchange for bandwidth and time in their channel. Both connect to a third box, the financial system, the banks, when the airtime distributor settles up with the mobile network operator. Now, as long as that connection to the third box is there, then – a payments expert would say – this is just a system for distributing a product paid for in money, and it is not in itself a new channel for the transit of money.

We have known for several years now that people use airtime itself as a currency, however. They do not have to 'cash out' or turn airtime back into state-issued money in order to

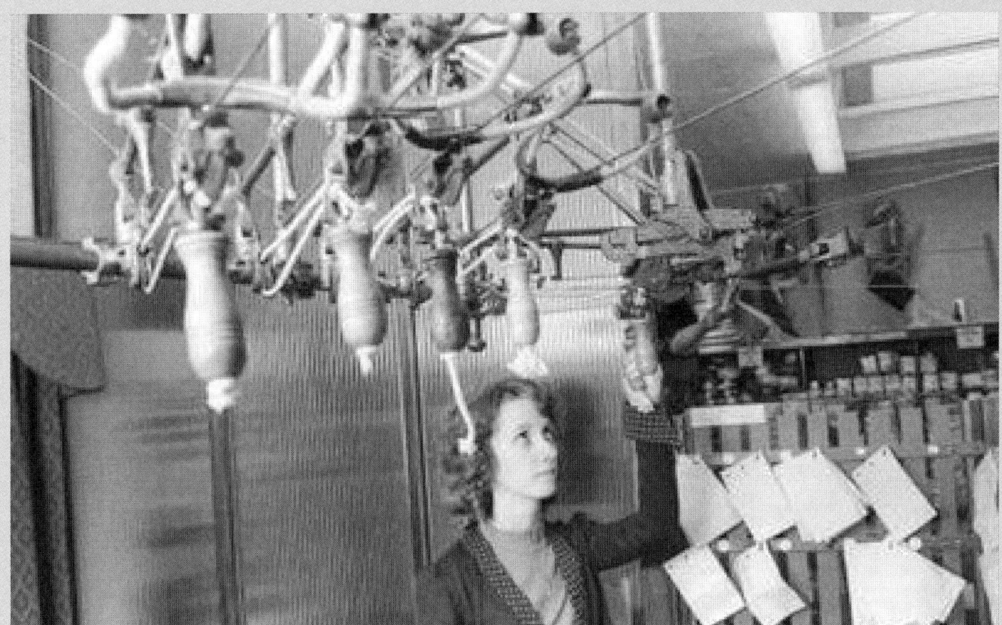

Figure 1

Anscombes Cash Railway, Anscombes Department Store, Harpenden, 1974.

Image courtesy of St Albans Museum. With thanks to Jane Guyer and her work on cash railways for inspiring the image selection.

exchange airtime credits with each other, or use them in something we can call barter if it makes us feel better but really is basically the use of airtime in lieu of state-issued currency.

In lieu of. This is a regulator's words. If the freight carried over a system is used in lieu of money, then the system is 'dangerously close' in form and function to a payment rail. Dangerously, because in that case, the state has an obligation to treat it as a regulated entity, make sure it is licensed, and levy fines or prison time or both if it is operating in violation of statute.

The state continues to do a very good job of ensuring its currency's place in the hierarchy of money. (Dwolla, for a time the only payments company that allowed a person to trade US dollars for Bitcoins, 'rides the rails' of the Automated Clearing House. Its Bitcoin account was seized in May 2013 by the US Department of Homeland Security for being an unlicensed money service business. As I said: the state continues to do a good job indeed.)

Now, let's say you are trying to set up an alternative rail. What do you have to do to comply with the state's desire to control its position in that hierarchy? Aside from registration and payment of fees for licensing, your chief obligation is to create and maintain records. Records-keeping. Transactional databases.

That starts to make things interesting.

Payment regulations in the global North suture any potentially alternative currency riding any potentially alternative rail into the rest of 'the economy' by requiring transactional records. In the United States, you are even supposed to report barter income, in a US dollar equivalent, on your federal income tax returns. Says the Internal Revenue Service: 'it's never too soon, or too late, to start good recordkeeping habits. You should keep all receipts, payment information and tax information in one location to make filing your taxes easier when the time comes.'[1]

Money, of course, is nothing but a bookkeeping operation.

So what happens if people, systems, infrastructures start up their own set of transactional databases? And then seek to trade against the obligations represented in those databases with their own token? In that situation, the distinction between network infrastructure maintaining the transactional database and the token built on the obligations recorded therein – also maintained in the same network infrastructure – starts to collapse.

When I see the market today, I see a proliferation of such transactional databases, privately held though – it turns out – subject to government scrutiny, not as entirely walled off as we might have thought. When Edward Snowden revealed that the US National Security Agency had entered into agreements with the main internet service and telecommunications companies like Google and AT&T to view information in their databases, the big news was privacy, surveillance, government abuse of power. As I write, some companies are fighting the US government in court so that they may disclose government data requests.

The sleeper story is the potential for money making in these networked systems of transactional data. Not monetisation of the data, or profit-making; but the making of a set of alternative, private currencies carried over closed-loop, alternative rails.

The gatekeeper – the regulator – would say: you can make alternative tokens using Facebook or set up a currency based on your reputation in an online marketplace or connections in a computer-mediated social network. I don't care about whether that new token actually serves as a store of value – that's not my job. You are free to speculate on and trade with anything you like. But as soon as you have a secondary market in that token – trading tokens for US dollars or trading tokens for other tokens – then you're entering my domain. Then you are a payment system. Then I want to see your records because then, and only then, you have become an infrastructure for the transmission of value. A rail.

From the regulator's point of view, such a system would be merely a new channel. Ultimately, no matter what you call it, the code going through that channel remains the same, even if it looks different: if it is traded with other codes, state-issued or otherwise, it is serving in lieu of money. Payment is therefore the choke-point for the definition of money.

The problem is – and we know this from semiotics, we know this from communications theory, we know this from Actor Network Theory and from civil engineering – the channel never just carries the code. It is not a simple intermediary or bridge. There are holes in it, portals and switches and connections all over the so-called system. There are also toll-seekers and toll-takers at every junction. There is noise on the line. Rails and channels work as intermediaries only when they can filter out that noise and transit freight or fluid seamlessly, smoothly, silently.

Ever heard a silent railway or aqueduct?

Perhaps we need to hear rather than see the market and money.

Notes

1 IRS Video, *Do You Barter?* (with transcript) available at http://www.irsvideos.gov/SmallBusinessTaxpayer/BusinessIncome/DoYouBarter, accessed 21 September 2013.

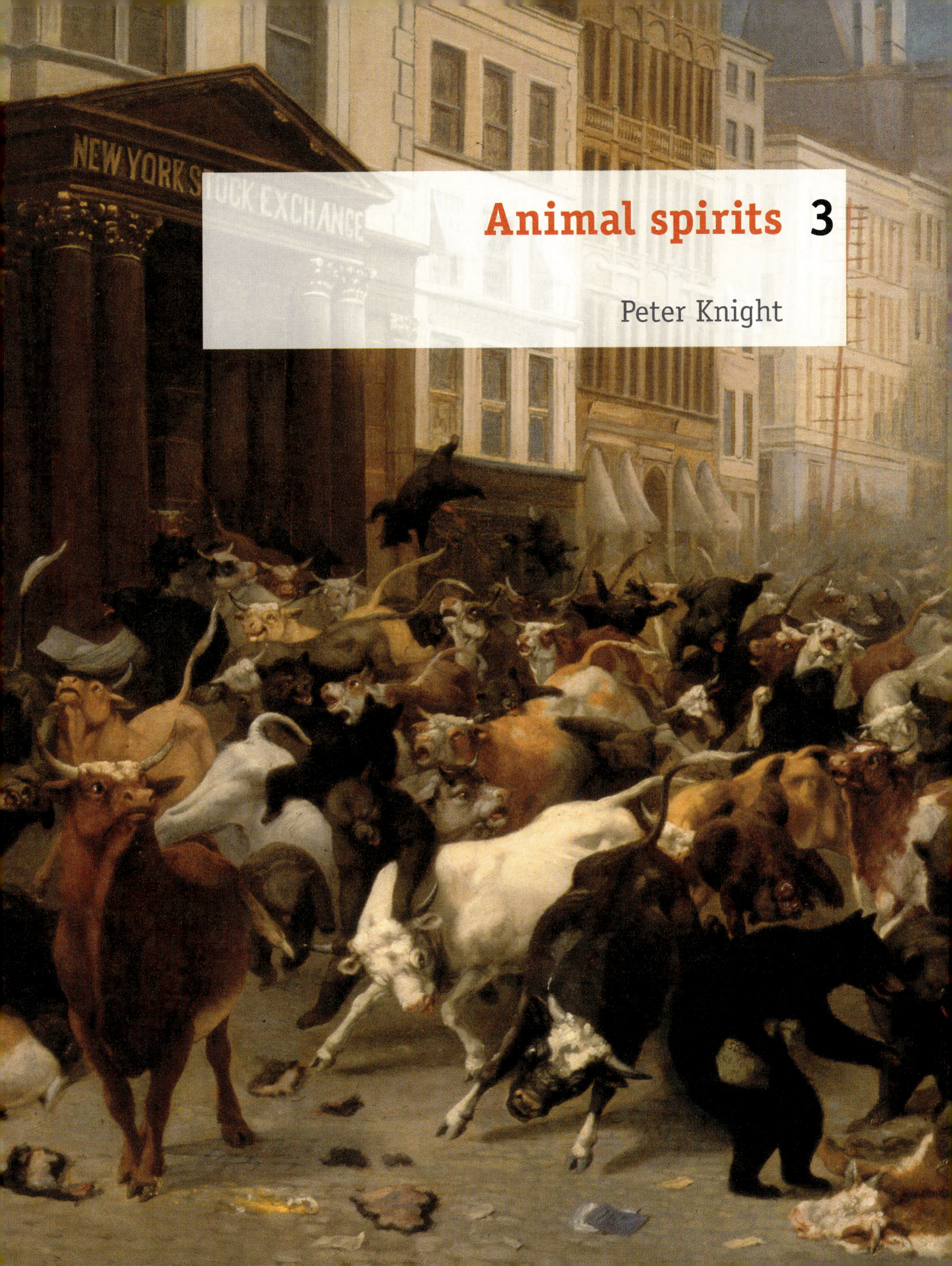

Animal spirits 3

Peter Knight

Animal spirits

Peter Knight

As the financial market shifted from the daily theatre of an actual marketplace in the eighteenth century to an increasingly anonymous, disembodied and deterritorialised circuit of exchange in the nineteenth century, it became harder to imagine – let alone depict – in its entirety. The 'Framing finance' and 'Money shot' sections of this book (Chapters 2 and 4 respectively) demonstrate how one strain of visual imagery has engaged repeatedly with the very idea of the increasing abstraction of finance. In contrast the 'Animal spirits' section considers a different strand of figural shorthand, one that asks not what or where the market is, but rather *who* the market is. At times an individual speculator – heroic or villainous – has been made to stand in visually for the vast confusion of the entire market, representing the animating spirit that operates the economic machinery and makes it tick. At others the focus has been not on an individual titan or devil standing behind the spectacle of finance and pulling its strings, but on the dissolution of individual rationality in the madness of crowds during a panic. Market players, both insiders and outsiders, have at times come to be seen as a herd of wild beasts moved by those 'animal spirits' of nervous excitement that, in J.M. Keynes's famous phrase, make financial capitalism tick.[1] Finally, the market itself has come to be thought of as a person, more often than not an omniscient but irascible deity who must be placated at all costs.

Figure 1

Wind-Kraamer en Grossier ('The Wholesale Wind-Peddler's Fair'), from *Het groote Tafereel der Dwaasheid* ('The Great Mirror of Folly') (Amsterdam, 1720).

The speculator

There is a long tradition of embodying the complexity of the market in an individual, from satirical prints of the archetype of the deceptive stockjobber in the eighteenth century, to lionising portraits of the Napoleons of Wall Street in the late nineteenth century, and through to the personification of the treachery of finance in the shape of, for example, Bernie Madoff in the crisis of 2008. *Het groote Tafereel der Dwaasheid* ('The Great Mirror of Folly'), a Dutch collection of satirical prints and writings published as an immediate response to the financial crises that spread across Europe in 1720 as a result of the collapse of the South Sea Bubble, included cartoons such as *Wind-Kraamer en Grossier* ('The Wholesale Wind-Peddler's Fair') (Figure 1). A speculator, seated on a cloud with a heavenly head blowing hot air that emerges as if out of his posterior, is accompanied by a man using a pair of bellows to send aloft a cat floating from four balloons. The 'wind-peddler' distributes paper securities in an image that suggests the very essence of inflationary bubbles. *Anatomie Der Wind-Negotie* ('Anatomy of the Wind Trade'), another broadside from the same volume, depicts the autopsy of a merchant who has died of wind, the prostrate figure embodying the dangers of a speculative economy (Figure 2).

In contrast a French cartoon of 1784 instead depicts the type of the 'Spéculateur' as a wretched specimen who has fallen on hard times, presumably as a result of being seduced into unwise financial dealings (Figure 3).

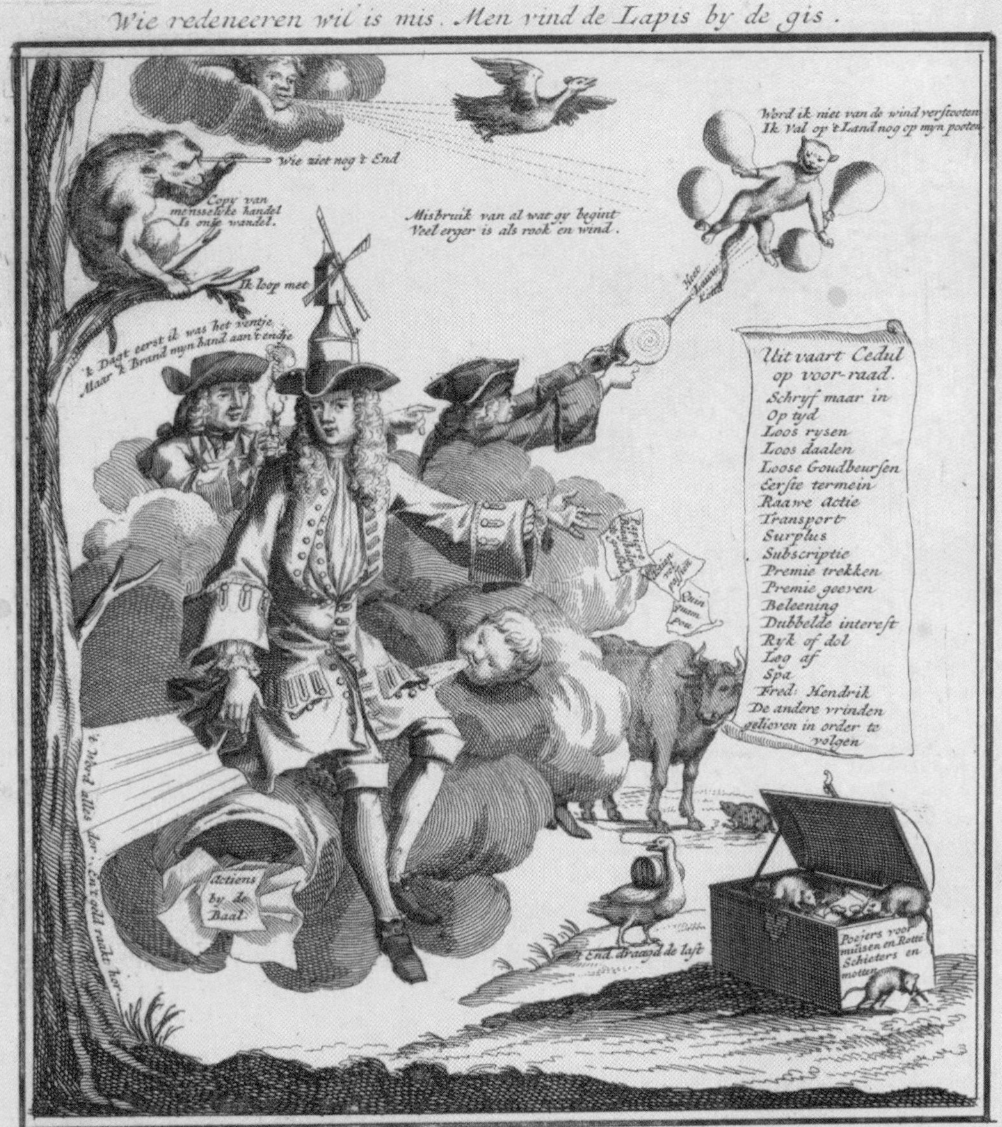
Wie redeneeren wil is mis. Men vind de Lapis by de gis.
Wie ziet nog 't End
Copy van menschelyke handel Is onse wandel.
Misbruik van al wat gy begint Veel erger is als rook en wind.
Word ik niet van de wind verstooten Ik Val op 't Land nog op myn pooten
Ik loop mee
'k Dagt eerst ik was het ventje, Maar 't Brand myn hand aan 't endje
Uit vaart Cedul op voor-raad.
Schryf maar in
Op tyd
Loos rysen
Loos daalen
Loose Goudbeursen
Eerste termein
Raawe Actie
Transport
Surplus
Subscriptie
Premie trekken
Premie geeven
Beleening
Dubbelde interest
Ryk of dol
Leg af
Spa
Fred: Hendrik
De andere vrinden gelieven in order te volgen
Actiens by de Baal
't End draagd de last
Poejers voor muisen en Rotte Schieters en motten
KERMIS WIND-KRAAMER EN GROSSIER
Wind is 't begin; wind is het end;
Myn kussen en myn fondement:
Wie zou van Nooren en van Lappen,
Als windverkoopers, nu veel snappen!
Een Modese afgod van de Wind
Een ryke klater goudmyn vind:
Dog niemand wil daar meer naar steeken;
Nog van verlauwden handel spreeken:
't Welk menig dolkop hollen dee
Naar buurman Rykert over Zee,
Die de afgevalle patriotten
Geen voet wou wyken in't bedotten;
En vies van Misselyke ziep,
Naar 't onbekende Zuiden liep;
Daar hy gelukkig ging ontdekken
Utopia, of 't hol der gekken.
Een ander buur draafd naar 't nieu West,
En droomd goude eyren uit dat nest
Te lichten; iets dat daar niet in is:
Inbeelding thans het grootst gewin is.
Daar hebje nu de drie grossiers,
Gevolgd van veele winkeliers,
Of kraamers, al zo fel in't blaasen
Straks heb je 't goojen met de glaasen
'k Moet lachen: wat of 't bier al doet?
Zeid de verkeerder: o! 't was goet,
Quam hier de Esopise verdichting
Voor veele baselaars tot stichting;
De pad zich groot maakt by de koe;
Maar barst van wind, door blaasen moe.
Q: Verwoude

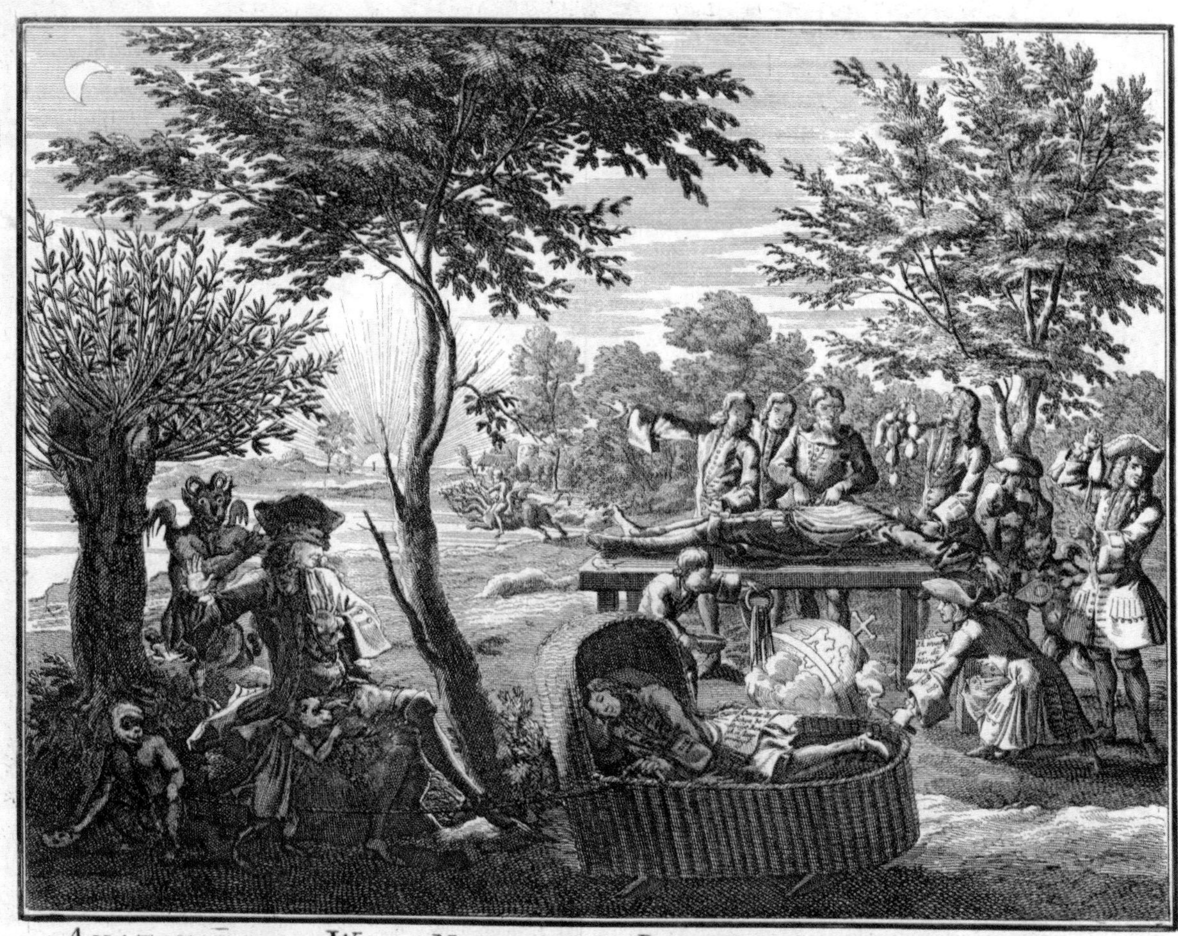

ANATOMIE DER WIND-NEGOTIE, OF BOMBARIO VOOR DEN DROMMEL.

Een Actie-Heer, die d' Actie-wind
Had by Scheeps-ladings ingeslagen,
Leid hier nu Stom, en Doof, en Blind,
En zonder ergens naar te vragen;
Geen wonder, want hy is van kant,
Daar één van Hipokrates bazen,
In 't zoeken van zyn ingewand,
Niets vind dan risten Varkens-blazen,
En oordeeld op zyn kunst gewis,
Dat hy van Wind gesturven is.

Daar word 'er een in slaap gewiegt,
Die toe gedekt met de Actie-deken,
Niet denkt dat hem 't Bedrog bedriegt;
Wyl Lauw de Wereld aan komt steken
Met 't vuur van Waan en Dolligheid,
't Geen deftig smookt, daar ondertuszen
Eenvouwdigheid te loos misleid,
't Met weinig water uit wil bluszen;
Want Monsieur Drommel helpt die kwant,
Waar door de Wereld raakt in brant;

Terwyl den Nikker zyn Monfreer,
Ten dienst van zyn getrouwe vrinden,
Niet minder mede is in de weer,
Om Loshards oogen te verblinden,
Terwyl dat de Aap zyn zakken plukt,
Om zoetjes 't geld daar uit te pluizen;
En zo die aanslag hem mislukt,
Dan naar Vianen te verhuizen,
Daar hy het groot geselschap vind,
Van Actie-Heren zonder splint.

Daar Held Bombario ter vlugt,
Zig op zyn Hofstee gaat bedekken,
Beängst, Bekommerd, en Bedugt,
Dat eens een party Actie-gekken,
Door 't geld verlies als desperaat,
Hem van elkand'ren mogten scheuren,
En 't zou niet voegen by zyn staat,
Hoewel het wel eens kon gebeuren;
Dies rend hy op zyn Hydra voort,
Tot 't eind Hem, en zyne Acties smoord.

Figure 2

Anatomie Der Wind-Negotie ('Anatomy of the Wind Trade'), from *Het groote Tafereel der Dwaasheid* ('The Great Mirror of Folly') (Amsterdam, 1720).

© Trustees of the British Museum.

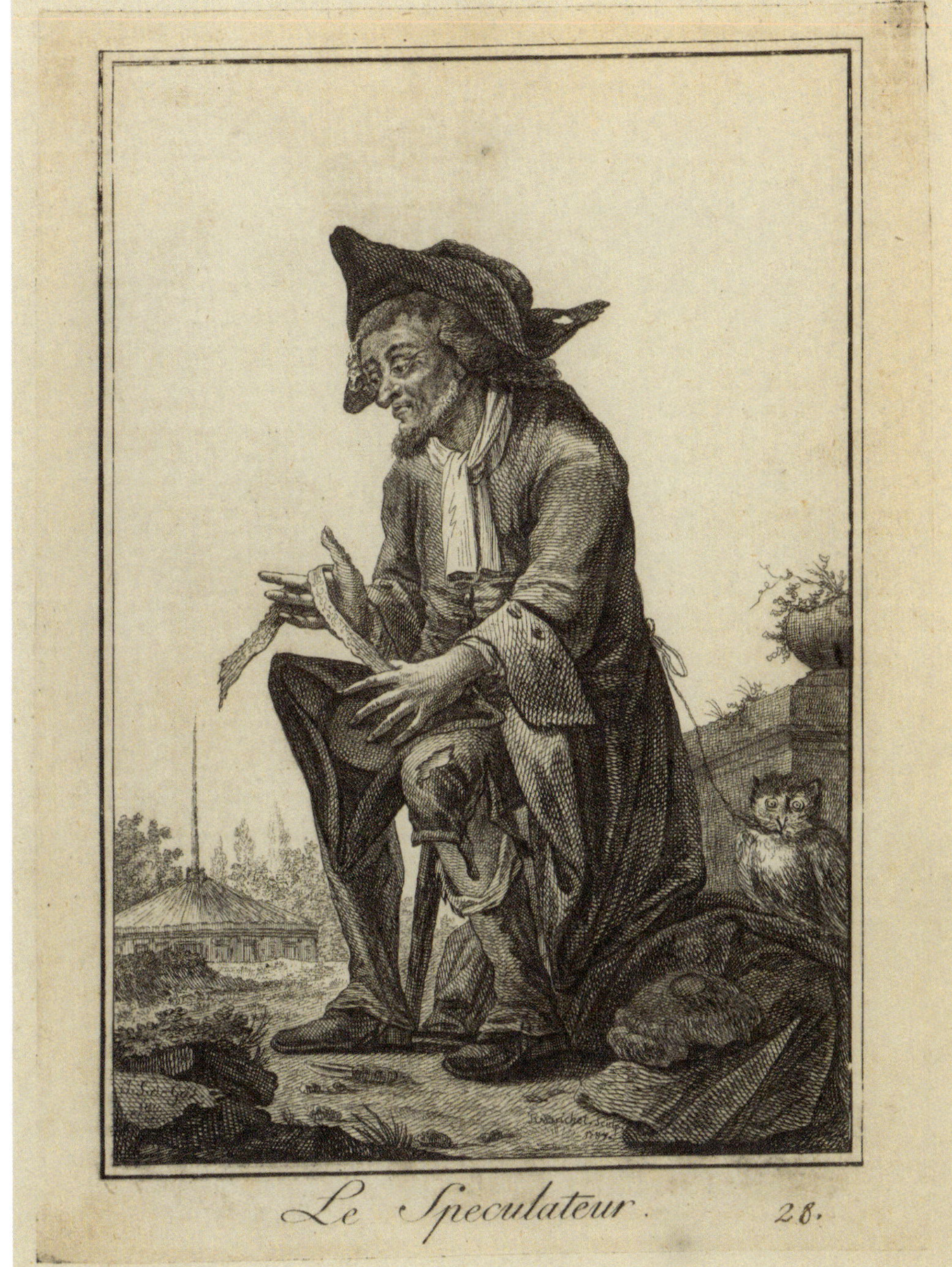

Figure 3

Robert Brichet, *Le Spéculateur*. Plate 28 from *Exercises d'Imagination de Différents Caractères et Formes Humaines* (Augsburg, 1784–85).

Bleichroeder Print Collection, Kress Collection. Baker Library Historical Collections, Harvard Business School (olvwork308310).

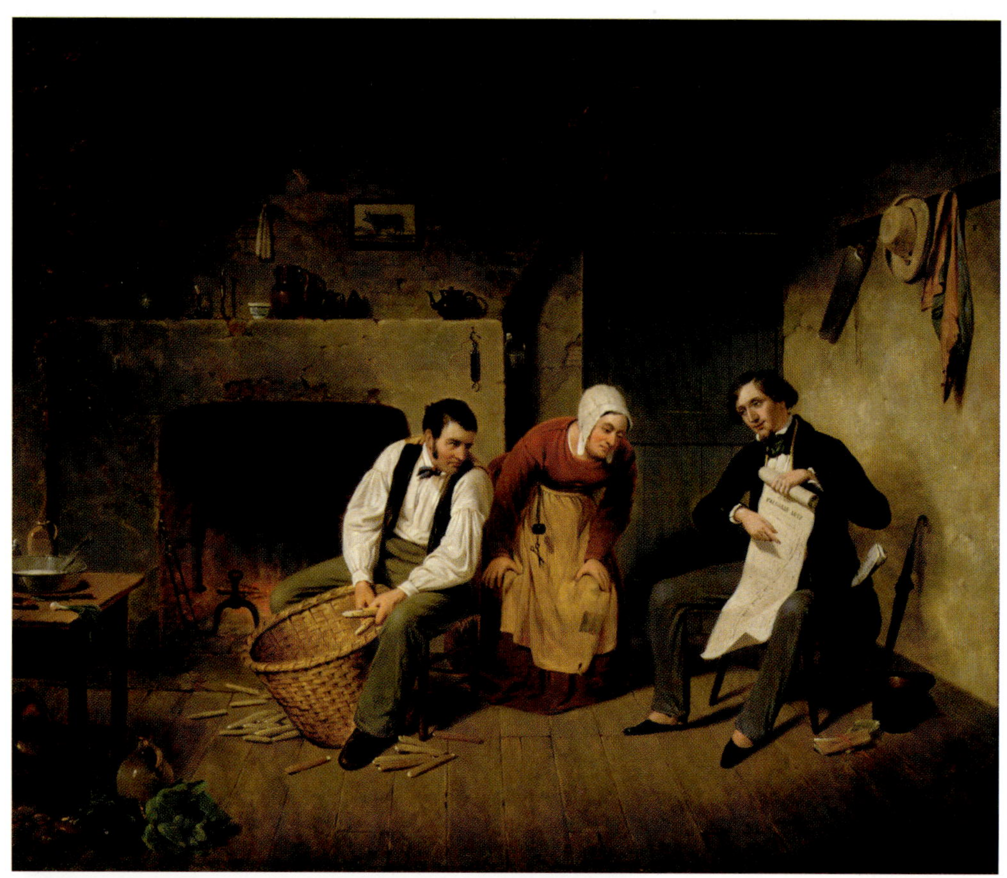

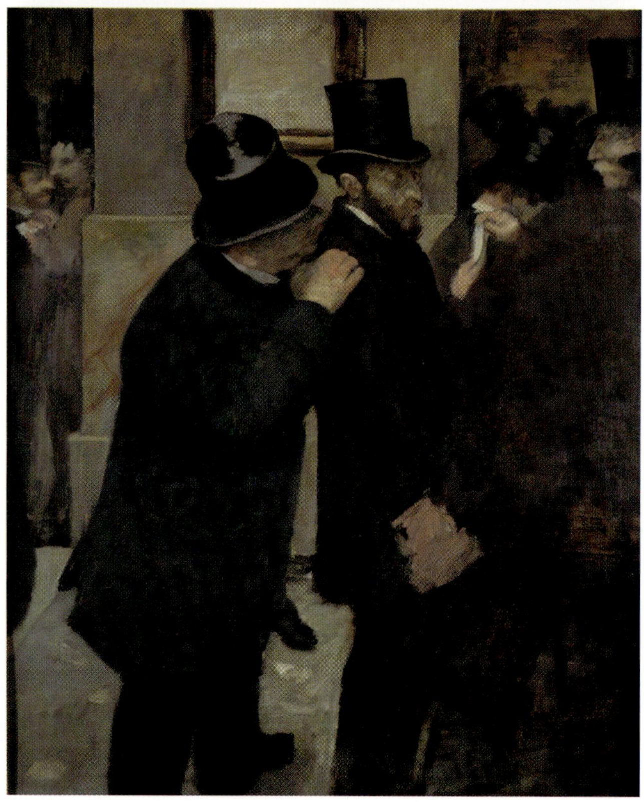

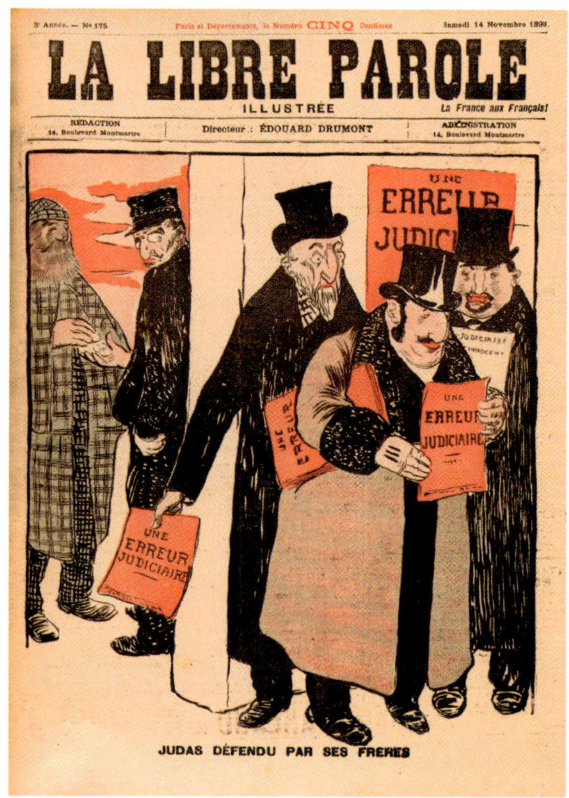

3e Année. — No 175 | Paris et Départements, le Numéro CINQ Centimes | Samedi 14 Novembre 1896.

LA LIBRE PAROLE

ILLUSTRÉE

La France aux Français!

REDACTION
14, Boulevard Montmartre

Directeur : ÉDOUARD DRUMONT

ADMINISTRATION
14, Boulevard Montmartre

JUDAS DÉFENDU PAR SES FRERES

Figure 4

Francis William Edmonds, *The Speculator* (1852).

Smithsonian American Art Museum.

Figure 5

Edgar Degas, *Portraits, At the Stock Exchange* (1879). Paris, Musée d'Orsay.

Figure 6

Judas défendu par ses frères (*Judas Defended by His Brethren*) *La Libre Parole* (no. 175, 14 November 1896).

Dreyfus Collection, David M. Rubenstein Rare Book & Manuscript Library, Duke University.

When not a buffoon or a degenerate, the figure of the speculator in the eighteenth century – as a stand-in for the market as a whole – was seen as a dangerous threat to the social order. The possibility of the sudden reversal of the natural hierarchy through the sudden creation or panicked loss of great fortunes was equated with the immoral risks of gambling, and more often than not the speculator was simply depicted as an outsider (as Dutch or French in British depictions in the eighteenth century, for example).[2] In the American painter Francis Edmonds's *The Speculator* (1852) (Figure 4), a simple country couple are distracted from their humble productive labour of shucking corn into a hand-woven basket by a foppish city slicker who had entered this sentimental space to tempt them with real estate speculation (the paper he unfurls before the couple and the viewer of the painting offers '1000 Valuable Lots on Rail Road Ave.').[3]

The hearth and the emblematic labour of self-sufficiency is at the visual and symbolic centre of this depiction of the classic rugged individualism of the nineteenth-century American frontier, but an outsider in the frame draws the attention of the couple and the painting's audience toward the seductive possibility of getting 'something for nothing', wealth generated from the speculative increase of value on paper. The actual market might be thousands of miles from this frontier homestead, but the temptation of speculative capitalism – personified by the anonymous stranger who might turn out to be a con man – invades this domestic haven. Edmonds indeed had a keen sense of the ligatures of finance that stretch from the rural backwater to Wall Street: not only was he an accomplished genre painter, but he also served on the board of the New York and Erie Railroad in the 1840s (the line that came to be known as the 'Scarlet Woman of Wall Street' for its seemingly endless financial scandals). Edmonds was also treasurer of the Mechanics' Bank in New York from 1839 to 1855, a period between the two great financial panics of 1837 and 1857, in which ordinary Americans struggled to stay afloat in the turbulent seas of mercantile capitalism. The realism of the painting's Dutch-inspired still life elements (e.g. the cabbage, cooking pot and glass jar in the left foreground) contrast with the gesture towards *trompe l'oeil* with the railroad real estate plan that the speculator unfurls.[4]

If the market is at times depicted in the guise of an archetypal speculator, who is figured as an outsider, then it comes as little surprise to find that satirical cartoons and paintings in the eighteenth and nineteenth centuries repeatedly fall back on the traditional prejudiced association of Jewishness with financial treachery. Even Degas' painting *Portraits, At the Stock Exchange* (1879) has recognisably anti-Semitic overtones, with its depiction of the Jewish banker Ernest May (Figure 5).

The hint of anti-Semitism in the painting is made manifest in *Judas défendu par ses frères* (*Judas Defended by His Brethren*) (Figure 6), a satirical print published in the journal *La Libre Parole* in 1899 that visually references the Degas composition in making its anti-Semitic anti-Dreyfusard attack (Degas himself was in the anti-Dreyfusard camp). Although

May was an art collector and benefactor to the artist, Degas' caricaturish rendition not only emphasises the central figure's stereotyped Jewish features but also constructs a scene suggestive of a shadowy financial conspiracy in which a whispered rumour is passed over May's shoulder and a note is slid into the latter's hand from the figure on the right, while a second pairing are glimpsed in close consort in the background.

Figure 7

Edgar Degas, *A Cotton Office in New Orleans* (1873). Pau, Musée des Beaux Arts.

This work is in contrast to Degas' earlier painting *A Cotton Office in New Orleans* (1873) (Figure 7) that presents speculative capitalism as a far less sinister affair, with the cotton traders as relaxed and self-possessed bourgeois gentlemen. Although there is a serenity and smoothness in the rendition of the individual traders (Degas' concession to the taste of his prospective buyer was a more finished *facture* than the original sketch version), the composition is oddly asymmetrical. The businessmen (several of whom are portraits of Degas' own family members) are spatially dispersed and seemingly isolated from one another as they are each absorbed in their own contemplation. In this way the painting evokes not so much the local, personal and kinship interaction of the small-scale family firm as the emergence in the nineteenth century of a geographically dispersed and impersonal global financial market for cotton futures.[5] The other difference between the two paintings, of course, is that at the centre of the earlier painting is the actual physical material of raw cotton itself, whereas in the latter one all we have is the suggestion of the ethically murky exchange of insider information. In between the two paintings being executed the bank owned by Degas' father had fallen on hard times, and Degas' own faith in the value of speculative capitalism had been shaken when his risky venture to sell *A Cotton Office in New Orleans* to a Manchester textile manufacturer had fallen through when the latter's business floundered in the financial crash of 1873, a global crisis that also saw the demise of the cotton factor business run by Degas' uncle that was the model for *A Cotton Office*.[6] Degas himself became embittered about the way that artists were forced to think of paintings as speculative commodities, just like cotton itself: 'It's as if pictures were being painted by stock exchange players, by friction from people avid for profit'.[7]

Figure 8

King's Views of the New York Stock Exchange (New York: Moses King, 1898), p. 1.

During the course of the nineteenth century the image of the stock broker slowly became more respectable, as speculation in the market was rhetorically distinguished from gambling. The idea of the stock market as a legitimate space of economic endeavour was in part created by those who wanted to think of themselves as financial professionals able to perceive opportunities and shoulder risk, and who were to be distinguished from the reckless amateurs taking a punt. The image these stock market insiders wanted to present to the public was one of prudence, efficiency and moral rectitude, downplaying the traditional archetype of the stockjobbing villain. Popular manuals on investment such as Samuel Nelson's *ABC of Wall Street* (1900), for example, preferred to show Wall Street as a calm zone, with its leisurely vistas of Wall Street, Broad Street and the exterior of the New York Stock Exchange (NYSE) building, along with depopulated views of the interior of the Exchange with its architectural harmony and dignified decoration that gives no hint

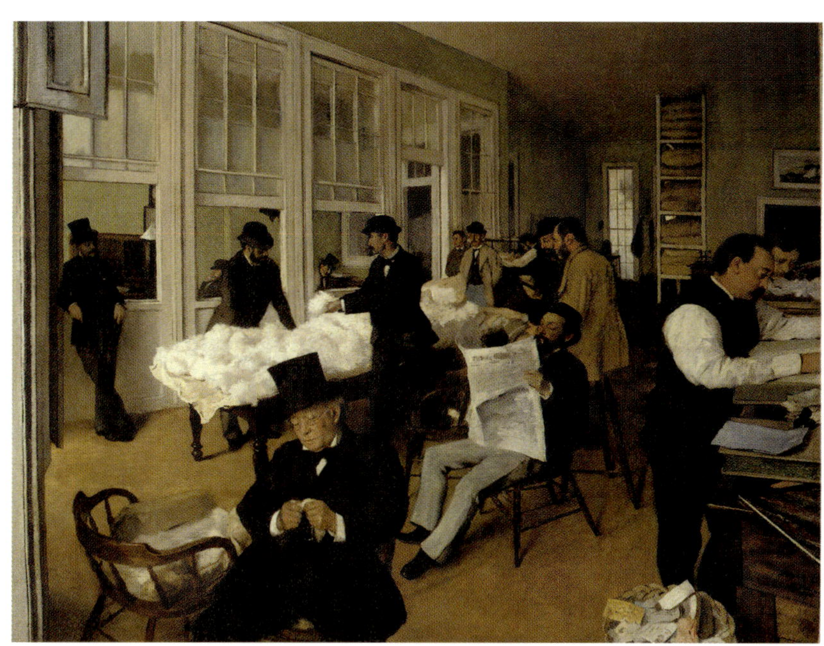

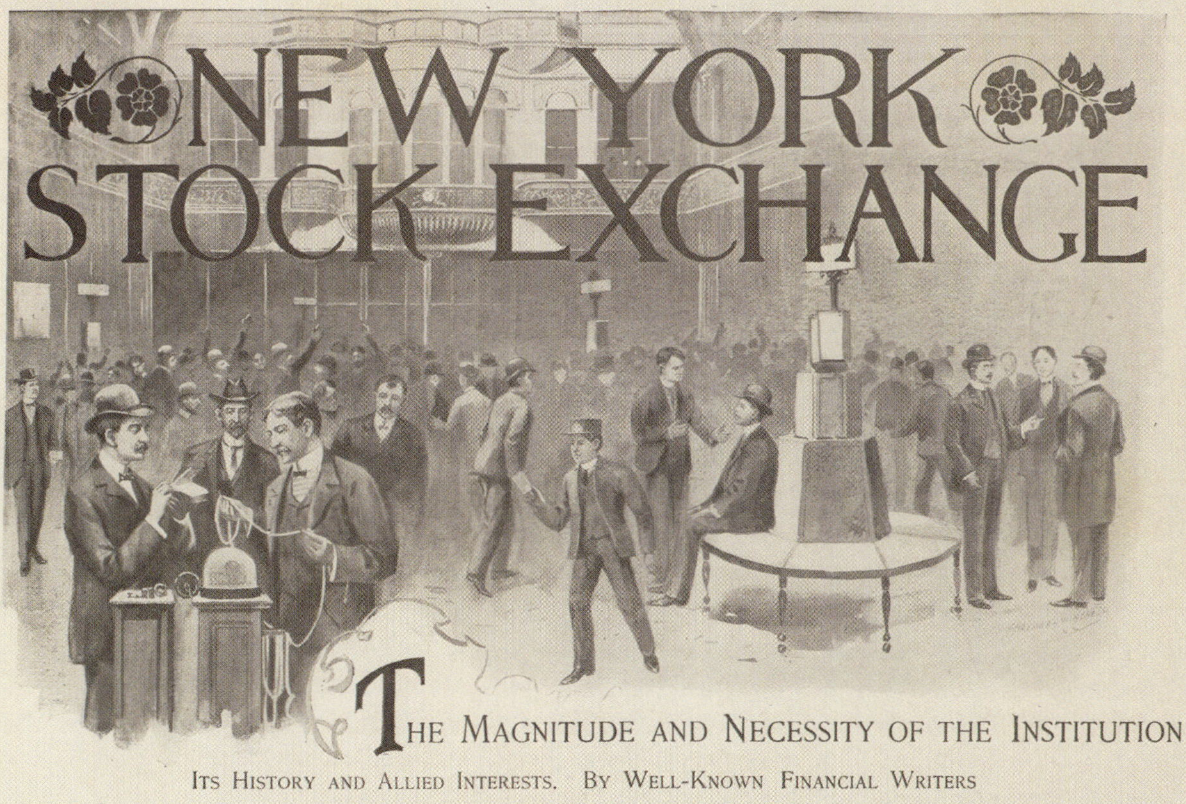

NEW YORK STOCK EXCHANGE

THE MAGNITUDE AND NECESSITY OF THE INSTITUTION

ITS HISTORY AND ALLIED INTERESTS. BY WELL-KNOWN FINANCIAL WRITERS

ILLUSTRATED WITH SIXTY-FIVE VIEWS AND ABOUT FIVE HUNDRED AND TWENTY-FIVE PORTRAITS

EDITED, PUBLISHED AND COPYRIGHTED, 1897, BY MOSES KING

ASSOCIATE EDITORS: COL. A. B. DE FRECE, PH.D., AND HENRY E. WALLACE

THIS simple account of "Wall Street" and of the Stock Exchange, with its accompanying illustrations, is intended for the millions of people through-

Treasury of the United States is now. The latter building succeeded the Congress Hall built for the meeting of the first Congress, on the balcony of which, of the frenzied activity that takes place there.[8] Picture books such as *King's Views of the New York Stock Exchange* (1898) by Moses King, a publisher of travel guide books, likewise included vistas of Wall Street and its most important buildings that are either devoid of people, or with merely a smattering of bourgeois city folk (both men and women) promenading or driving by carriage in the vicinity. King's book also contains depictions of the interior of the Stock Exchange, with, for example, austere photographs of the Bond Room and Main Room cleared of the typical signs of chaotic business that struck most visitors to the exchange.

The only view of the trading floor in action that the volume does include is not a photograph but an artist's rendering, as the illustration for the lead article in the volume on 'The Magnitude and the Necessity of the Institution' (Figure 8). Unlike popular descriptions of the mayhem on the floor of the NYSE visible from the Visitors' Gallery, this fantasy representation shows an orderly scene, with a cluster of men calmly reading the stock ticker in the foreground, two brokers chatting alone at one of the posts (one of them even sitting down), and only in the distant background are a couple of men hazily shown raising their arms to bid stocks, but without the sense of frenzy that usually characterises such scenes. This is unsurprising because King's volume was less a guide book than a promotional tome designed to be presented to clients as a gift. Although the lead article begins by announcing that '[t]his simple account of "Wall Street" and the Stock Exchange, with its accompanying illustrations, is intended for the millions of people throughout the country who are deeply interested in the "Street", and who hardly know what it looks like, what it really is, or who its leaders are at this time', the frontispiece tellingly includes a panel announcing that it is 'Presented with the compliments of …'[9] However, the vast majority of the 1,050 illustrations that the cover proclaims are not of Wall Street in general but are uniform oval photographic portraits of past presidents, officers and current members of the New York Stock Exchange, flattering images that in reality tell readers more about the moustache fashions of the Gilded Age New York *haute bourgeoisie* than about the workings of the Exchange and 'what it really is'.

If *King's Views* presented to potential investors an idealised rendition of the work of Wall Street through the medium of dignified portraits of its elder statesmen, in contrast a privately printed and distributed collection of caricatures of leading Exchange figures in 1904 showed instead how the nation's financiers pictured themselves when they were not having to appeal to ordinary mortals. The images show the members of the Exchange as hearty fellows, referencing their individual passions for, say, carriage driving, hunting or yachting, but always with the ticker, the tape or other symbols of their occupation woven into the image. The caricature of Alfred M. Judson, for example, shows him riding the stock ticker as if a horse (it also resembles a phallus) (Figure 9), while the portrait of Charles E. Knoblauch shows him as a cowboy astride a submissive bull, bear and lamb simultaneously, with a stock ticker strapped to his back like a rifle (Figure 10).

Figure 9

Portrait of Alfred M. Judson, in George E. Croscup (ed.), *Stock Exchange in Caricature: A Private Collection of Cartoons, Caricatures and Character Sketches* (New York: A. Stone, 1904).

Harvard College Library.

Figure 10

Portrait of Charles E. Knoblauch, in George E. Croscup (ed.), *Stock Exchange in Caricature: A Private Collection of Cartoons, Caricatures and Character Sketches* (New York: A. Stone, 1904).

Harvard College Library.

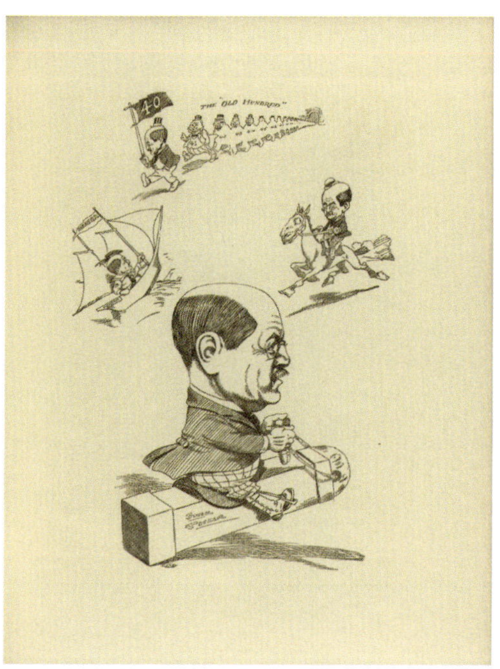

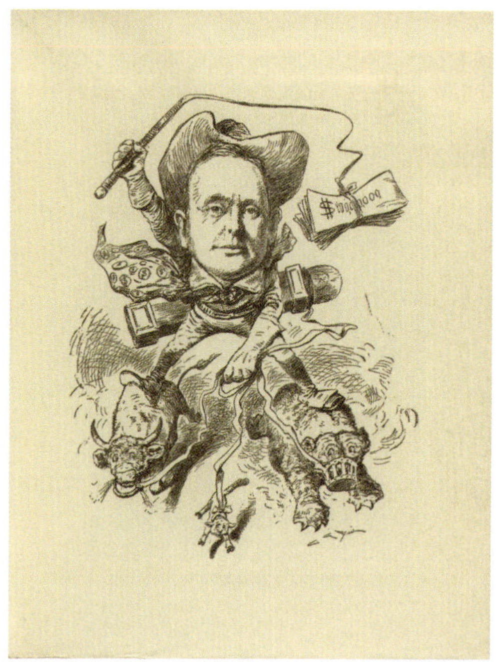

Despite efforts by Wall Street practitioners in the late nineteenth and early twentieth century to redefine the popular image of finance, the American public continued to focus on prominent individuals as the embodiment of the stock market.[10] Visual and verbal portraits of robber barons such as Daniel Drew, Jim Fisk, Cornelius Vanderbilt and Jay Gould in the 1870s and 1880s and John D. Rockefeller and J.P. Morgan in the 1890s and 1900s dominated the public imagination of the market, as 'giants' that loomed over Wall Street, in the view of a satirical cartoon of 1903 (Figure 11).

Jay Gould, for example, had himself painted as a respectable and kindly bourgeois businessmen (Figure 13) by the German-British Royal Academician Sir Hubert von Herkomer (ironically best known now as the painter of *Hard Times*, a searing portrayal of rural poverty). The public, however, thought of the notorious stock market manipulator as the 'Mephistopheles of Wall Street', a cold and calculating devil manipulating the market with sublime ease.

A satirical illustration from *Judge* magazine of 1886, for example, calls to account the outrageous claim made by Gould that he never speculated (Figure 12).[11] The cartoon shows Gould seated in the bell jar of a gigantic ticker machine and unseen by the frenzied stock market players beneath, dictating market prices directly onto the ticker tape itself. Gould is thus rendered as the very personification of market manipulation, with stock prices moved not by the Smithian 'invisible hand' of supply and demand, but by the visible hand of the Mephistopheles of Wall Street himself. (The cartoon thus ironically confirms Gould's

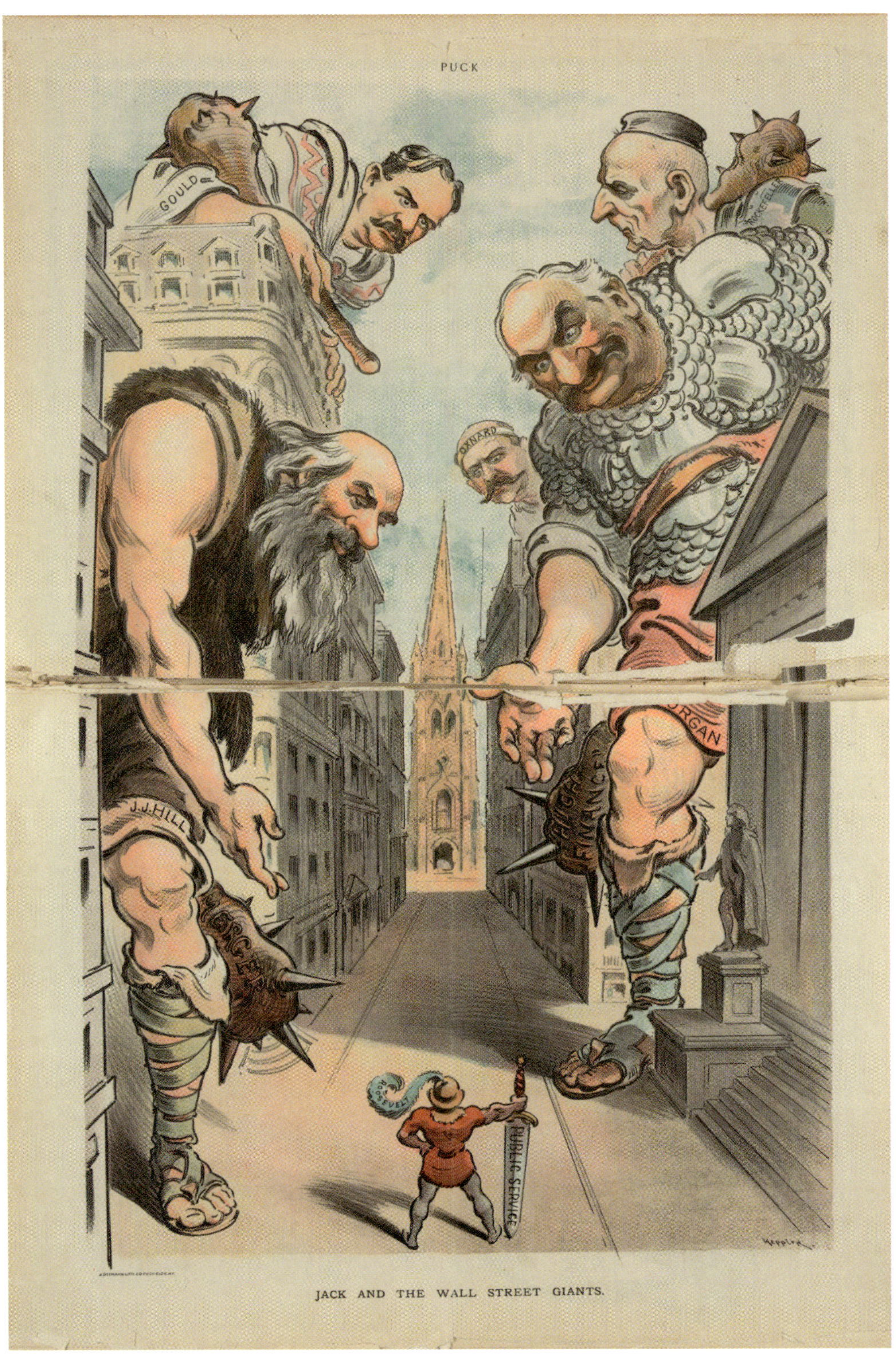

Figure 11

Jack and the Wall Street Giants, *Puck*, v. 54, no. 1402 (13 January 1904).

Prints & Photographs Division, Library of Congress, LC-DIG-ppmsca-25813.

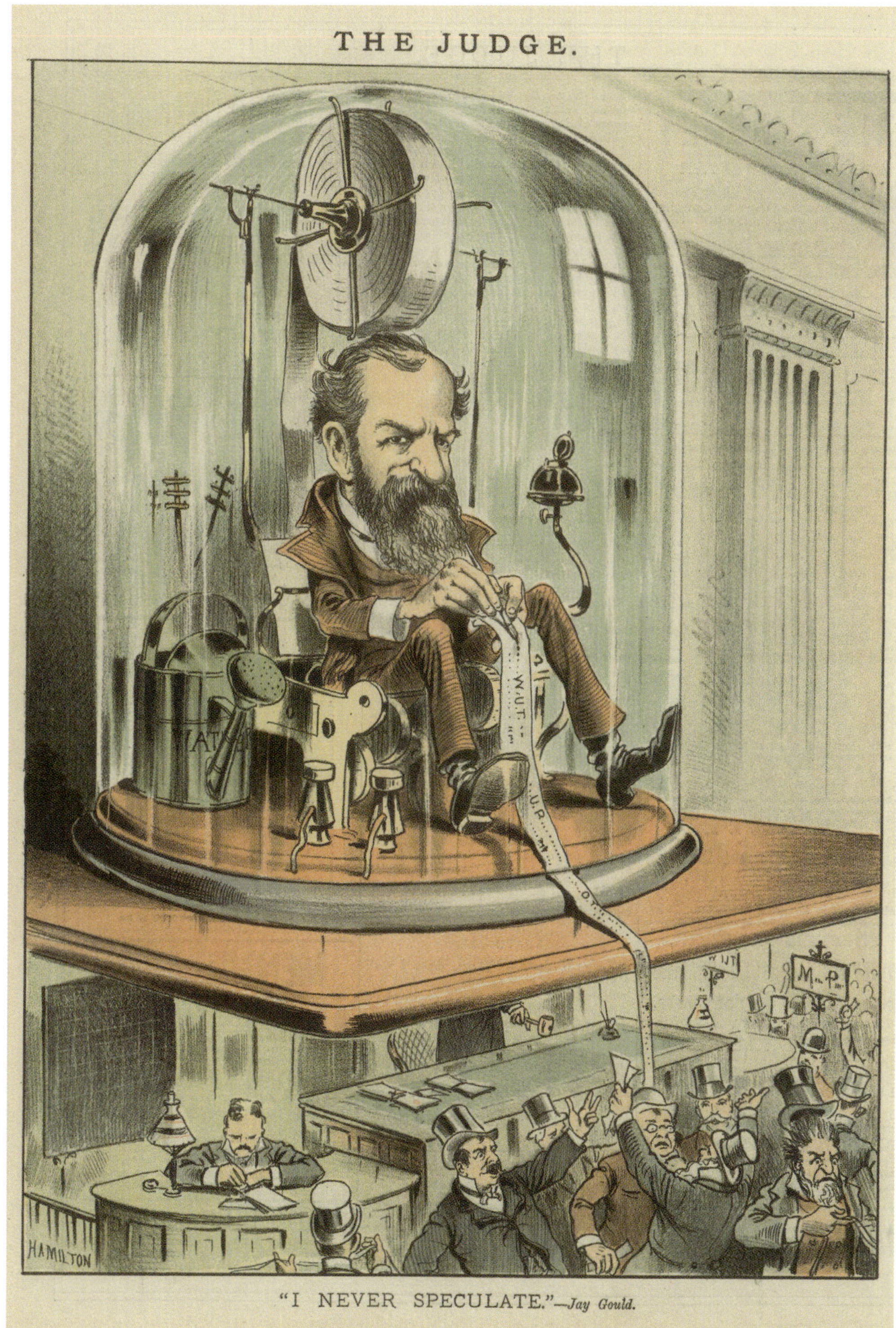

Figure 12

Grant E. Hamilton, '"I Never Speculate" – Jay Gould', *Judge* 9 (9 January 1886): back cover.

Harvard College Library.

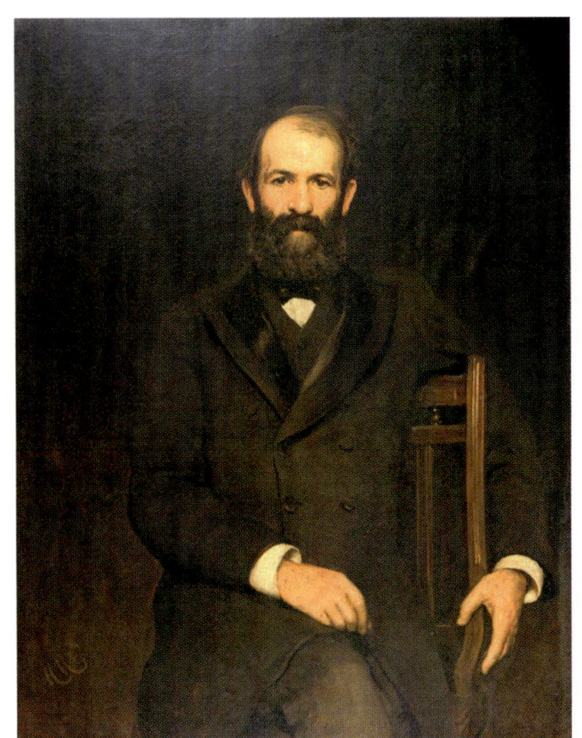

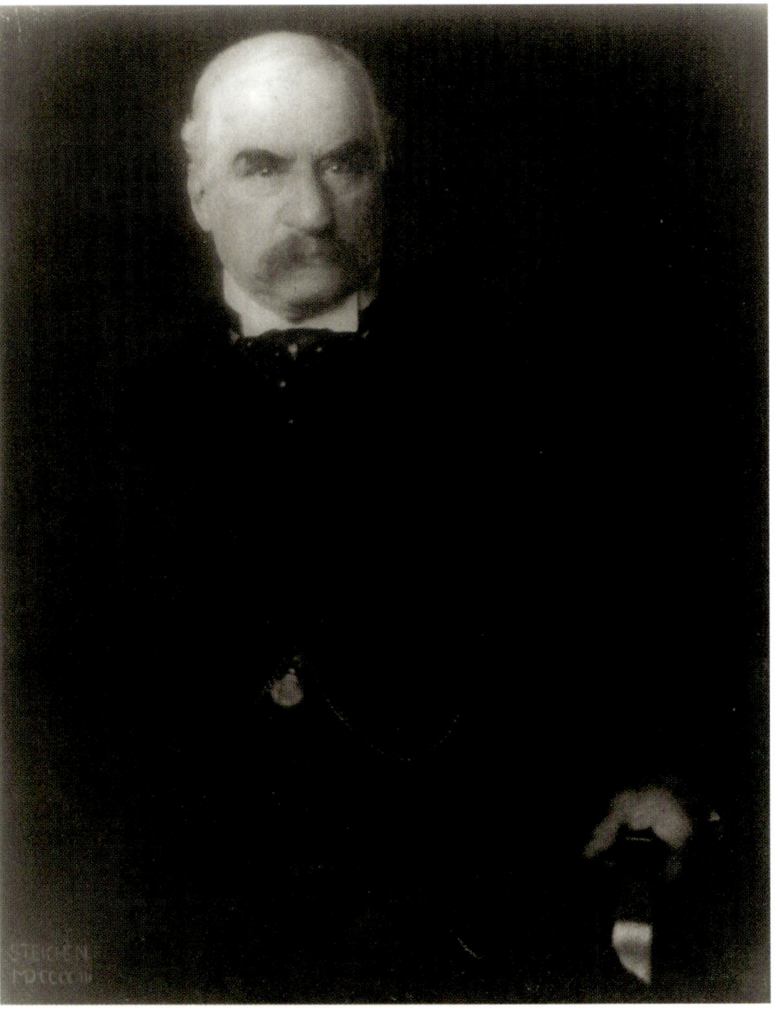
STEICHEN

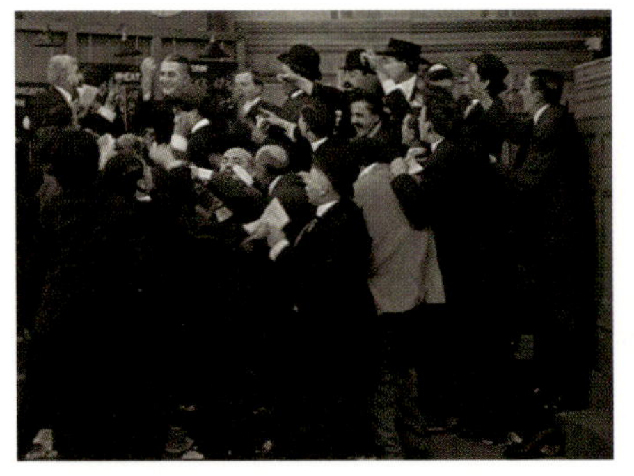

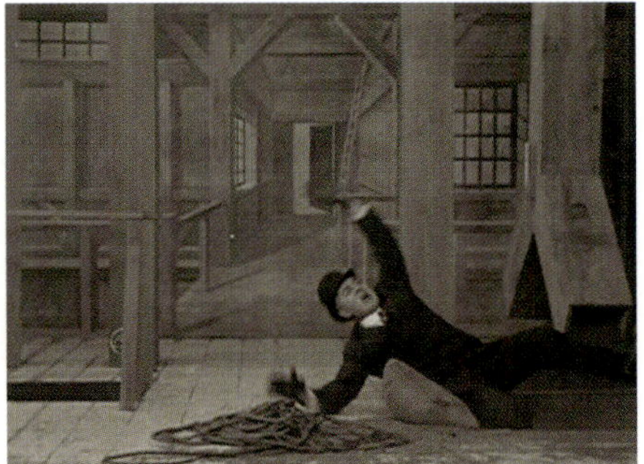

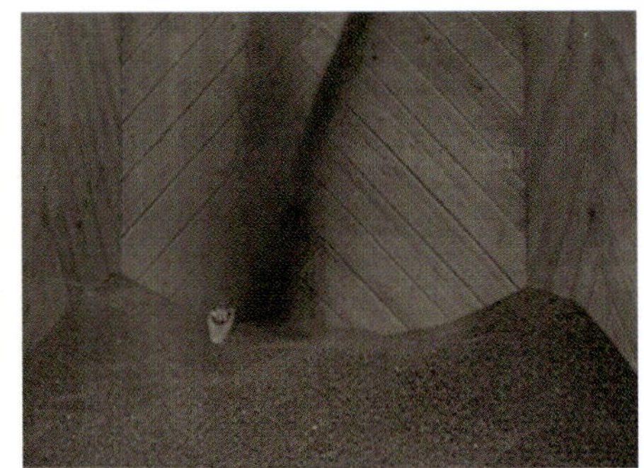

Figure 13

Hubert von Herkomer, *Portrait of Jay Gould* (1883).

Image courtesy of Lyndhurst, Tarrytown, NY.

Figure 14

Edward Steichen, *J. Pierpont Morgan, Esq., 1903* (printed 1909–10). Gum bichromate over platinum print. Alfred Stieglitz Collection, 1949. Washington DC, National Portrait Gallery, Smithsonian Institution.

scandalous denial: he would have no need to engage in risky speculations if he were able to accurately predict price movements because he was creating them himself.)

There is a similar fixation on the hand of the market manipulator in a famous photograph of the notoriously camera-shy J.P. Morgan (Figure 14). In 1903 the painter Fedor Encke commissioned Edward Steichen to taken some photographs as an aid to his portrait, as his subject Morgan was always too busy to sit for the painter. The atmospheric lighting carefully orchestrated by Steichen in a sitting lasting just three minutes resulted in a photo that shaped the public's view of Morgan for generations to come. Not only do Morgan's eyes stare fiercely out of the gloom, but the light falling on the arm of the chair gripped by the subject's hand looks uncannily as if Morgan is brandishing a dagger at the viewer.[12]

The naturalist writer Frank Norris likewise focuses on the actual hand of the grand market manipulator in his short story 'A Deal in Wheat' (1902) and his novel *The Pit* (1903), both of which tell a version of the doomed attempt to corner the market in wheat in the Chicago pits in the 1890s. In *A Corner in Wheat*, D.W. Griffith's 1909 silent film adaptation of Norris's short story, the domineering market titan is shown in one scene personally raising his hand in the wheat pit to accept all offers from the frantic floor traders. In the most iconic scene of Griffith's short film, the Machiavellian speculator – who is informed by telegram that 'You have control of the entire market of the world' – is seen accidentally tumbling into the grain elevator that he is showing off to visiting ladies (Figure 15). As he drowns in his own wheat only his hand is visible above the rising tide of produce.

Projecting the market

When they were not evoking the inscrutable mysteries of Providence, popular explanations for sudden market movements that created or wiped out fortunes tended from the eighteenth century onwards to rely on the idea of plotting and scheming behind the scenes by powerful 'insiders', seeing the conspiring agency of a hidden hand in place of the abstract convergence of aggregate supply and demand that constituted the 'invisible hand' of more respectable economic theory. This way of thinking about the market was reflected in many of the satirical cartoons of the period that depicted the conspiring hand of the robber barons, such as a *Puck* cartoon depicting J.P. Morgan as a bullish figure blowing worthless soap bubbles of 'inflated value' eagerly chased by the diverse crowd (Figure 16). These forms of popular visual protest fed into populist agitation against Wall Street corruption that captured centre stage in the Pujo Committee hearings in Congress in 1913.

Figure 15

A Corner in Wheat (dir. D.W. Griffith, 1909).

The late nineteenth century also saw several new popular explanations arise for the movement of stock market prices. The forerunners of 'technical analysts' or chartists, some market watchers began to claim that they could identify regular patterns in the otherwise seemingly unpredictable market fluctuations, although early works such as Samuel Benner's *Prophecies of the Future Ups and Downs in Prices* (1876) had more in

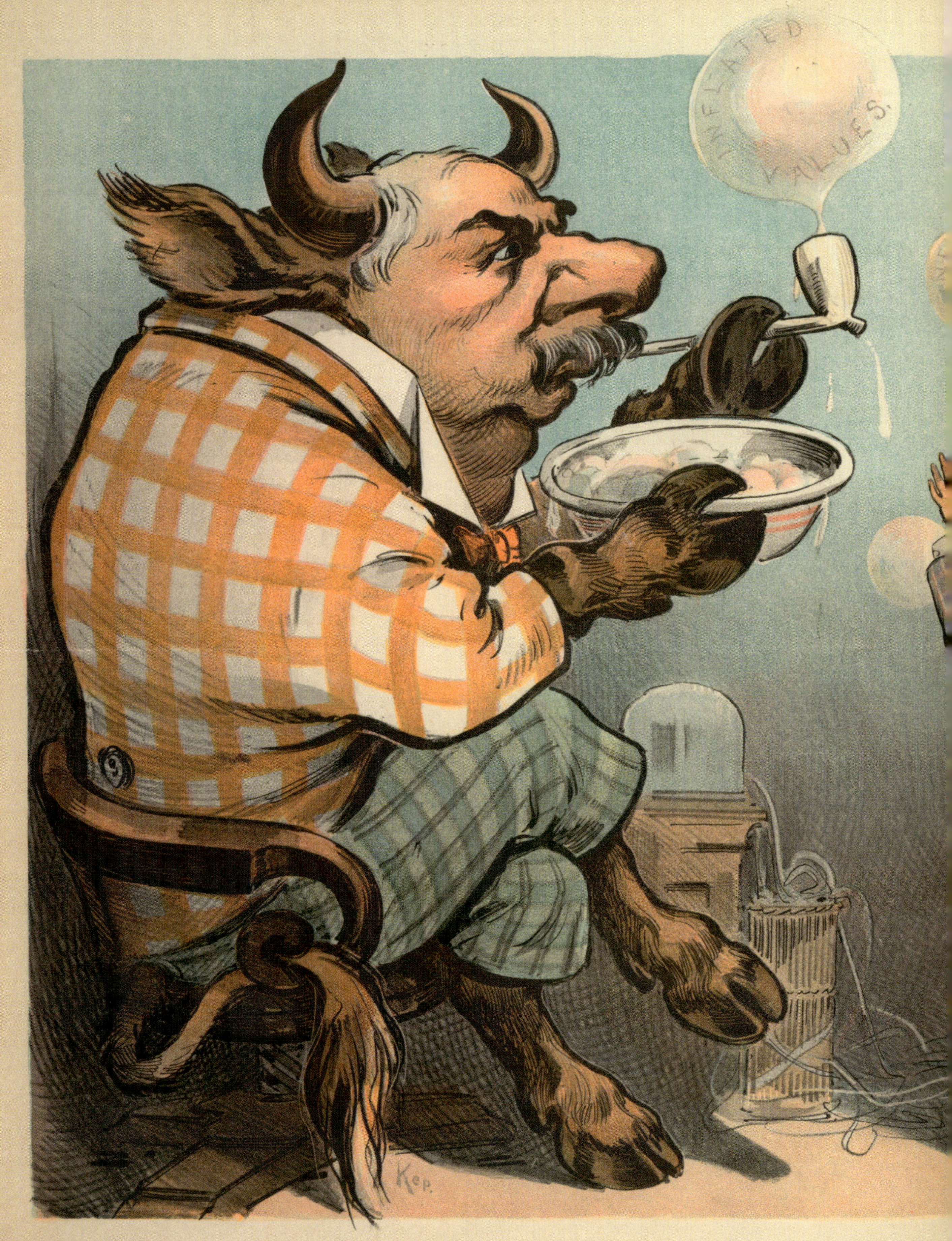

WALL STREET BUB

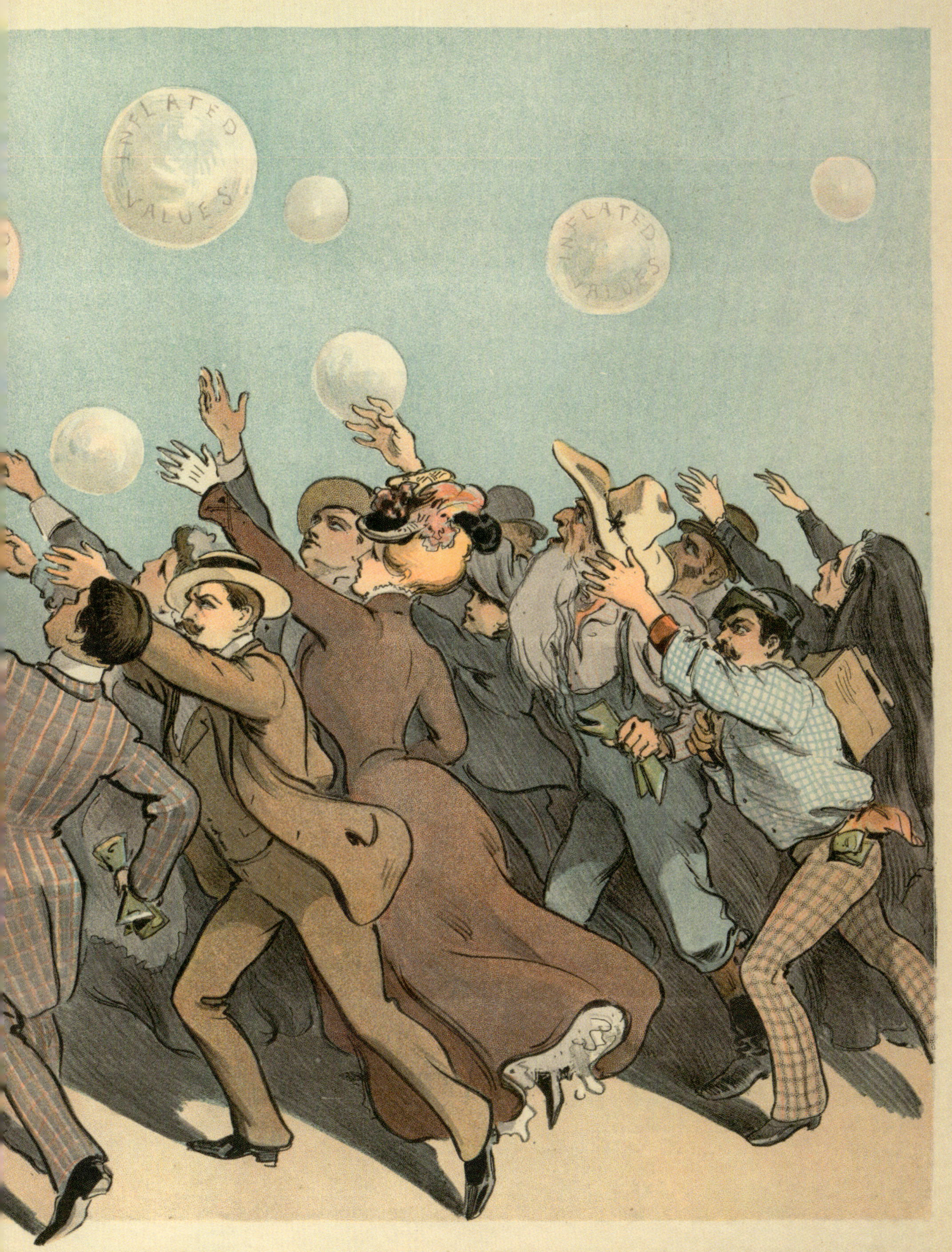

ALWAYS THE SAME.

common with the tradition of farmers' almanacs for predicting the weather than with the science of meteorology.

Other observers of the market began to locate the explanation for the many financial panics that repeatedly struck both sides of the Atlantic in the course of the nineteenth century in the emotional state of individual stock market participants. Talk of panics, depressions, exhilaration and mania was used to describe not merely the emotional state of those playing the market but the emotional state of the market itself. As noted in Chapter 2, 'Framing finance', illustrations accompanying the emerging genre of popular Wall Street fiction in the late nineteenth century often focused on crucial scenes in which the speculating protagonist reads his fate on the stock ticker. Although many of these scenes focus on the stock ticker itself as the medium of the market, some emphasise the emotional register of those reacting to the ticker, from the sangfroid of the masterful market player to the intense fear of the victim entranced by a panic. On the one hand financial traders are figured as the epitome of economic rationality, able to make dispassionate calculations and becoming machine-like in their reading of the tape. On the other hand, they are represented as being hypnotised by the tape, entering into a divine communion with what Slavoj Žižek has termed the 'mysterious spectral agency' of the market's Invisible Hand.[13]

For ordinary investors, the market held them in even more powerful sway. A photograph in a promotional brochure for the Haight & Freese bucket shop, for example, shows off its well appointed quotation board, but it also reveals its patrons sitting in rows mesmerised by the endlessly changing prices. The photograph suggests similarities with another new communal viewing technology of the later nineteenth century: the moving pictures. As with movie audiences, the experience of watching the market by watching the quotation board involved not just becoming emotionally invested in the highs and lows but being gripped by the sheer movement of the unfolding spectacle of endlessly changing numbers.[14] And, like the cinema, it was an experience of isolated, immersive identification with what was represented on the tape that nevertheless took place within a collective setting, a place in which insider knowledge and camaraderie (but also perhaps hysteria) could be shared with fellow viewers.[15] Although until World War I very few Americans actually invested in the stock market (the estimated number of Americans who owned stocks or bonds was less than 1 per cent of the total population), bucket shops and popular financial reporting made market watching a popular activity, creating a very different optic on the market than the one provided by the satirical cartoons discussed above.[16]

Nineteenth-century written and visual portraits of speculators raised the question of whether dramatic fluctuations in the market were an aggregated effect of the emotional turmoil of individual financial players, or whether market watchers read into the market a projected confirmation of their own emotional state. As Audrey Jaffe observes in her

PREVIOUS SPREAD

Figure 16

Udo J. Keppler, *Wall Street Bubbles: Always the Same*, *Puck*, v. 49, no. 1264 (22 May 1901), centrefold.

Prints & Photographs Division, Library of Congress, LC-DIG-ppmsca-25531.

study of the idea of the statistically 'average man' in Victorian culture, the trajectory of the impersonal stock market graph is often 'assimilated to a narrative of feeling':

> universally apprehended as a picture of emotions—a snapshot of the national (or global) mood – it is understood to swing (for example) between elation and depression, optimism and alarm. Looking to the numbers to see how we feel, we both personalize them – render them a projection of our individual and collective narratives – and depersonalize them, conceding our authority to know ourselves to an abstract system that seems to have captured this knowledge.... Is the market a projection of the man, or is the man a projection of the market?[17]

Even in their most abstract, depersonalising form, then, the graphs of stock market prices tempt readers into an affective identification that is often registered by the insistent personification of financial data: when we read the market, what we in fact are reading is a fantasy projection of our collective self. Jaffe finds this blurring of emotional internalisation and projection at work in contemporary adverts for financial services companies, with one example (a television advert for CNBC in 2000) quite literally projecting stock market data onto the heart of the railway commuter, like a financial ECG. Lynn Hershman Leeson's *Synthia Stock Ticker* (2000–02) provides a witty take on the conflicted nature of the stock market as both emotional internalisation and projection. It consists of a stock ticker bell jar, in which the traditional telegraphic mechanism is replaced by screen showing 'Synthia', a virtual person who reacts emotionally to a live data feed of stock prices from the Dow Jones and NASDAQ, the favoured exchange of the dotcom boom and bust around the turn of the millennium. The name Synthia recalls Robert Smitley's joking evocation in his book *Popular Financial Delusions* (1933) of 'Cynthia Speculation', a twentieth-century reworking of the familiar eighteenth-century trope of Lady Credit as a personification of the seductive lure and feminising irrationality of the market.[18] Leeson's stock indicator ironically displays the seductive but supposedly fickle and overly emotional face of speculation that results from a lapse from masculine objectivity. *Synthia Stock Ticker* internalises impersonal stock data which triggers the emotional reaction. Yet the synthetic female figure on display also serves as a reminder of the visual projection of idealised women as a male viewer's fantasy, a concern that chimes with Leeson's other works exploring gender politics in the increasingly blurred interface between the real and the virtual world (most notably with her long-term construction of 'Roberta Breitman' as a fictional persona).

Madness of crowds

If one way of conceptualising the movement of the market has been to focus on the emotion of individual speculators (both in itself and as a stand-in for the market as a whole), then another strand has located its explanation in the peculiar dynamic of crowds. Although Charles Mackay first formulated the notion of mass delusions in the context of market behaviour in his *Extraordinary Popular Delusions and the Madness of Crowds* (1841), popular imagery of finance had long drawn attention to the chaotic dynamic surrounding the stock markets of London, Paris and Amsterdam. Since the Renaissance the market had been conceived of as a kind of theatre, a place of carnivalesque public spectacle that was outside the bounds of normal social rules.[19] In the cartoon *Arlequyn Actionist* from *Het Groote Tafereel der Dwaasheid*, for example, Scaramouche and Harlequin hold back a stage curtain revealing to the viewer the bawdy bedlam on rue Quinquempoix in Paris, in which stock certificates are issuing forth from the bare behind of one of the jobbers in the midst of the clamouring crowd. The implication is that the stock jobbers are merely enacting out a scene written by someone unseen, unwittingly caught up in a drama they cannot control. *The Bubblers bubbl'd*, a cartoon from the English version of *The Great Mirror of Folly*, depicts the stock jobbers passing stock certificates that flutter down from above from one to another in a circle, as part of a demented dance that they cannot escape, as they try and pass the worthless paper to the greater fool behind them (Figure 17).

Figure 17

The Bubblers bubbl'd or the Devil take the Hindmost, print made by James Cole from original in *The Great Mirror of Folly* (1720).

In many of these eighteenth-century satirical cartoons the compulsive behaviour of the speculating public itself becomes a spectacle. Investors are shown possessed by a collective mania, losing the sense of self-possession that was supposedly vital to a functional polity. *The Bubblers Medley or a Sketch of the Times: Being Europe's Memorial for the Year 1720*, for instance, depicts a disordered crush of bodies in 'Change Alley in London and rue Quinquempoix in Paris, conjuring up the spectre of the libidinous irrationality of an unregulated crowd (Figure 18). At the same time, however, the *trompe l'oeil* form of the *Bubblers Medley* draws attention self-reflexively to the duplicitous nature of representation, and the 'trickery, artifice and the kind of fictions that lay at the heart of stockjobbing'.[20]

In the late nineteenth century the work of emerging crowd psychology theorists such as Gustave Le Bon and Gabriel Tarde gave weight to explanations of financial panics that focused on the peculiar dynamic that turned seemingly rational individuals into an unthinking and unpredictable herd, unthinkingly apeing one another in a vicious spiral of contagious mimesis. In contrast to the oddly static portrayal of Wall Street during the panic of 1857 in James Cafferty and Charles Rosenberg's painting *Wall Street, Half Past Two O'Clock, October 13, 1857* (Figure 19) many illustrations from the late nineteenth century emphasise the sheer chaos of the stock market during a panic, both on the trading floor and in the public space surrounding the exchanges. Although by this time the widespread use of the stock ticker meant that 'the market' was no longer located in a single place, illustrators – when they did not focus on an emblematic individual conquering or being controlled by the market – fixated on the spectacle of the madness of crowds, as if the market as a whole could be viewed from the Visitors' Gallery of the New York Stock Exchange. For example, in 'The Recent Panic Scene in the New York Stock Exchange On

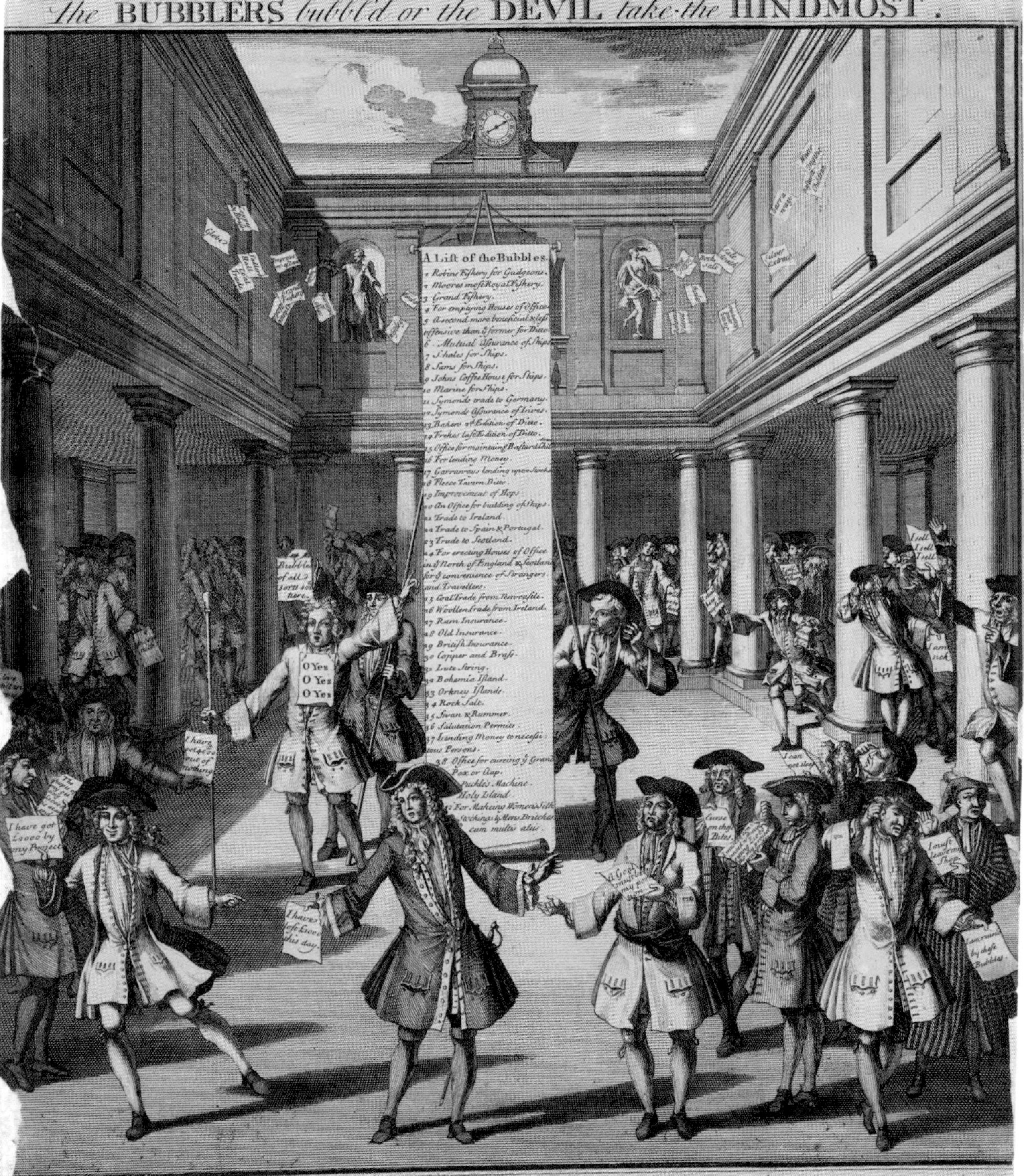

Come all ye mony'd Bites & Culls,
Dukes Commoners and Nobles,
Who stray alike from reason's rules,
To deal in Stocks and Bubbles;
Behold your sundry Pictures here,
Amidst a Reigning folly:
And see what Asses men appear,
When jobbing in Change Ally.

Here Whig and Tory, Rich & Poor,
All Languages and Nations
Jabber, as if at Babels Tow'r,
To shew their sev'ral passions;
Some laugh that win, some curse y^t lose
Some Coughing, others Sneezing,
Some stink of Garlick, some of Toes
Whilst others fart with Squeezing.

Here Fortune does her smiles dispen
Like other jilting Witches,
But often frowns on men of Sense,
To pleasure Fools with Riches;
Our Trade we shun, to South we run,
We bubble and are Bubbles;
In Stock we're Rich, by stock undon
O. Britain mourn thy troubles.

J. Cole Sculp.

Sold by the Printsellers of London & Westminster.

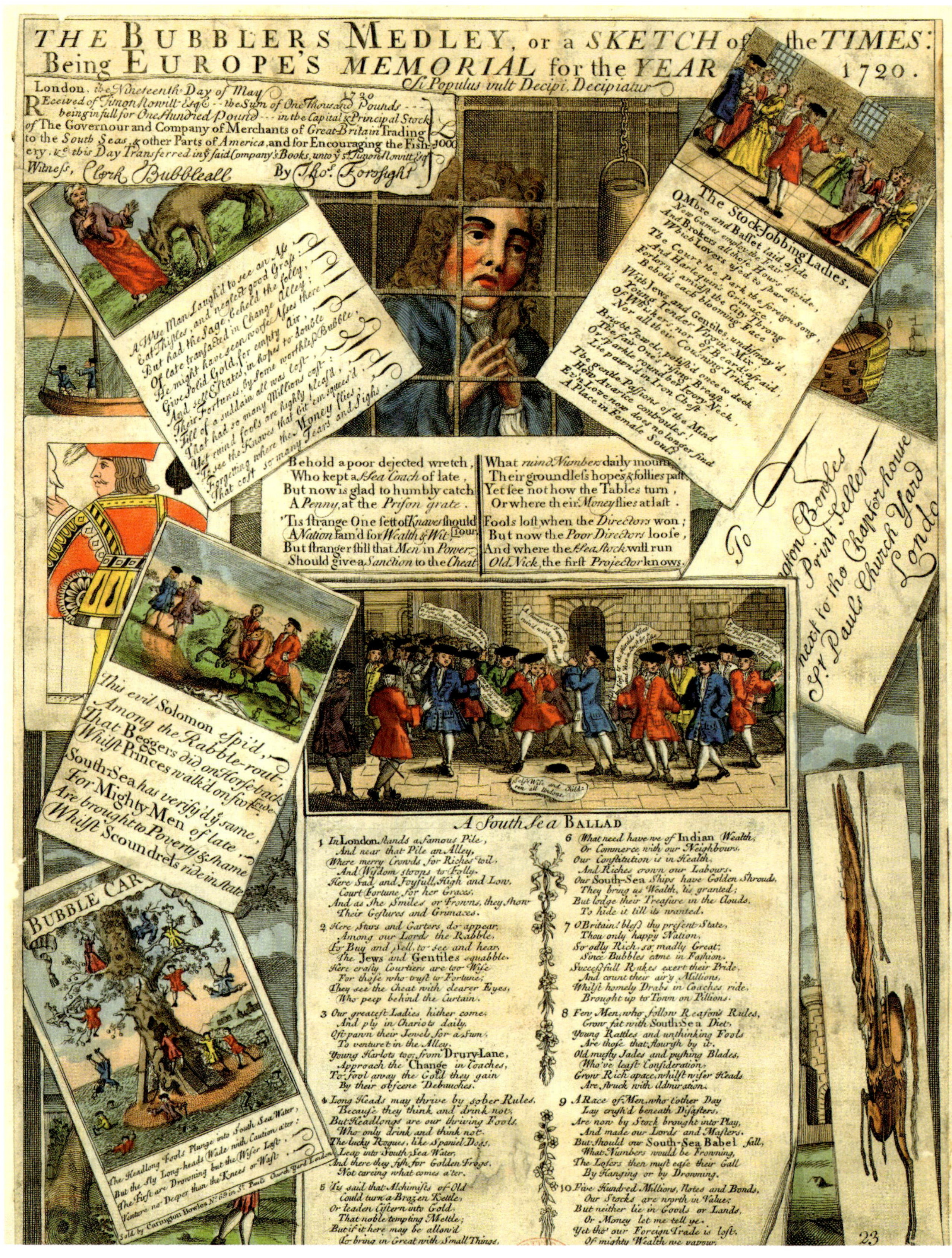
THE BUBBLERS MEDLEY, or a SKETCH of the TIMES:
Being EUROPE'S MEMORIAL for the YEAR 1720.
Si Populus vult Decipi, Decipiatur
Witness, Clerk Bubbleall
The Stock-Jobbing Ladies.
Behold a poor dejected wretch,
Who kept a Sea Coach of late,
But now is glad to humbly catch
A Penny, at the Prison grate.
'Tis strange One sett of Knaves should [f]our,
A Nation fam'd for Wealth & Wit;
But stranger still that Men in Power,
Should give a Sanction to the Cheat.
What ruin'd Numbers daily mourn
Their groundless hopes & follies past,
Yet see not how the Tables turn,
Or where their Money flies at last.
Fools lost when the Directors won;
But now the Poor Directors loose,
And where the Sea Stock will run
Old Nick, the first Projector knows.
This evil Solomon espi'd,
Among the Rabble-rout,
That Beggers did on Horse back ride,
Whilst Princes walk'd on foot.
South-Sea has verify'd ye same,
For Mighty Men of late,
Are brought to Poverty & Shame
Whilst Scoundrels ride in state.
A South Sea BALLAD
1 In London stands a famous Pile,
And near that Pile an Alley,
Where merry Crowds for Riches toil,
And Wisdom stoops to Folly.
Here Sad and Joyfull, High and Low,
Court Fortune for her Graces,
And as She Smiles or Frowns, they show
Their Gestures and Grimaces.
2 Here Stars and Garters do appear,
Among our Lords the Rabble,
To Buy and Sell, to see and hear,
The Jews and Gentiles squabble.
Here crafty Courtiers are too Wise
For those who trust to Fortune;
They see the Cheat with clearer Eyes,
Who peep behind the Curtain.
3 Our greatest Ladies hither come,
And ply in Chariots daily,
Oft pawn their Jewels for a Sum,
To venture't in the Alley.
Young Harlots too, from Drury-Lane,
Approach the Change in Coaches,
To fool away the Gold they gain
By their obscene Debauches.
4 Long Heads may thrive by sober Rules,
Because they think and drink not;
But Headlongs are our thriving Fools,
Who only drink and think not.
The lucky Rogues, like Spaniel Dogs,
Leap into South-Sea Water,
And there they fish for Golden Frogs,
Not careing what comes a'ter.
5 'Tis said that Alchimists of Old
Could turn a Brazen Kettle,
Or leaden Cistern into Gold,
That noble tempting Mettle;
But if it here may be allow'd
To bring in Great with Small Things,
6 What need have we of Indian Wealth,
Or Commerce with our Neighbours,
Our Constitution is in Health,
And Riches crown our Labours.
Our South-Sea Ships have Golden Shrouds,
They bring us Wealth, 'tis granted;
But lodge their Treasure in the Clouds,
To hide it till its wanted.
7 O Britain! bless thy present State,
Thou only happy Nation,
So odly Rich, so madly Great;
Since Bubbles came in Fashion.
Successfull Rakes exert their Pride,
And count their airy Millions,
Whilst homely Drabs in Coaches ride,
Brought up to Town on Pillions.
8 Few Men, who follow Reason's Rules,
Grow fat with South-Sea Diet,
Young Rattles and unthinking Fools
Are those that flourish by it.
Old musty Jades and pushing Blades,
Who've least Consideration,
Grow Rich apace, whilst wiser Heads
Are struck with Admiration.
9 A Race of Men, who t'other Day
Lay crush'd beneath Disasters,
Are now by Stock brought into Play,
And made our Lords and Masters.
But should our South-Sea Babel fall,
What Numbers would be Frowning,
The Losers then must ease their Gall
By Hanging or by Drowning.
10 Five Hundred Millions, Notes and Bonds,
Our Stocks are worth in Value;
But neither lie in Goods or Lands,
Or Money let me tell ye.
Yet tho' our Foreign Trade is lost,
Of mighty Wealth we vapour,
23

Figure 18

The Bubblers Medley, or a Sketch of the Times: Being Europe's Memorial for the Year 1720 (1720).

Figure 19

James H. Cafferty and Charles G. Rosenberg, *Wall Street, Half Past Two O'Clock, October 13, 1857* (1858).

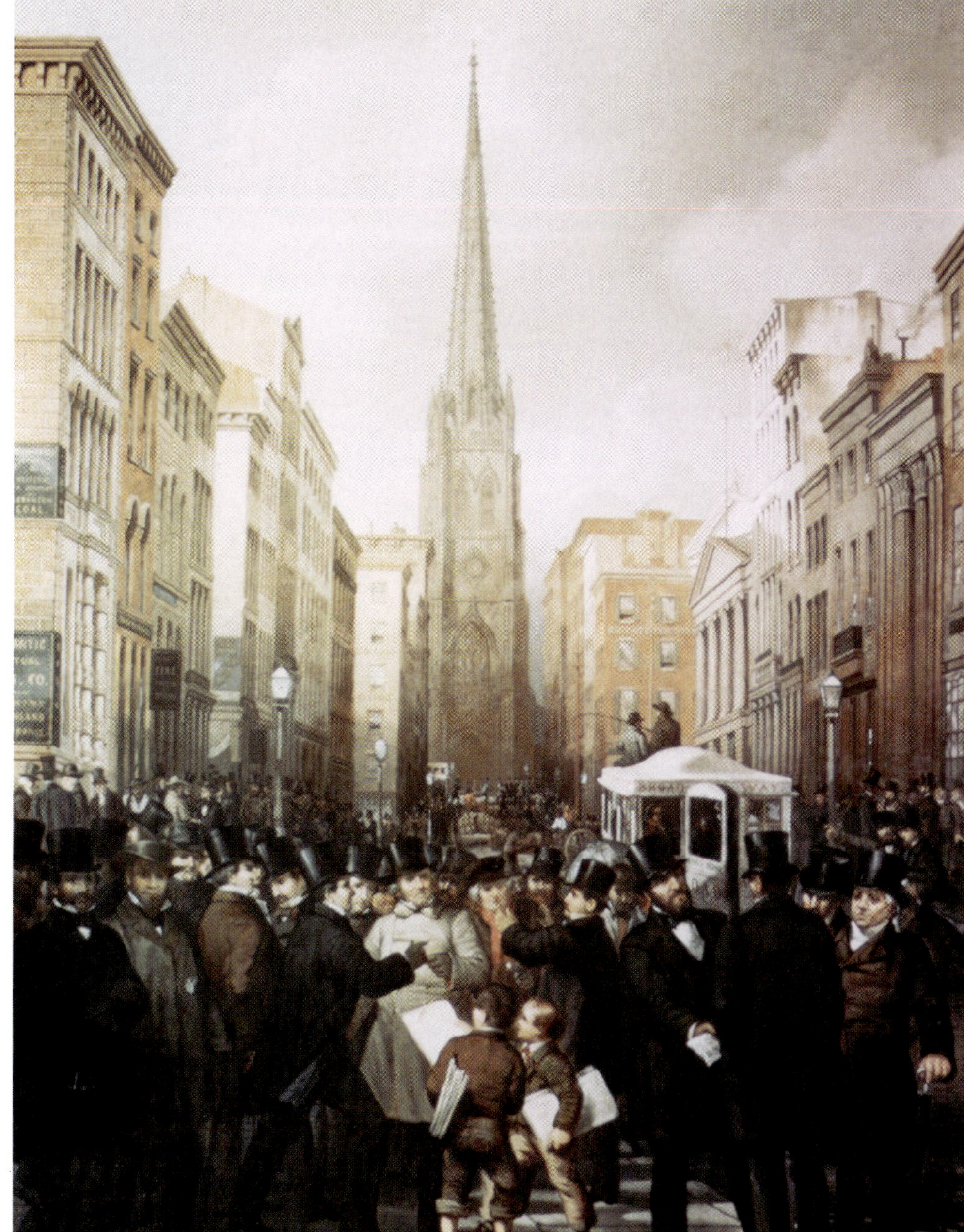

the Morning of Friday, May 5th', published in *Frank Leslie's Illustrated Newspaper* in 1893, vignettes of individual brokers in extremes of emotion in the foreground blur into an indistinguishable whirl of heads and hands in the background (Figure 20).

Bestial finance

Many nineteenth-century depictions of financial panics draw attention to the animal, herd-like behaviour of market crowds, in which the violence of the struggle for financial survival on the floor of the exchange resembles the Darwinian jungle. As Sarah Burns notes in her study of animal imagery in nineteenth-century depictions of finance:

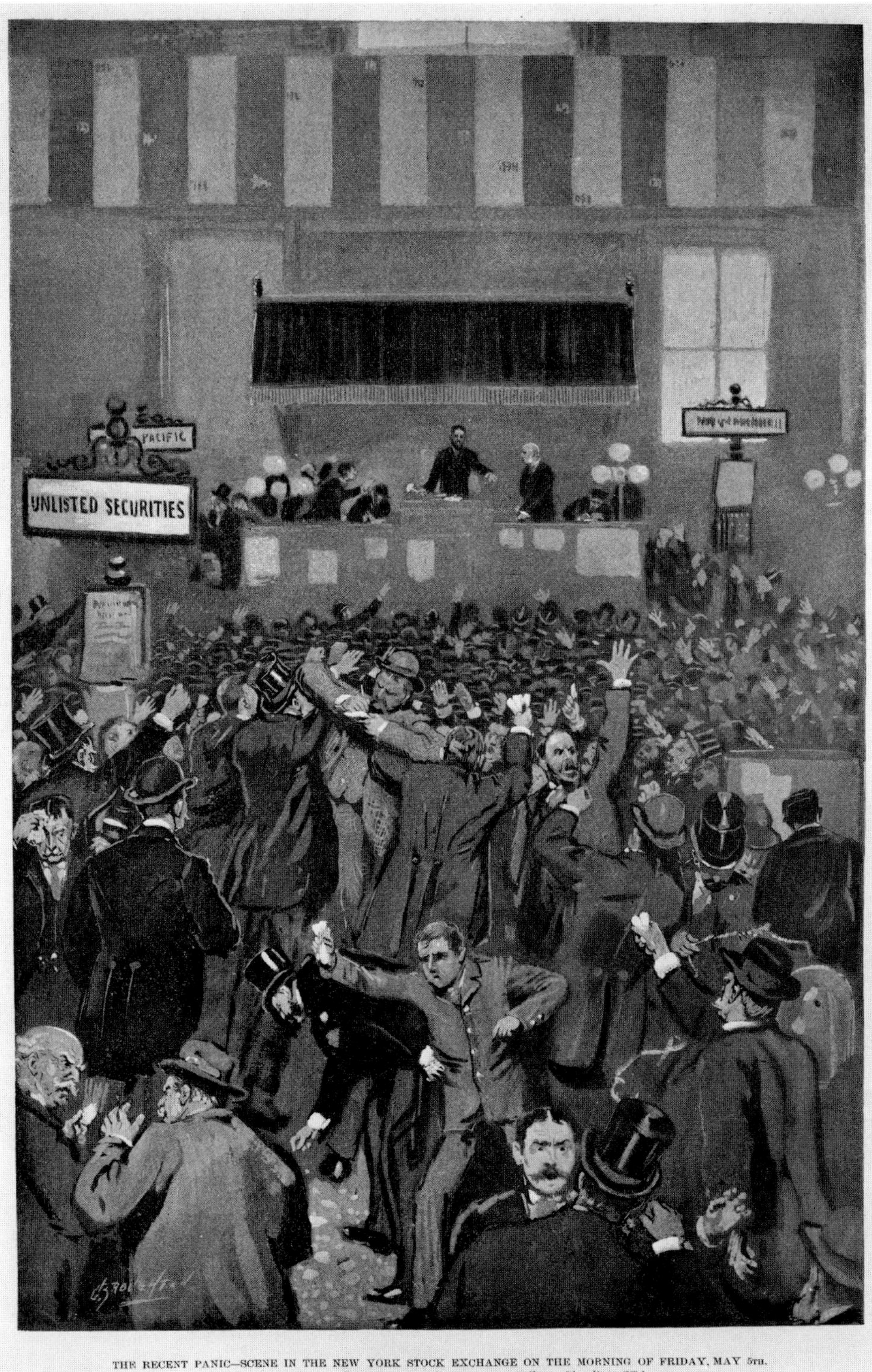

Figure 20

'The Recent Panic Scene in the New York Stock Exchange on the Morning of Friday, May 5th.', *Frank Leslie's Illustrated Newspaper* (18 May 1893).

Prints & Photographs Division, Library of Congress.

> To outsiders, Wall Street was a mysterious, powerful, dangerous place. It had its own esoteric rituals, traditions, and language. It was the site of deception, destruction, and extinction. It was also a wilderness of confusion, where men became beasts and beasts became men ... In contemporary reports about Wall Street, the same metaphors occurred time after time: rat-pit, insane asylum, bedlam, circus, carnival, menagerie, den of wild beasts. The stock exchange was a place where nature ruled, emotions burst out of control, and men, driven by the raw force of their animal spirits, metamorphosed into bears, bulls, vultures, foxes, lions, tigers, and hyenas.[21]

These nineteenth-century depictions of finance drew on a long tradition of characterising the market in bestial terms; indeed, the *Oxford English Dictionary* dates the first emergence of the term 'bear' in relation to stock markets to the 1710s (the association of the term with short selling was apparently based on the proverb 'to sell the bear's skin before one has caught the bear'). More generally, in eighteenth- and nineteenth-century political cartoons animal imagery featured regularly as a visual shorthand, drawing on the classical tradition of animal fables, with political and financial actors taking on the roles and appearance of foxes, wolves, lambs and other emblematic creatures such as the English bulldog, the American eagle or the Republican Party elephant.[22] By the turn of the twentieth century these depictions of a financial bestiary had become ritualised. W.A. Rogers' cartoon *Great Activity in Wall Street*, for example, features anthropomorphised bulls, bears and lambs (naive investors, ready to be 'fleeced'), dressed up in the latest fashions, and all following one another in a merry dance (Figure 21). The suggestion is that what looks to the outsider like 'great activity in Wall Street' is merely an endless and highly ritualised circle of buying and selling governed by the fixed behaviour of the different market 'beasts'. In a neat doubled metaphor *The Triumph of the Bear in the Wall Street Arena*, a *Puck* magazine cover from 1903, has market bulls and bears dressed as Roman gladiators (Figure 22). Although bull and bear imagery was most common, other animal metaphors were deployed. Another *Puck* cover from 1913, for instance, features J.P. Morgan (complete with a bulbous, purple nose) as a monstrous spider representing 'flim-flam finance' at the centre of the web of Wall Street, an idea familiar to many satirical cartoons of the muckraking era that picture corporations as octopuses, and their financial leaders as giants astride the nation, or spiders at the centre of a web (Figure 23). In this case however, the caption informs us that 'the flies got wise', with the public keeping clear of the web.

The most notable portrayal of bestial finance is undoubtedly William Holbrook Beard's painting *The Bulls and Bears in the Market* (1879) (Figure 24), which references what had become the standard way of describing those who gambled, respectively, on a rising and a falling market. However, Beard's painting also marked a new departure, not least because it weds the visual allegory of political cartoons to the dramatic narrative and realism of late nineteenth-century high art. Beard had already made a name for himself as an accomplished painter of humorous, anthropomorphic scenes, including several involving gatherings of rapacious and Bacchanalian bears in the woods.[23]

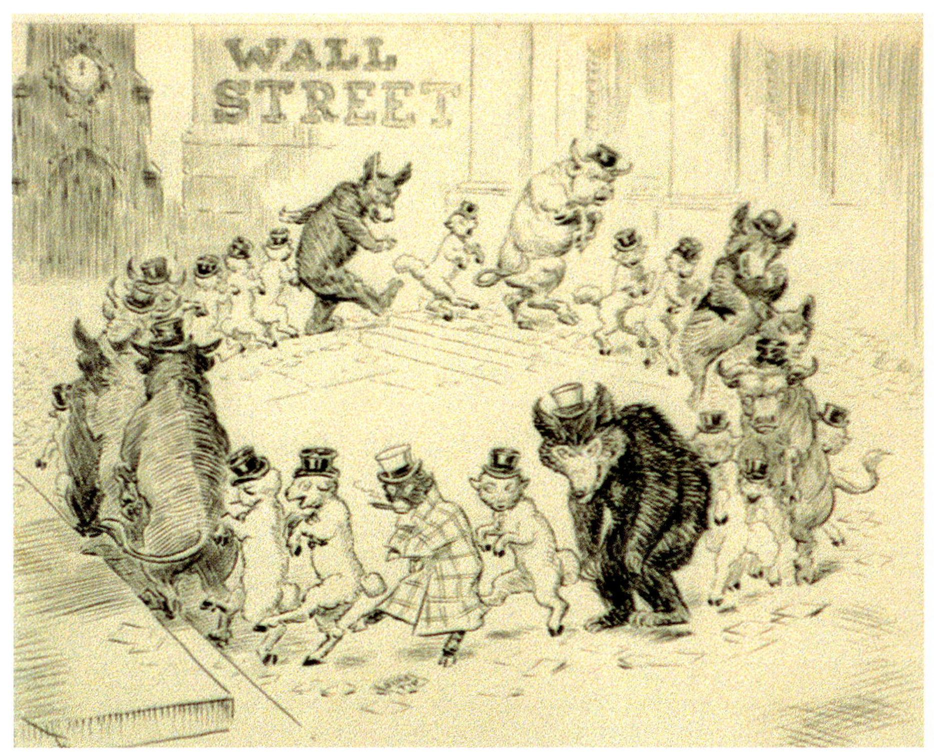
WALL
STREET

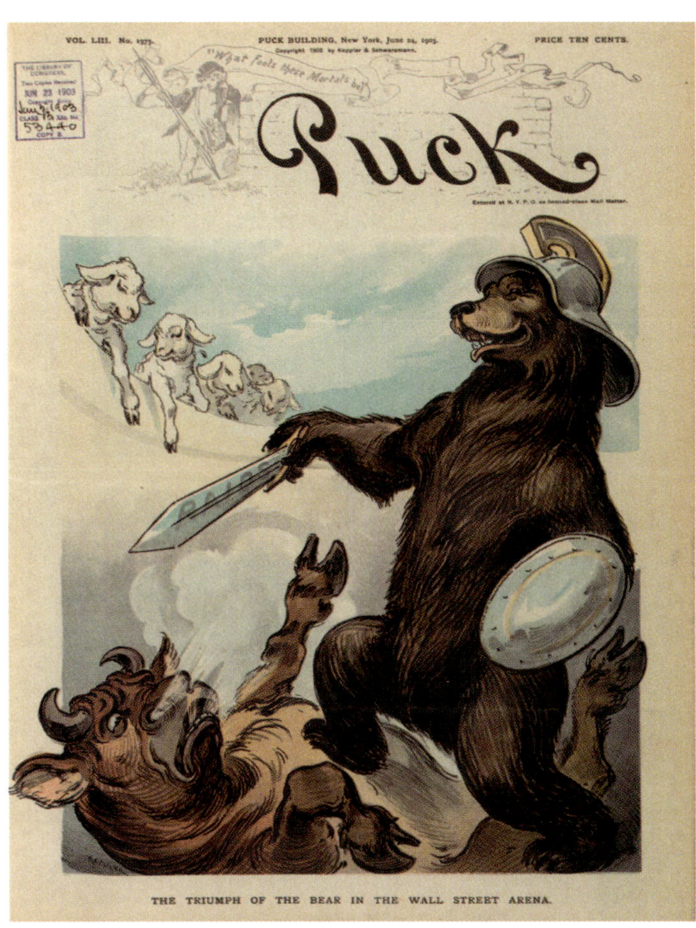
VOL. LIII. No. 1373.
PUCK BUILDING, New York, June 24, 1903.
PRICE TEN CENTS.
"What fools these Mortals be!"
Puck
THE TRIUMPH OF THE BEAR IN THE WALL STREET ARENA.

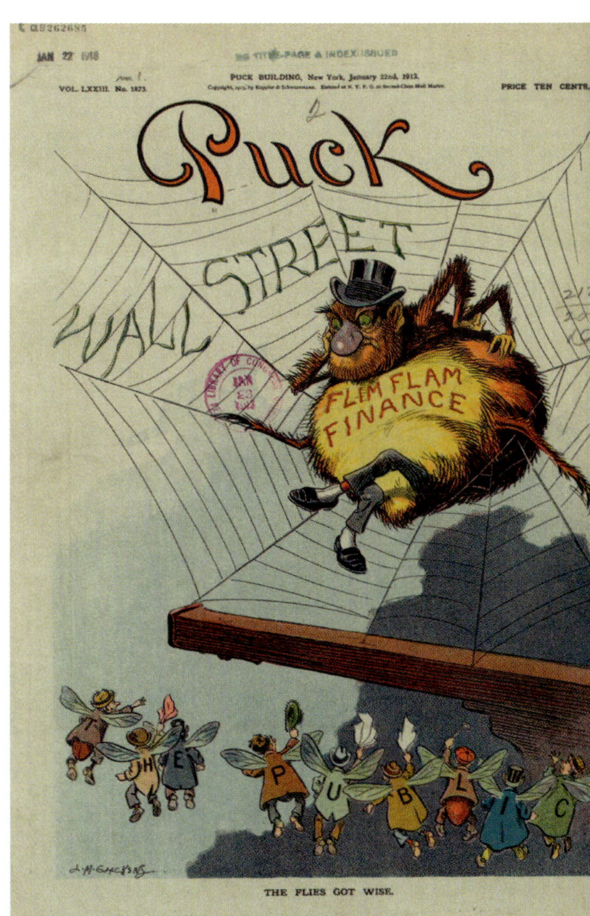
VOL. LXXIII. No. 1873.
PUCK BUILDING, New York, January 22nd, 1913.
PRICE TEN CENTS.
Puck
WALL STREET
FLIM FLAM FINANCE
THE
PUBLIC
THE FLIES GOT WISE.

Figure 21

W.A. Rogers, *Great Activity in Wall Street*, *New York Herald*, 19 March 1908, p. 7.

Prints & Photographs Division, Library of Congress, LC-DIG-ds-00117.

Figure 22

Udo J. Keppler, *The Triumph of the Bear in the Wall Street Arena*, *Puck*, v. 53, no. 1373 (24 June 1903), cover.

Prints & Photographs Division, Library of Congress, LC-DIG-ppmsca-25752.

Figure 23

L.M. Glackens, *The Flies Got Wise*, *Puck*, v. 73, no. 1873 (22 January 1913), cover.

Prints & Photographs Division, Library of Congress, LC-DIG-ppmsca-27912.

FOLLOWING SPREAD

Figure 24

William Holbrook Beard, *The Bulls and Bears in the Market* (1879).

Collection of The New York Historical Society.

Although the bears in those earlier images referred obliquely to professional speculators, in *The Bulls and Bears in the Market* there is no doubting that the subject is Wall Street: the stampeding herd of bulls and bears, tearing the flesh from one another, rush past the clearly demarcated classical façade of the New York Stock Exchange, threatening to overwhelm the viewer. If the cause of the devastating panic of 1873 is to be found anywhere, this painting suggests, it is not in the moral failings of ordinary citizens or even in the political machinations of Washington (as popular explanations for previous panics had insisted), but in the heart of Manhattan's financial district. The canvas combines a melodramatic panorama of the chaotic struggle between the bulls and bears with realistic attention to the details of horns, fangs and hooves. It also couples animal brutality with recognisably human expressions, poses and actions, such as the bear trying to lasso a bull in the background on the right hand side. Beard thus re-literalises the metaphor of social Darwinism: here in lower Manhattan the law of the jungle reigns, with the bulls and bears personifying those 'animal spirits' of greed, fear, panic and exuberance deemed to be ruling the market, and familiar from other exposés of the era into the 'men and mysteries of Wall Street'.[24]

The popular tradition of using a bestial taxonomy to make sense of market behaviour was eclipsed in the twentieth century by the rise of professional economics, and in particular its emphasis on the efficiency and rationality of the market. The figure of *Homo economicus* that emerged from orthodox economic theory was not an actual man (let alone a wild beast) but a calculating machine, a robot that endlessly maximised utility. Despite its ubiquity in economic discourse, the economic abstraction of *Homo economicus* does not lend itself to easy depiction in the way that the vernacular rhetoric of bulls, bears and lambs had once done. However, since the 1990s and particularly since the 2008 crash there has been a return to the visual and verbal language of 'animal spirits', as the myth of the rational market in general and the fiction of *Homo economicus* in particular have begun to seem suspect in light of copious evidence from behavioural economics that individuals, institutions and indeed the entire financial system do not always follow the dictates of rationality. *Animal Spirits*, George A. Akerlof and Robert J. Shiller's book on the crash, is the most prominent of these recent returns to the Keynesian phrase and its wider evocation of zoological explanations for market failure.[25] The book's cover image by the *New Yorker* cartoonist Ed Koren features a troop of furry creatures hanging from a stock market chart as if it were a jungle vine, elated when riding a rising trend, and anxious or dejected when clinging precariously to a plunging line. Likewise newspaper articles by Shiller on the theme of 'animal spirits' include illustrations of bankers-as-animals, in the shape of a wolf, a tiger and a shark.[26] The return to a bestial imaginary with the rise of behavioural finance also chimed with more populist explanations for the financial meltdown of 2008 as the result of the voracious and near animalistic greed of bankers. However, as Paul Crosthwaite has argued, the portrayal of economic man as a wolf or a shark (or a gecko, in Stone's film *Wall Street*) might help chip away at the dominant

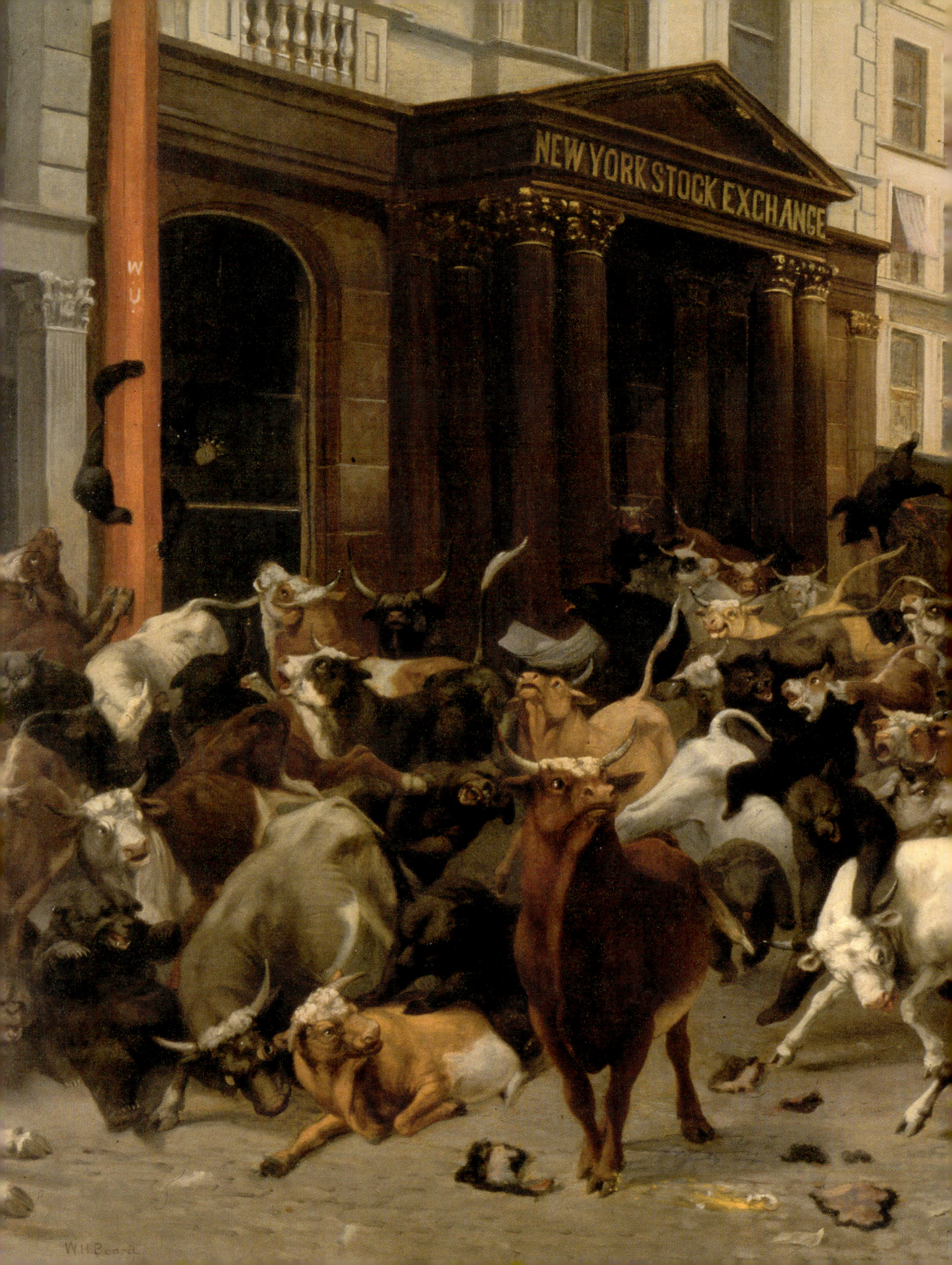
NEW YORK STOCK EXCHANGE
W.U.
W.H.Beard

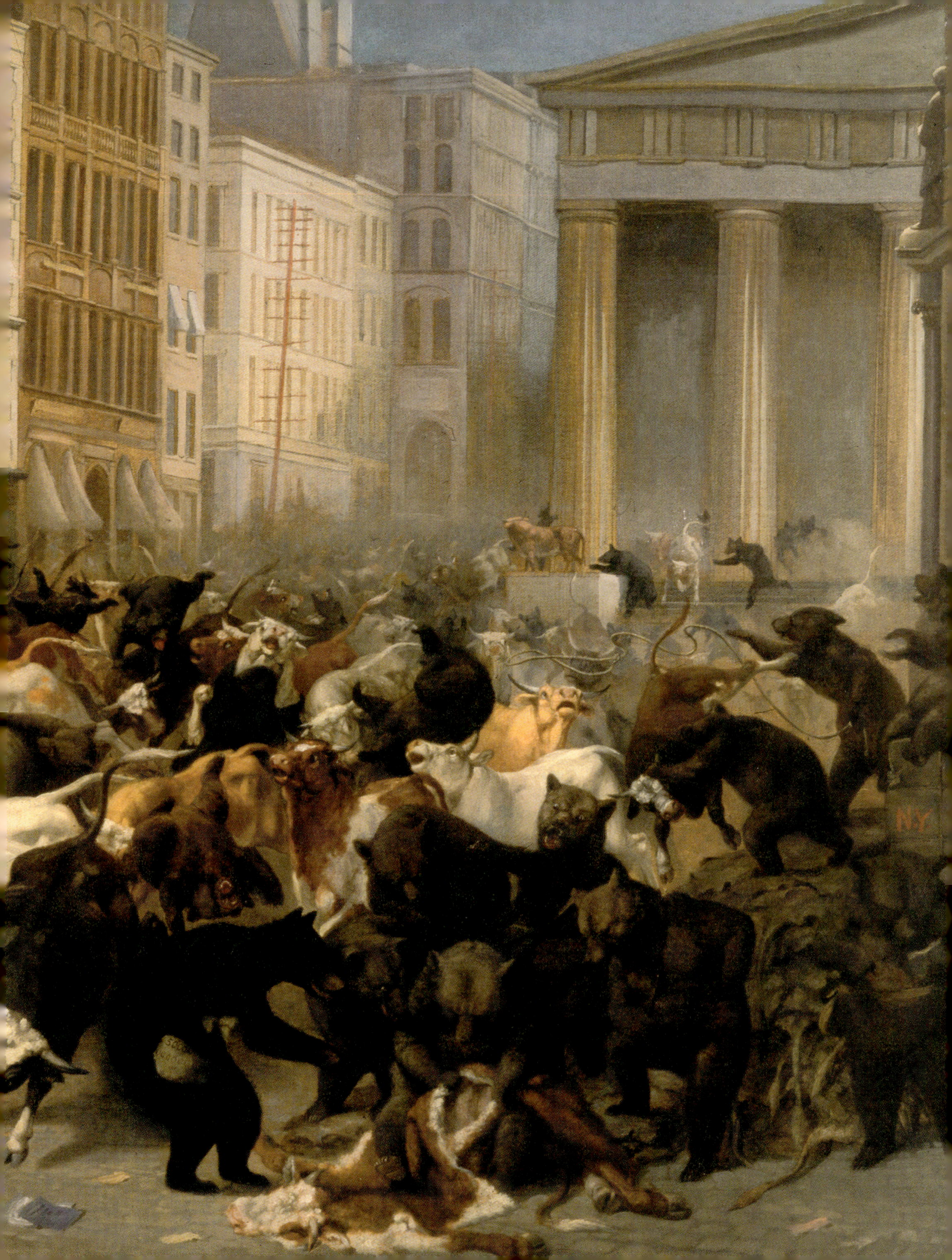
N.Y.

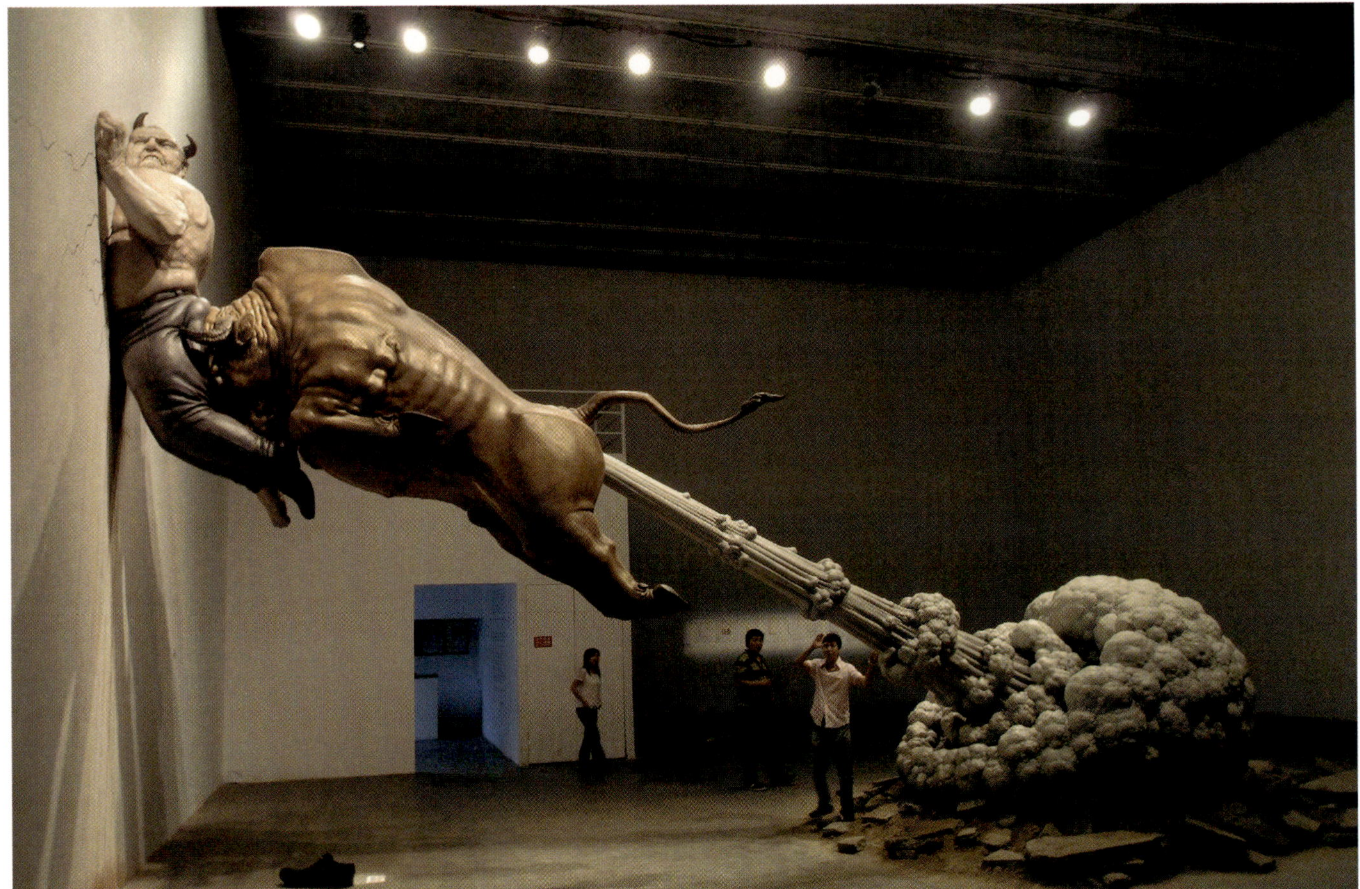

Figure 25

Chen Wenling, *What You See Might Not Be Real* (2009).

AP Photo/Ng Han Guan.

myth of the rational market, but in turn it carries its own ideological baggage, making a particular form of economic behaviour seem 'natural' rather than immoral, and therefore immune to popular contestation.[27]

Although the broad trajectory of modern and postmodern visualisations of finance is towards greater abstraction, there is nevertheless a persistent reliance on anthropomorphic allegories. For example, with its stylised lion's head, etched with fierce, imperious expression, and four aggressively posed human legs, the creature depicted in Gordon Cheung's *Lion Dance 2* plays on Western fantasies and fears of China that now increasingly presides over the terrain of global finance (Cheung is discussed in Chapter 2). At the same time, by tapping into a Chinese mythological tradition in which animal figures carry a dense array of symbolic meanings, Cheung's work recalls the allegorical style of eighteenth-century visual responses to the South Sea Bubble. Chen Wenling's striking sculpture *What You See Might Not Be Real* (2009) plays with the return to 'animal spirits' explanations in the wake of the 2008 crisis (Figure 25). It features a massive, muscled bull goring a comedy version of a hyper-masculine broker (supposedly Bernie Madoff), complete with horns, and who has literally 'lost his shirt'. The bull market is turbo-charged, with a vast cartoon cloud of rocket exhaust exploding out of its behind. The implication is that if you perceive the market through the explanatory lens of bestial finance, what you see might not always be real.

The market as god

So far this chapter has explored the way that representations of finance have focused on the emotions and passions of the people caught up in the market, both singly and as part of a crowd. This tradition of highlighting the 'animal spirits' involved in finance has offered a partial corrective to the myth of the rational market. We have seen how market players have been imagined as conspiring Jews, as financial titans, as wracked by panic and elation, as part of a hysterical crowd, and even as bulls, bears and wolves. Another way of thinking about the market, however, has concentrated not on the people within the market, but on the way that the *market itself* might be though of as a person, animal or machine. The markets (particularly after 2008 the bond markets that determined the levels of sovereign debt) are at times figured as unpredictable animals, at times 'nervous' or 'skittish', liable to 'stampede', and in permanent need of being 'reassured'. The figuration of the market as creature of uncertain origin or shape has a long tradition: Marx compared capitalism to a vampire; today we are surrounded by zombie banks; and the *Rolling Stone* journalist Matt Taibbi famously called Goldman Sachs a 'great vampire squid wrapped around the face of humanity'.[28] At other times, however, the market is presented as an omniscient, omnipotent and yet inscrutable deity, whose wrath must be appeased by propitiatory measures (which usually seem to mean austerity cuts and other neoliberal reforms), but whose Delphic pronouncements can only be interpreted by its special priests and prophets. Neoliberal theory has characterised the market as a vast, impartial, and incomparable information-processing machine, but at times this way of thinking about the market has shaded into a fetishised rendering of the market as an irascible god whose whims and moods must be divined from the signs that surround us: 'The Market, we are taught, is able to determine what human needs are, what copper and capital should cost, how much barbers and CEOs should be paid, and how much jet planes, running shoes, and hysterectomies should sell for. But how do we know The Market's will?'[29] The market is the name we give to the unimaginable. Like the gods of ancient Greece, it is a fantasy projection, a mystified personification of powerful forces that cannot be explained but which seem to control everything we do.[30]

There is a long tradition of allegory, personification and deification in thinking about the market, most notably with the Roman goddess Fortuna symbolising the role of chance in human fate, in the shape of a female deity, or, in Daniel Defoe's sexualised personification of the spirit of finance, 'Lady Credit'. For example, Hans Sebald Beham's engraving *Fortuna* (1541) shows the goddess with a wheel of fortune upon which a mere mortal perilously sits (Figure 26). In Thomas Cleland's cover drawing for the inaugural issue of *Fortune* magazine (1930, barely six months after the Wall Street crash) the wheel of fortune has now become a giant industrial wheel (Figure 27). Or, for example, an illustration from *Puck* magazine in 1909 shows *Dame Rumor* as a withered crone, sitting upon a stock ticker amid the noxious fumes of 'Inside Information' (Figure 28).

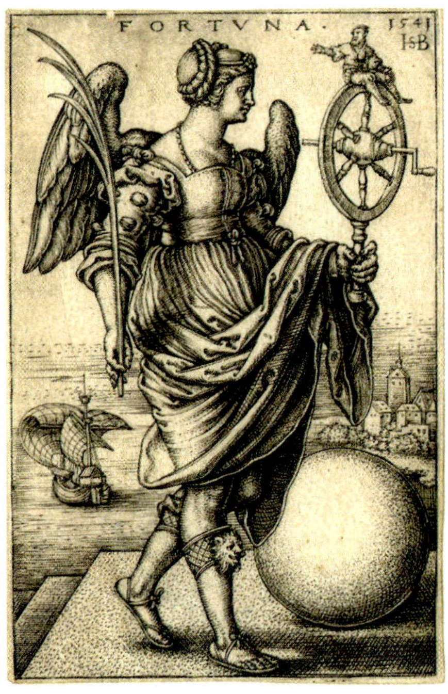

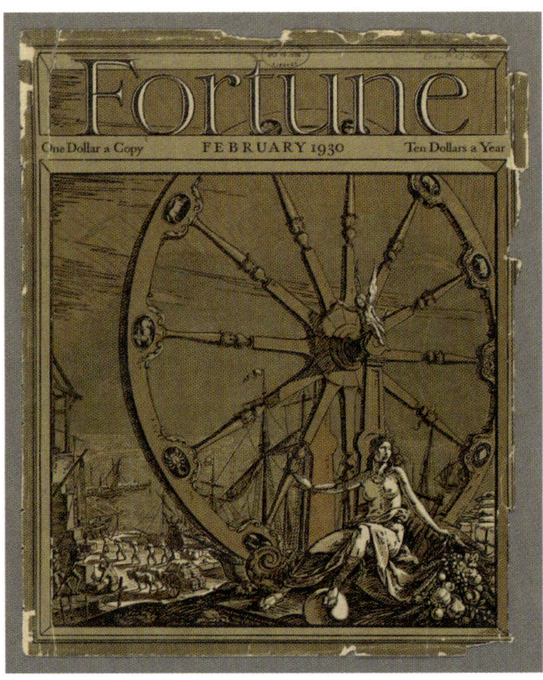

Figure 26

Hans Sebald Beham, *Fortuna* (1541).

© Trustees of the British Museum.

Figure 27

Thomas Cleland, *Fortuna and the Business Cycle*, *Fortune Magazine* vol. 1, no. 1 (February 1930), cover.

Harvard College Library.

Figure 28

Udo J. Keppler, *Dame Rumor*, *Puck*, vol. 66, no. 1697 (8 September 1909), centrefold.

Prints & Photographs Division, Library of Congress, LC-DI.

Despite this tradition of allegorical portrayals of elements of finance such as credit, fortune and rumour, the notion of the market as a divine person does not lend itself readily to direct visualisation. At best, 'market fundamentalism' has relied at times upon substitutions, such larger-than-life market titans as the saintly prophets of profit, or visual allusions to the market as itself a larger-than-life being.[31] An advert for investment firm State Street's Standard & Poor's Depositary Receipts (SPDR) product, for example, represents the market as Gulliver when he is a giant among the Lilliputians, with ordinary humans clinging desperately onto his coat-tails, accompanied by the strap line, 'If you can't beat the market, join it.' It is arguable, however, that the very impossibility of visualising the market in its entirety (in the advert, we cannot see the giant's head) is in part what lends the neoliberal fantasy of the all-knowing market its power, its capacity to generate a sense of ubiquitous yet 'headless' power, as Goldin+Senneby's installation project reminds us. On the one hand, the notion of the market as a person imbued with 'animal spirits' holds out the possibility of comprehending in a single image the impossible totality of global finance. On the other, the impossibility of giving visual shape to that idea collapses 'the market' back into a fetishised abstraction, the inscrutability of which serves to maintain the troubling suggestion that finance is best left to the technocratic 'experts' who constitute its priesthood.

PUCK

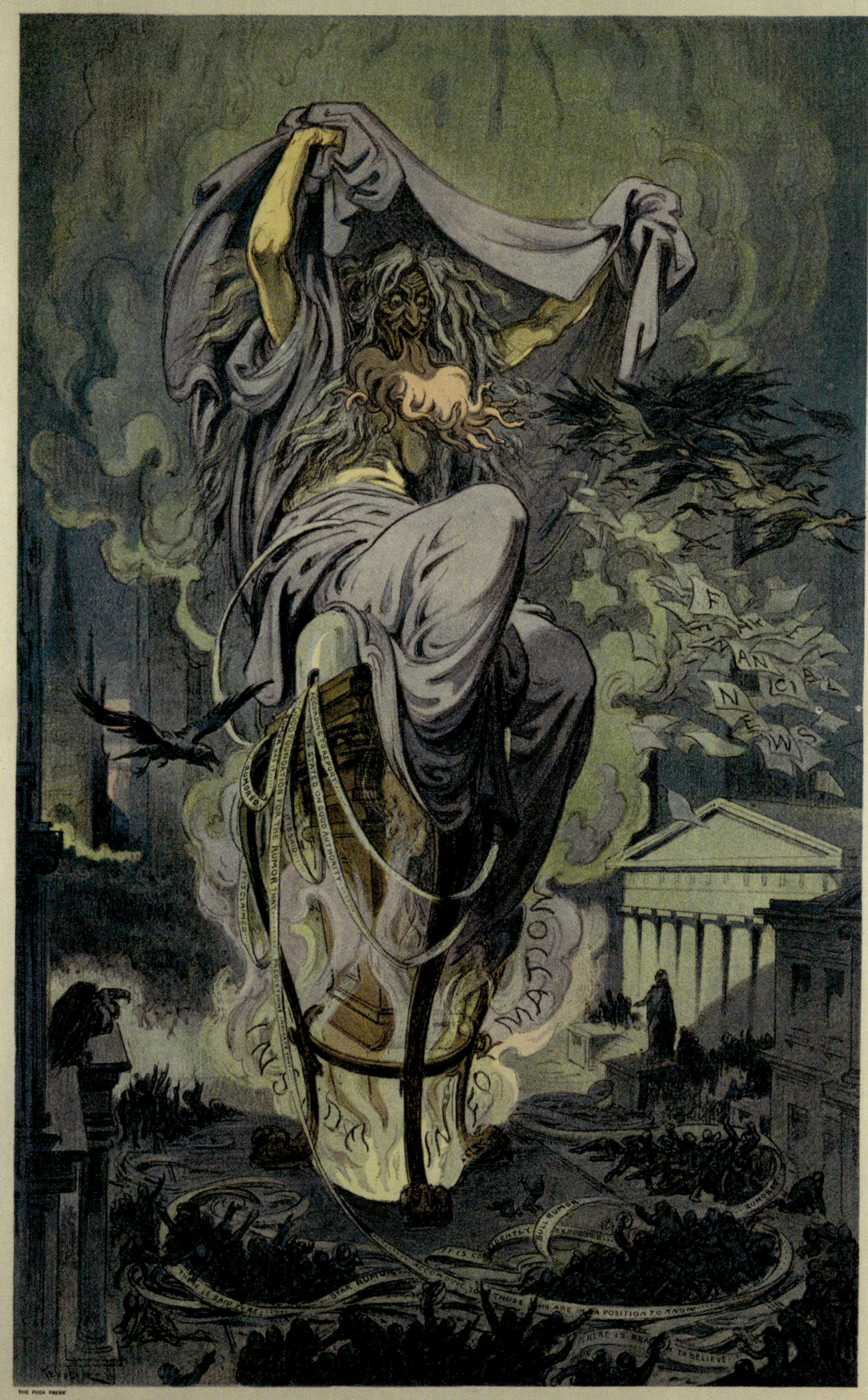

DAME RUMOR.

THE WITCH OF WALL STREET.

Notes

1 For a discussion of the origin of Keynes's phrase, see Paul Crosthwaite, 'Animality and ideology in contemporary economic discourse: Taxonomizing Homo Economicus', *Journal of Cultural Economy* 6:1 (2013): 94–109.

2 On the changing social status of the speculator, see Alex Preda, *Framing Finance: The Boundaries of Markets and Modern Capitalism* (Chicago: University of Chicago Press, 2009), pp. 53–81.

3 See Leo G. Mazow and Kevin M. Murphy, *Taxing Visions: Financial Episodes in Late Nineteenth-Century American Art* (University Park, PA: Palmer Museum of Art, Pennsylvania State University, 2010).

4 On the development of realism in American literature as a counter-weight to the feared erosion in a speculative economy of tangible and lasting value, see Andrew Lawson, *Downwardly Mobile: The Changing Fortunes of American Realism* (Oxford: Oxford University Press, 2012); and on *trompe l'oeil* paintings of money in American art see Walter Benn Michaels, *The Gold Standard and the Logic of Naturalism* (Berkeley, CA: University of California Press, 1987).

5 For more on this interpretation of the painting, see Robert L. Herbert, *Impressionism: Art, Leisure, and Parisian Society* (New Haven, CT: Yale University Press, 1988), pp. 52–5; Carol Armstrong, *Odd Man Out: Readings in the Work and Reputation of Edgar Degas* (Chicago: Chicago University Press, 1991), pp. 32–4; and Marilyn A. Brown, 'An entrepeneur in spite of himself: Edgar Degas and the market', in Thomas L. Haskell and Richard F. Teichgraeber III (eds), *The Culture of the Market: Historical Essays* (Cambridge: Cambridge University Press, 1993), pp. 270–1.

6 For a more detailed account of these paintings see Marilyn A. Brown, *Degas and the Business of Art: 'A Cotton Office in New Orleans'* (College Park, PA: Penn State University Press, 1994).

7 Brown, *Degas*, p. 118.

8 Samuel Armstrong Nelson, *The ABC of Wall Street* (New York: S.A. Nelson, 1900).

9 *King's Views of the New York Stock Exchange* (New York: Moses King, 1898), p. 1.

10 On the public relations efforts of the New York Stock Exchange, see Julia C. Ott, *When Wall Street Met Main Street: The Quest for an Investors' Democracy* (Cambridge, MA: Harvard University Press, 2011).

11 On the American public's imagination of Gould, see Richard R. John, 'Robber barons redux: Antimonopoly reconsidered', *Enterprise & Society* 13 (2012): 1–38.

12 Steichen denied that was his intention, but the lighting for the image was rehearsed in advance with a janitor sitting in for Morgan. See Abigail Tucker, 'J.P. Morgan as cutthroat capitalist', *Smithsonian* (January 2011), www.smithsonianmag.com/history-archaeology/J-P-Morgan-as-Cutthroat-Capitalist.html, accessed 2 August 2013.

13 Slavoj Žižek, *The Ticklish Subject: The Absent Centre of Political Ontology* (London: Verso, 1999), p. 339.

14 For a Lacanian reading of investors' affective identification with securities, see Karin Knorr Cetina and Urs Bruegger, 'The market as an object of attachment: Exploring postsocial relations in financial markets', *Canadian Journal of Sociology* 25 (2000): 141–68.

15 On the modes of perception instilled by new visual technologies in the nineteenth century see Jonathan Crary, *Techniques of the Observer: On Vision and Modernity in the Nineteenth Century* (Cambridge, MA: MIT Press, 1990); and Preda, *Framing Finance*, pp. 132–5.

16 For a summary of the varying evidence, see Ott, *When Wall Street Met Main Street*, p. 2.

17 Audrey Jaffe, *The Affective Life of the Average Man: The Victorian Novel and the Stock-Market Graph* (Columbus, OH: Ohio State University Press, 2010), pp. 64–5.

18 On Smitley's book see Urs Stäheli, *Spectacular Speculation: Thrills, the Economy, and Popular Discourse*, trans. Eric Savoth (2007; Stanford: Stanford University Press, 2013), p. 173. For a discussion of the feminised trope of credit, see ibid., pp. 171–94, and Marieke de Goede, *Virtue, Fortune and Faith: A Genealogy of Finance* (Minneapolis: University of Minnesota Press, 2005), pp. 21–46.

19 Jean-Christophe Agnew, *Worlds Apart: The Market and the Theater in Anglo-American Thought, 1550–1750* (Cambridge: Cambridge University Press, 1986).

20 Mary Poovey, *Genres of the Credit Economy: Mediating Value in Eighteenth and Nineteenth Century Britain* (Chicago: University of Chicago Press, 2008), p. 82.

21 Sarah Burns, 'Party animals: William Holbrook Beard, Thomas Nast, and the bears of Wall Street', *American Art Journal* 30 (1999): 9–35 (pp. 22–3).

22 For an overview of these tropes in economic imagery, see Mike Emmison and Alex McHoul, 'Drawing on the economy: Cartoon discourse and the production of a category', *Cultural Studies* 1 (1987): 93–111.

23 For details of these images, see Burns, 'Party animals'.

24 James K. Medbery, *Men and Mysteries of Wall Street* (Boston, MA: Fields, Osgood, 1870).

25 Robert J. Shiller and George A. Akerlof, *Animal Spirits: How Human Psychology Drives the Economy, and Why It Matters for Global Capitalism* (Princeton, NJ: Princeton University Press, 2009).

26 Robert J. Shiller, 'Animal spirits depend on trust', *Wall Street Journal*, 27 January 2009, and 'A failure to control the animal spirits', *Financial Times*, 8 March 2009.

27 Crosthwaite, 'Animality and ideology'.

28 Matt Taibbi, 'The great American bubble machine', *Rolling Stone*, 9 July 2009, www.rollingstone.com/politics/news/the-great-american-bubble-machine-20100405#ixzz2nwEHiAEw, accessed 20 December 2013.

29 Harvey Cox, 'The market as God', *The Atlantic Monthly* 283:3 (1999): 18–23.

30 Campbell Jones, *Can the Market Speak?* (Alresford, Hants.: Zero Books, 2013).

31 'Market fundamentalism' is a coinage of Thomas Frank in *One Market Under God: Extreme Capitalism, Market Populism, and the End of Economic Democracy* (New York: Doubleday, 2000). On the neoliberal fantasy of the limitless market, see Angus Burgin, *The Great Persuasion: Reinventing Free Markets Since the Depression* (Cambridge, MA: Harvard University Press, 2012), and Michael J. Sandel, *What Money Can't Buy: The Moral Limits of the Market* (London: Allen Lane, 2012).

Markets without people

Justin Fox

When artists depict financial markets, they tend to focus on the people – greedy people, sad people, conniving people, angry people. Animals make occasional appearances too, but usually to represent the 'animal spirits' that purportedly drive human behavior.

Serious academic study of financial markets, on the other hand, has long tried to take human beings out of the picture. The starting point for all economics is of course the dispassionate, somewhat inhuman being known as 'economic man', but in mainstream financial economics even this creature is quickly dispensed with. A small group of supremely rational and self-interested arbitrageurs are assumed to be so adept at sniffing out market inefficiencies and mercilessly exterminating them that one need pay attention only to market prices and their movements. ('Neoclassical finance is a theory of sharks', MIT finance professor Stephen Ross once wrote, 'and not a theory of rational *homo economicus*'.)

The attractions of this bloodless approach are clear enough. As the great British statistician Maurice G. Kendall proclaimed in announcing the results of an early 1950s investigation into wheat futures prices, 'the symmetrical distribution reared its graceful head undisturbed amid the uproar of the Chicago wheat-pit'. That is, graceful statistical laws appeared to describe market behavior so well that one could safely ignore all those clumsy, confusing humans who were doing the trading.

This impulse long predated Kendall. In 1900 a graduate student in Paris, Louis Bachelier, completed a doctoral dissertation that depicted price movements on the Paris Bourse in entirely mathematical terms, in the process prefiguring several great twentieth-century breakthroughs in statistical method. But Bachelier was careful to note that he did not think his models captured the entire reality of the market, just the probabilities at a 'given instant' in time. Go any farther into the future, and he didn't think his maths was much help.

By the 1950s, though, this modesty was evaporating. Lots of statisticians and economists could now do the sorts of calculations that Bachelier had pioneered, and they had discovered during World War II that their skills were of genuine value to the military and to manufacturers. With the war over, it was only natural that they started applying this approach to the data-rich environment of financial markets. The arrival of computers on university campuses in the early 1960s only added impetus.

So we got things like Modern Portfolio Theory, the Capital Asset Pricing Model, the Efficient Market Hypothesis, and the Black-Scholes Option Pricing Theorem. All were grand models that abstracted from the individual participants in a market to say big things about how markets operated. All were useful, and to some extent even right. But they missed a lot – most obviously the people.

That started changing a bit in the 1980s, as a small group of upstart scholars began importing observations from psychology into economics and finance. They were not discussing people so much as bundles of traits and quirks – the disposition effect, overreaction, overconfidence,

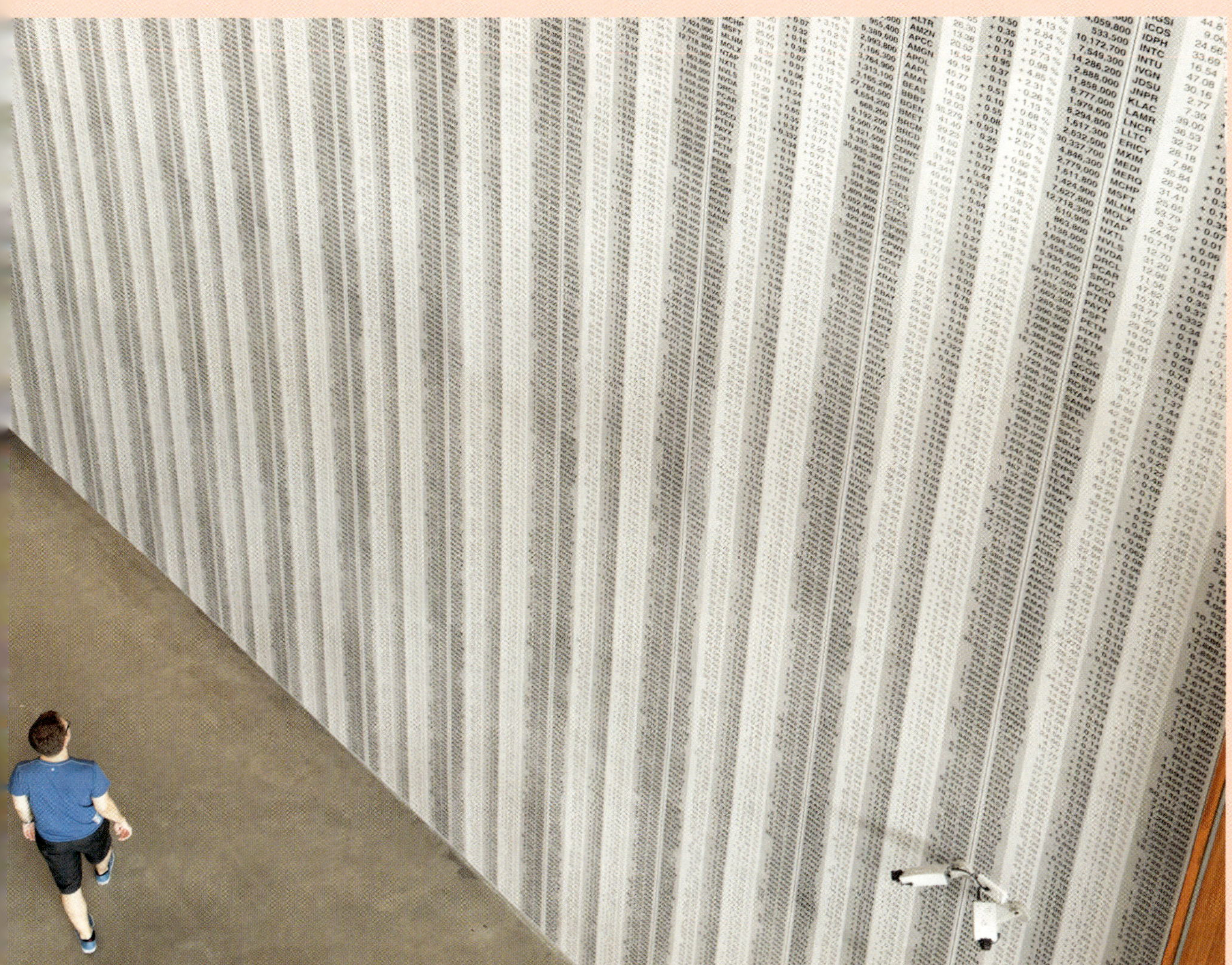

Figure 1

Claude Closky, 'Untitled (NASDAQ)' (2003). Wallpaper, silkscreen print. Exhibition view '21st Century, Art in the First Decade', Gallery of Modern Art, Brisbane, 2010. Curated by N. Chambers, A. Clark, T. Ellwood, S. Raffel, K. Weir.

Courtesy Claude Closky and Galerie Laurent Godin, Paris.

myopia, etc. But it was *something*. Another new line of research examined the incentives and constraints faced by the professional arbitrageurs (the sharks) who were supposed to keep markets in line. Yet another examined how even a market populated by only rational investors would still be tested by bubbles and crashes as long as there was disagreement and incomplete information.

Since the global financial crisis of 2008 there has been an understandable explosion of interest in how financial markets go wrong. But it is probably fair to say that the explanations that have gained the most traction among financial economists are those of the impersonal sort – liquidity traps, multiple equilibria, rational herds. The role of emotions, of culture, of *people* still get pretty short shrift.

Maybe that is as it should be. Much of the action on financial markets is now controlled by machines. It has to be – trading in stocks and some derivatives now often takes place at the sub-millisecond level. Humans simply cannot keep up; they just design the algorithms and get out of the way. This demands a different kind of artistic depiction, and it's beginning to get it, with an increasing number of images showing an abstract world of finance that is devoid of people. Still, if financial markets entirely lose their connection to people, exactly what purpose will they be serving?

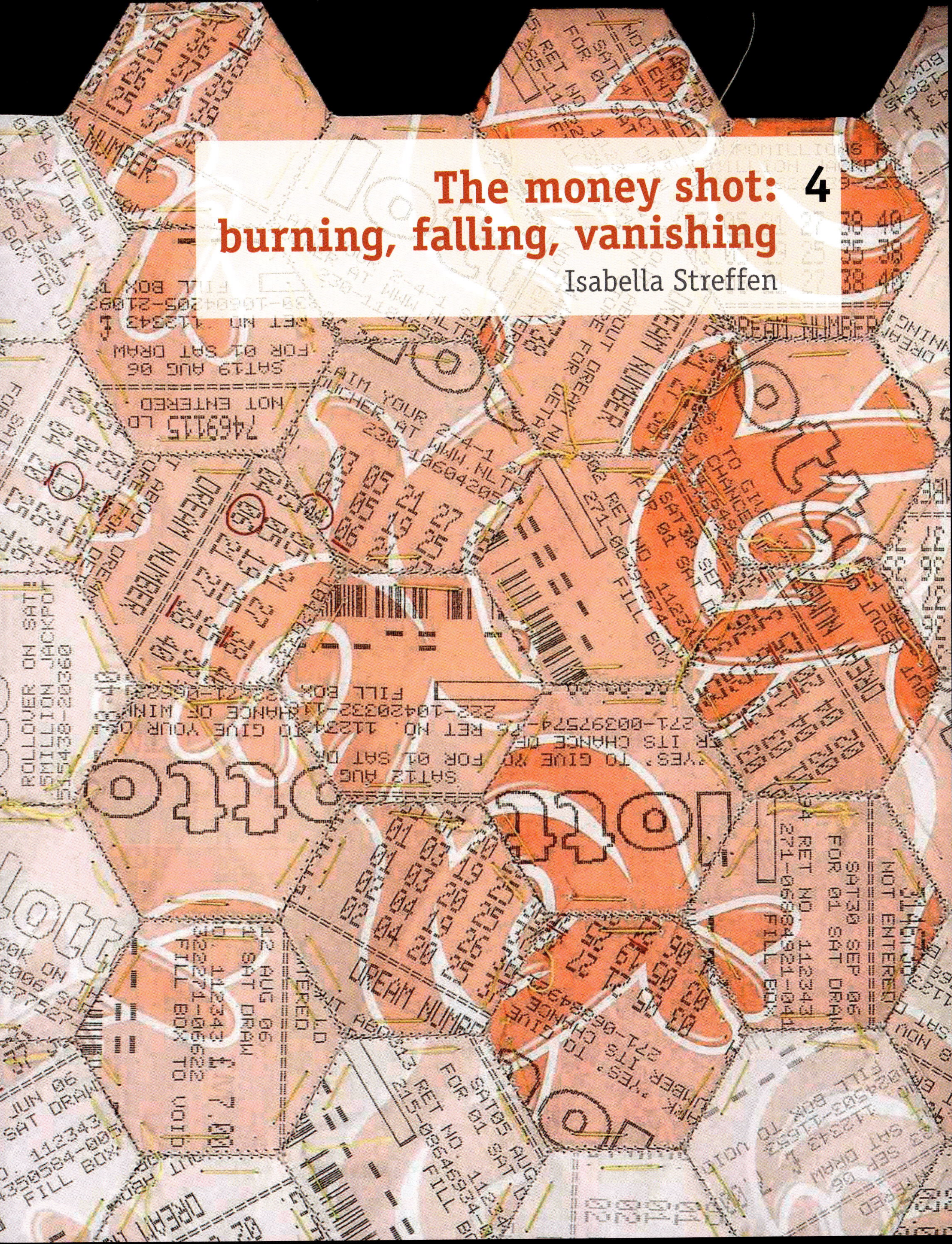

The money shot: burning, falling, vanishing 4

Isabella Streffen

The money shot: burning, falling, vanishing

Isabella Streffen

> When bankers get together for dinner, they discuss art. When artists get together for dinner, they discuss money. (Oscar Wilde)

There are millions of ways to burn a million quid or more in contemporary art. You can blow your money financing biennials, or launching a gallery, or purchasing art investment funds. You can buy a Richter,[1] or a sexual encounter with an artist,[2] or be part of a theatrical performance where you can bet long, short and hedge with actors performing as former fund managers.[3]

These most recent inter-twinings of art and money take place at a point in time where the ramifications of a lack of money in everyday life are particularly evident, both on an institutional and personal level. Following the failure of the market in 2008, the division of the field of art into those art works that are trophies for the 1% (if you like, signifiers of 'money to burn') and works that critique the precipitating financial and social instruments has never been more acute. But art is still a strong market (and easily discussed and reduced in those terms), with record-breaking prices offered up at auction, and unprecedented audience figures for blockbuster exhibitions. Max Haiven wonders about the cause of this (perhaps unexpected) blooming of interest, suggesting 'I think that, in a funny way, art is more important than ever, because art sort of insists that something *other* than money is valuable in this world'.[4] Peter Schjeldahl, writing about the recent $142 million sale of *Three Studies of Lucian Freud* by Francis Bacon at Christie's in New York is more trenchant: 'Desires occupy a scale between idle liking and ruinous passion. The present art market plainly won't quit until it hits the end of the line. So it has our attention. ... Art in today's market fascinates by performing like money itself, on a miniaturised stage: Mammon's Mini-Me'.[5]

In *Art and Money*, however, Marc Shell suggests that 'the tendency to merge money with art is often misinterpreted as essentially a late capitalist phenomenon', before stating categorically that 'an icon, like a coin is an instance of intellectual value invested or impressed in a material thing'. [6] Refusing utopian and psychoanalytic readings of the contemporary fascination with art and its value, Shell argues not only that representational practices are intrinsically hitched to systems of exchange, but that the key factor revealing our anxiety relating to the relationship between art and money is the idea of an ideal and a real thing: 'Money is thus understood as a manifestation of authority and substance, of mind and matter, of soul and body ... of inscription and inscribed. This makes money disturbingly close to Christ as a competing architectonic principle.'[7]

The relationship between the ideal and the real thing was particularly exposed during the 1960s and 1970s, as artists moved away from earlier forms of more traditional portraiture and the concerns with the surface of money and *trompe l'oeil* re-presentations that had been present in the work of money artists such as William Michael Harnett, John Haberle

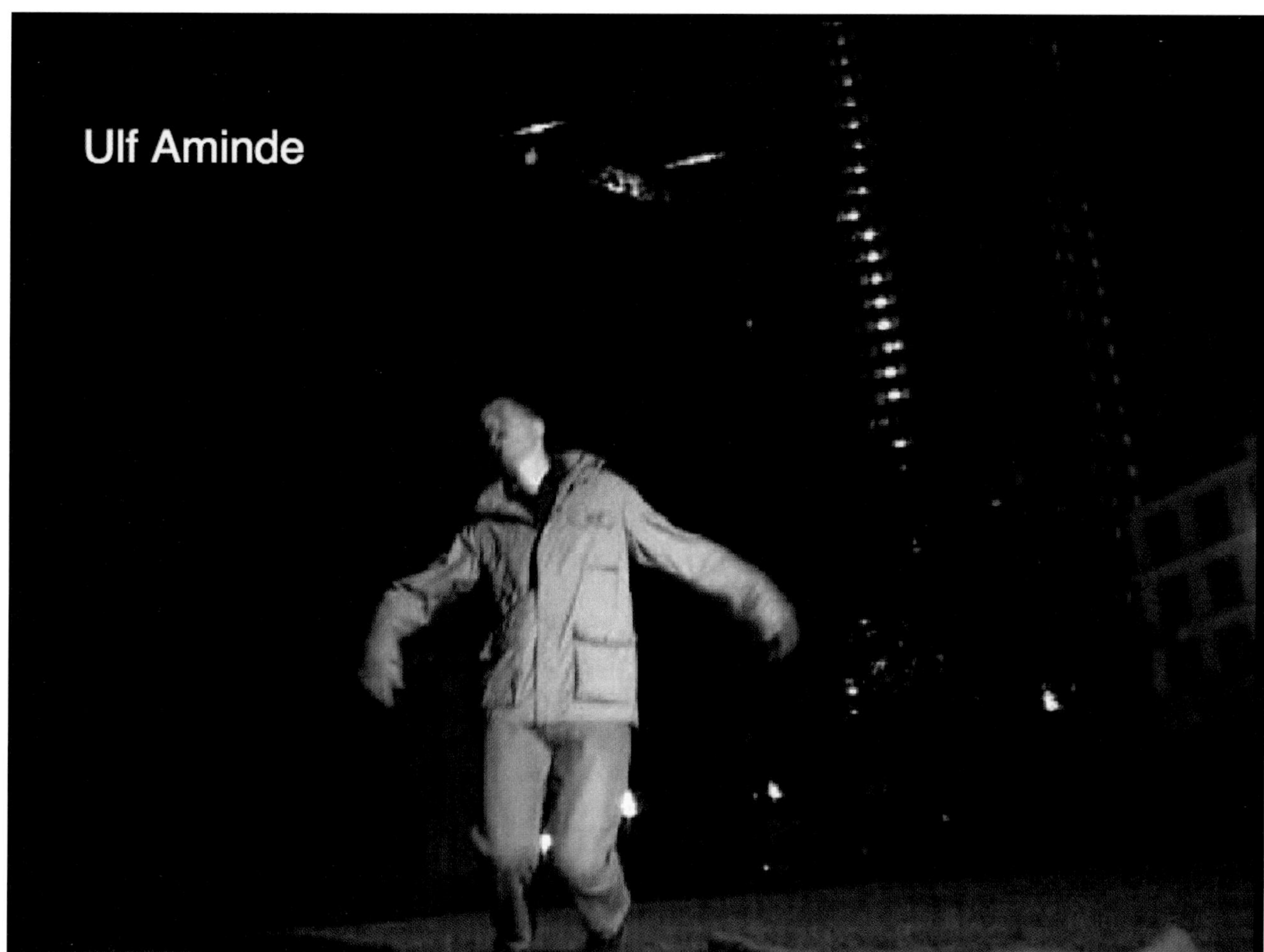

Figure 1

Ulf Aminde, *Schamdruck,* still from video (2009).

Image courtesy of the artist and Galerie Tanja Wagner, Berlin.

and Otis Kaye, towards more conceptual and often performative practices about finance and currency. These works, which often had their roots in post-Gold Standard changes in global and domestic economies, prefigure postmodern aesthetics with their focus on modes of production and technologies, the critique of the grand narrative, and questions of the organisation of knowledge. Mark Taylor describes the 'strangely characterless character' of this work and suggests that it engages with 'an inconspicuous crisis of representation, which occurs when the referents that once provided secure foundations for thought and action are "liquified" and begin to circulate freely in worldwide webs whose dynamics we do not yet understand'.[8]

Cildo Meireles' polemical *Insertions Into Ideological Circuits* is an important work that is situated within those strange webs of invisible exchange. Meireles is one of Brazil's most significant living artists and his works operate as a bridge, not only between the neo-concretism of the 1950s and the emergent conceptual art of the 1960s, but also between poetry and philosophy. He consistently explores the co-existence of freedom and control, taking a *contra* position against cultural, curatorial and artistic authoritarianism as he dissects and reformulates conceptual principles of art, politics and economics.

The *Insertions* consisted of two parts: the *Coca-Cola Project*, and the *Cédula* or *Banknote Project*. For the Banknote variant, subversive messages in English and Portuguese were

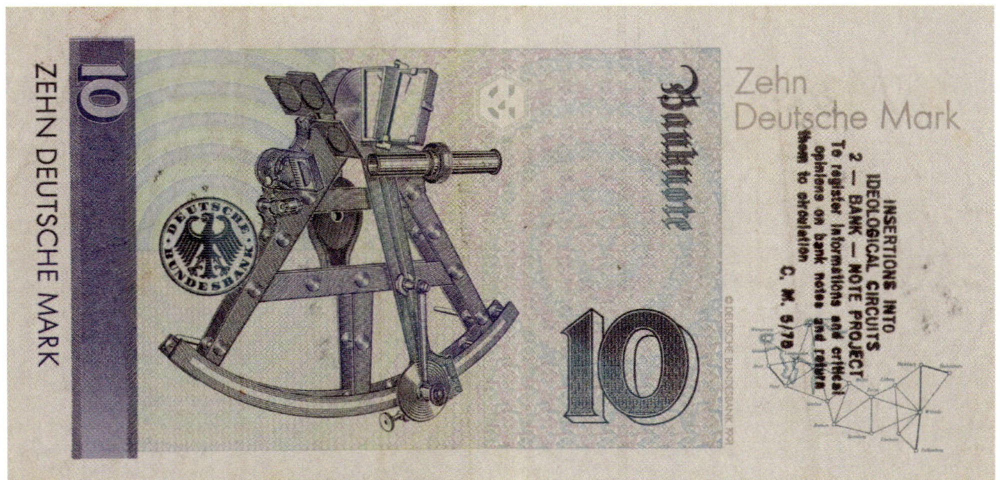

Figure 2

Cildo Meireles, *Insertions Into Ideological Circuits* (1970). Rubber stamp on banknotes.

rubber-stamped onto banknotes, which were then sent back into normal circulation. The title of the work was stamped on one side of the note, and the 'mobile graffiti' of political slogans appeared on the reverse.[9] The *Coca Cola Project* functions similarly, with transparent labels attached to Coca Cola bottles that were then returned to the Coca Cola factory for re-use. Meireles frequently rejects the interpretation of his work as political but his usual preference for the poetic does not apply with this work, which he categorically positions as a guerilla tactic of political resistance. The work only operates when the notes are in circulation.

Meireles aimed to create a system that did not depend on centralised control for the circulation and exchange of information in response to Brazil's militarised, oppressive political system that was essentially opposed to broadcast and print media. He duly set out his position: in society, there are certain mechanisms for circulation, and these circuits clearly embody the ideology of the producer:

> the insertions are a negation of authorship, of copyright. They aren't works of art, they are propositions for action and participation. Nor are they a form of multiplied art – or whatever you want to call them (multiples or editions). I never sold any of my Inserçőes em Circuitos Ideológicos. Anyone can make them, albeit not for commercial purposes. Actually my Inserçőes bothered me. At the time I thought that the artist's problem was whether or not to be in the Sau Paulo Biennial, for example. The problem was: could my work be in the Biennial? Could I explain the Inserçőes being part of museum collections, as works of art? I soon understood, though, that they weren't souvenirs or editions. They were actually examples of action. So, in spite of the impasse, I continued to create works. After all, conflict is the best camouflage.[10]

The challenges of censorship enacted by the repressive military dictatorship (1964–85) resulted in a further radicalisation of the political context of Meireles' work and a sharper political demand within the work to expose the social mechanisms that articulate the circulation of consumer goods and information. *Insertions* was included in Kynaston McShine's ground-breaking 1970 *Information* exhibition at the Museum of Modern Art in New York which established Conceptual art as a dominant tendency in the United States.[11] In his introductory text to the show, McShine identifies the key features of the exhibition as being art that reaches out to a wider audience, art that provides a refreshing experience and art that is participatory.[12] *Insertions Into Ideological Circuits* certainly fits each of these categories, and the terms may perhaps herald the emergence of relational art in the 1990s.

As financial instruments and concepts become increasingly abstracted, dematerialised, and *non-human*, artists have sought out the visceral, the affective, and the *rematerialised*. And it is the strategy of rematerialisation that emerges in the 1980s that structures many artists' responses to finance. This rematerialisation is often realised in a highly visually seductive form, as this chapter will show, alluding to the properties of the art works even as those works themselves are dematerialised.

This chapter proposes that there are three broad aspects of rematerialisation dominating the way in which finance is thus visualised by contemporary practitioners: the tropes of burning and falling; the staging of disappearances and reappearances; and the promises and implied lies of contracts. What these strategies have in common is anxiety – not just anxiety about monetary fragility or value – as a symptom of a prevalent condition of groundlessness. In her 2011 text *In Free Fall: A Thought Experiment on Vertical Perspective*, film-maker and philosopher Hito Steyerl explores the implications of falling towards an unstable ground, summing up a sense of the contemporary moment:

> We cannot assume any stable ground on which to base metaphysical claims or foundational political myths. At best, we are faced with temporary, contingent, and partial attempts at grounding. But if there is no stable ground available for our social lives and philosophical aspirations, the consequence must be a permanent, or at least intermittent state of free fall for subjects and objects alike.[13]

Burnings and fallings: Ulf Aminde, K Foundation, Geraldine Juárez

The burning of legal tender banknotes is frequently construed as a form of madness, so unlikely does it seem that the destruction of currency can be a rational act. Many artists have defaced currency, but comparatively few have completely destroyed it (and perhaps more importantly, the promise of what it could possibly buy, even if it does not) on a grand scale.

Beginning on a cold, rainy August night in 1994 in a boathouse on the Scottish island of Jura, one of the most notorious artworks of the 1990s began to unfold.[14] Journalist Jim Reid had accompanied Jimmy Cauty and Bill Drummond of the K Foundation, and

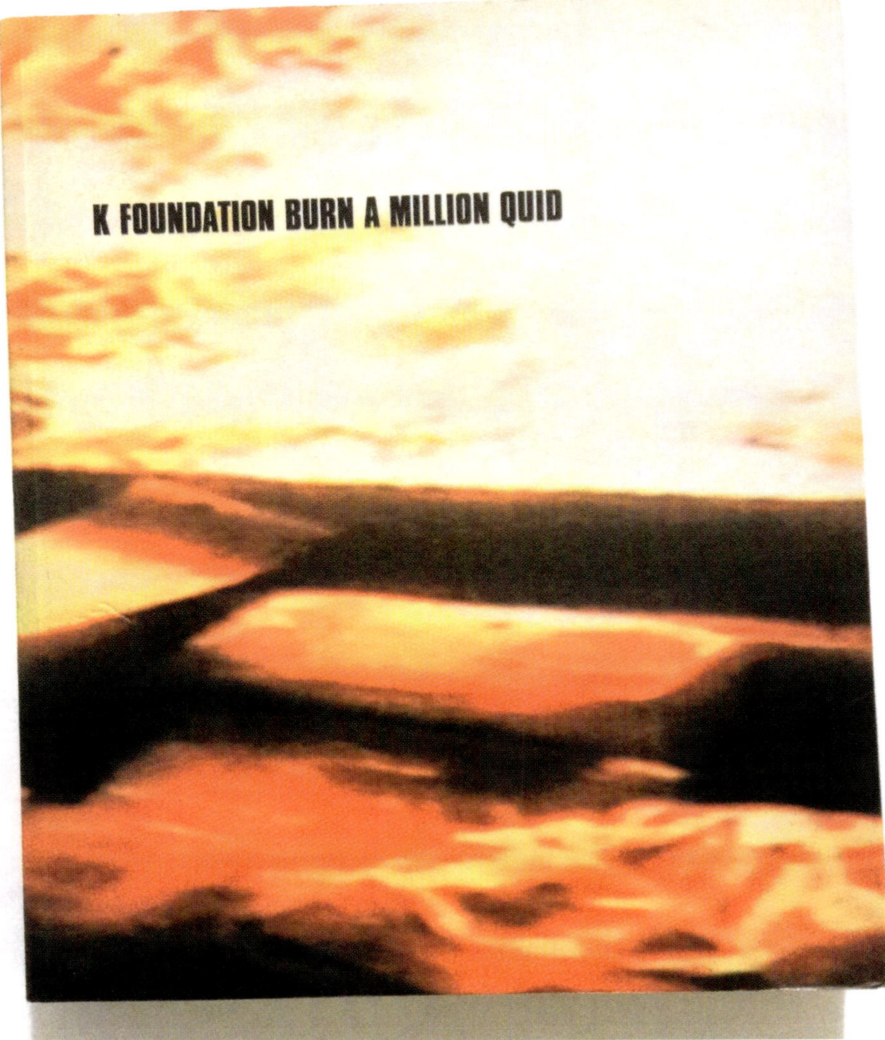

Figure 3

Isabella Streffen, *Appropriating A Million Quid* (2014). Still from video.

Courtesy the artist with acknowledgements to the K Foundation.

their colleague Alan Goodrick (known as Gimpo) on a bizarre mission. His testimony in the *Observer* newspaper was the first public statement on a project that has been dogged by questions of veracity and intent from the beginning. As an anonymous commentator remarked, 'it's a powerful statement to burn our motivation'.[15]

In that dark boathouse between 12.45 and 2.45am, the K Foundation burned a million pounds in the form of twenty thousand £50 notes.

The K Foundation grew from Drummond and Cauty's successful career in popular music as the KLF. During the opening years of the 'roaring nineties' – a period in which deregulation, a decline in income inequality and falling unemployment combined with low inflation to pave the way for an unprecedented economic boom, as well as the burgeoning shoots of global neoliberal hegemony – the KLF was one of the biggest selling popular music acts in the world, with their distinctive pure trance sound bringing success in Europe and the United States.[16] Their work was always charged with a focus on ideas which seemed to resist the traditional signs of success in that field (flashy cars, designer clothes and supermodel girlfriends), and soon engaged with the art world by making an award of £40,000 to Rachel Whiteread as 'worst artist' on the occasion of her winning the Turner Prize. Not satisfied by goading the art establishment, and heralding their retirement from music with the Surrealist gesture of leaving a dead sheep at a pop awards ceremony, they used their money to pursue their interest in money:

> What Cauty and Drummond were primarily concerned with was money: money as art, art as money. The possibility of meaning beyond money. To challenge the power of money. And if none of that makes sense, maybe that was the intention.[17]

A chain of events, discussions with galleries, and proposals outside of the art system ensued, before the pair resolved on their final action. Even then, it was not spectacularised, but hidden, concealed, unceremonious, off-the-cuff, as though they were determined to break the spell of the cold hard cash, and treat it as contemptuously as possible. They certainly conceived of the work as art, something which at the time was denigrated by critics and curators, who believed that any spectacle around the project would damage its impact, and that the cathartic experience of destroying it themselves reeked of self-indulgence and weakened its potential as an act of art.

Following the torpid burning the K Foundation returned to England, where Cauty destroyed what he thought was all the video and photographic evidence of the event. A media storm subsequently erupted, with a mixed response from members of the public who alternated between finding the action radical, poetic, profoundly meaningful, hideously selfish and irresponsible.[18] Gimpo's surviving film formed the basis of a series of screenings, and a brick made from the ashes was also exhibited, with a book finally published that showed some of the images, and contained comments from audiences at the screenings.[19] At a later point, Drummond and Cauty signed a self-imposed legal agreement not to discuss the event for twenty-three years. So *K Foundation Burns A Million Quid* has achieved mythic status: did it really happen and are the artists so scarred by the artwork that they cannot bear to discuss it?

It would be interesting to see what we would make of a burning on this scale during these post-crash times. Geraldine Juárez – born in Mexico City, 'de-schooled' in New York, based in Gothenburg, a fellow of FAT LAB and a founder member of DataSlöjd studio – has been profoundly influenced by the K Foundation in her approach to copyright.[20] Her 2012 work *Hello Bitcoin* could almost be seen as a response, but for the joyous anarchy of the video that culminates in the toasting of marshmallows over the remains of digital drives containing bitcoins.

Bitcoin is an open-source peer-to-peer electronic money and payment network, in existence since 2008. It is not backed by any sovereign government, and is described as a 'decentralised virtual currency'. Felix Martin argues that it is in many ways no different to older forms of currency, understood as simply an underlying system of credit

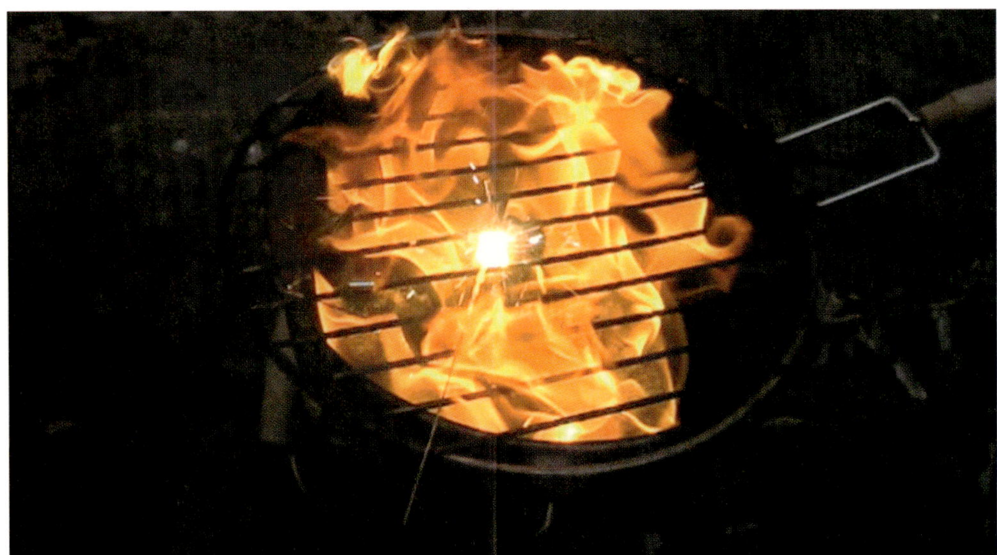

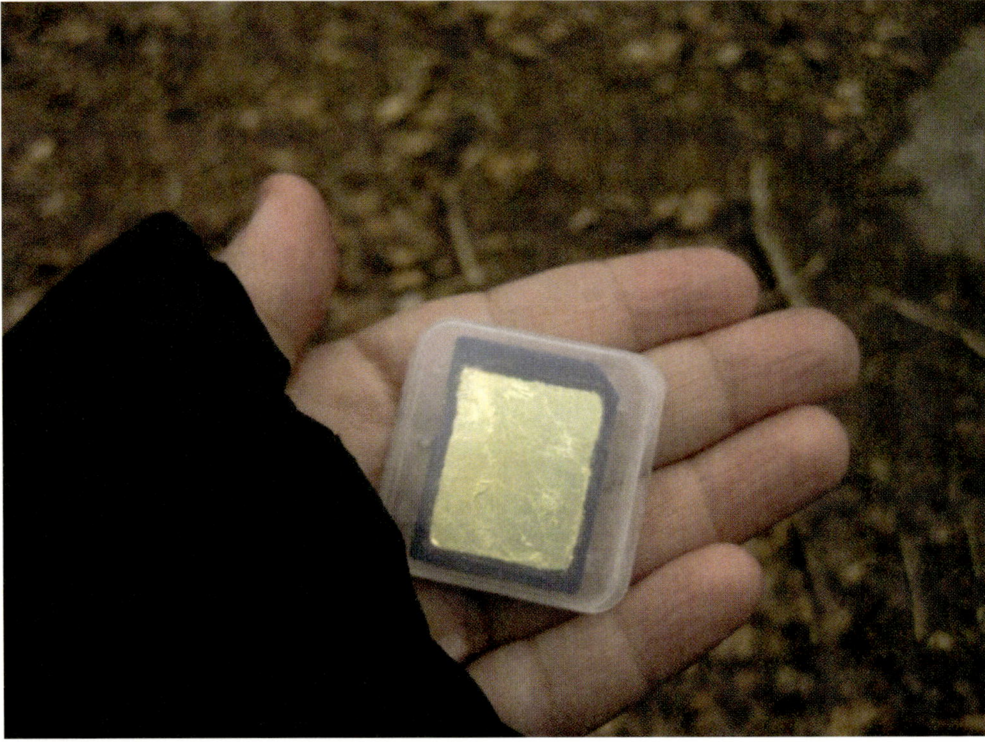

Figures 4 and 5

Geraldine Juárez, *Hello Bitcoin* (2012). Stills from video.

Image courtesy of the artist.

and clearing: 'all money is virtual, and always has been – because money is just a set of ideas'.[21] Money has existed for thousands of years, and the fact that most of the surviving artefacts are coins or tokens made from metal has given us the erroneous idea that the money is trapped within the coin like a bee in amber. It is a common perception that the coin is the essence of money. Martin traces the history of a number of alternative currencies in his book *Money: The Unauthorised Biography* to clearly demonstrate how the stone *feis* of Yap, the English Exchequer tallies (a wooden stick inscribed with details of payments) of the twelfth to the late eighteenth centuries, and the private IOUs that circulated as money during the Irish bank closure of 1970 could be 'tangible and visible record[s] of the outstanding credit that the seller enjoyed'.[22]

Juárez is dealing in bitcoins, which are objects of suspicion for many. Bitcoin was, however, established as money (however apparently unconventional) and it continues to function in that way. Angus Cameron (a collaborator of Goldin+Senneby) comments:

> Bitcoin's increasing integration into established financial and derivatives markets (it is always expressed as a metric of $US, for example) marks the difference between the creation of an electronic currency and the creation by contemporary artists of quasi-economies (both within and for particular artworks). Although artworks can become valuable assets, they do not circulate as money. Similarly, though Bitcoin is seen by some as a challenge to conventional monies, it does not carry any critique of the money economy – indeed it seeks only to extend such an economy and embed itself within it.[23]

The complex encrypted coding on which it is based is a deterrent for further engagement by the computer-timid. But Juárez is hardly that: as an accomplished hacker with a radical environmentalist practice, she gleefully wreaks havoc with the systems that come her way. In the 2013 project *Wealth Transfer* Juárez uses the pattern of stock market fluctuations as a musical waveform, pressing the output into a 10-inch vinyl record. The relationship with Autogena and Portway's *Black Shoals* is evident, yet *Wealth Transfer* and *Hello Bitcoin* effectively function as reprobate off-spring.[24] It is deadly serious work with a light, DIY, hacker ethic. It is difficult to imagine Juárez's methodology permitting her to negotiate with the stock exchange for classified information – as she says, she'd rather steal it: 'you need to get some material for free by any means. And this can be as broad as you want. Hacking, thieving, freecycling. You have to make an effort to avoid money exchange.'[25]

It is this 'freegan' approach that echoes the ethos of the K Foundation, and the seizing of established systems.[26] There is no controversy about Juárez's video, and the two burnings seem to speak to a broader trope of burning as a profound rejection of these systems. But burnings are haunted by the ghosts of images of 9/11, when burnings, fallings, banking and dematerialisation were irrevocably fused in the popular imagination. The power of the iconic images of that day – the Twin Towers ablaze, Richard Drew's *Falling Man*, interviews with Cantor Fitzgerald CEO Howard Lutnick – is such that they have been effectively repressed (indeed there is an informal concord not to show particular images of 9/11), only for them to return at the flickering edges of subsequent images of burning, falling and banking. Whether we see images of brokers sitting amongst the paper detritus of their trades in Aernout Mik's *Middlemen* (2001), or watch them on stage in Lucy Prebble's *Enron* (2009), our internal museum swiftly whisks us back to New York's devastation.

Berlin-based artist Ulf Aminde's 2009 work *Schamdruck (The Pressure of Pudency)* (see Figure 1) powerfully evokes the return of this particular idea of the real, as he stages confrontations of individual lifestyles amidst the towers of Frankfurt's banking district. Aminde does not make statements on globalisation and consumerism, opting instead for the participation of people or groups who are socially stigmatised by socio-economic mechanisms, in this case a female investment banker, a junkie and a male prostitute, all masked. The works are complex systems for examining how people 'develop very specific strategies to deal with the conditions of everyday life' and he uses this 'family' to explore, unscripted, the problems and conflicts that arise within the realm of finance and capitalism.[27] Aminde's use of non-actors ('authentic persons belonging to these scenes')[28] allows the drama of the piece to evolve, as a discussion of morality, responsibility and guilt leads first to an emotional confrontation, and then to a second, poignant, wordless video-loop: 'We simply asked a lot of people to lay down, at night, in the park, to lay down leisurely and lustfully in front of the camera, which was a beautiful alleviation of the heavy meaning, and all the things not verbally expressed in this family reunion'.[29]

Aminde's video is dark, made darker by its rendering in atmospheric black and white. There are tall buildings, skyscrapers, with over-exposed windows (the way the light blazes). All around, people are falling. Men and women of all ages, of all levels of formality, buckle at the knees and slide to the ground. There's an elderly man in a smart suit – all the signifiers of the classic, conservative banker. There's a thin blonde woman in fashionable clothing with a designer handbag. There are young men, in short sleeves, with cross-body bags, with sunglasses and trendy trainers. All of them are brought to the ground, felled, one might say, perfectly encapsulating the impact of a market crash in a visual vocabulary with which we are entirely historically familiar. The market falls. All manner of people have their legs kicked out from under them. It is a profoundly empathetic work, elegiac and elegant, with an unexpectedly disconcerting soundtrack uncomfortably echoing the sonic records extracted from the videotape of 9/11 taken by Jules and Gedeon Naudet.[30] Scalpel-sharp, the video shows repeated collapses that bring to mind not only the great financial falls, but the ruinous falling of buildings, the fall of empires, and most poignantly, the fall of bodies from the sky on 9/11. So our tropes of burnings and fallings play to our most atavistic fears, and we worry perhaps about paying for our funerals or the significance of our *petite mort*.

Vanishings and reappearances: Adam Hahn, Rhiannon Williams, RBS Collection

As the burnings and fallings of the previous section suggest both our imminent demise and our *petite mort*, the vanishing and reappearances (the sleights of hand of the accomplished magician) of the subsequent section call to our fascination with disappearance and our construction of it as a seductive delight. In *Why Hasn't Everything Already Disappeared?*, Baudrillard writes of our contemporary urge to reject the reality to which we are no longer in thrall, through embracing a strategy of disappearance.[31] The works of Rhiannon Williams and Adam Hahn exemplify this in contrasting ways.

My Loss Is My Loss is a consideration of desire and disappointment. Every week since 2002, Williams has purchased lottery tickets to the value of £10, always using the same set of numbers. The missing tickets are her small-scale wins. The rest have been cut into neat hexagonal patches, and sewn into a paper quilt, reinforced with a layer of birthday and Christmas cards to support the fragile structure. Thus, Williams's personal narrative is woven tightly into her broader critique in an extraordinary collection of loss. Williams stages a disappearance as an appearance as she invokes the 'little moment of fantasy and potential' of the new lottery ticket: 'it faces our ambiguities around appropriate uses for money and is perhaps a distasteful record of how I have spent my money, time and labour; I gamble, I lose, I work with my loss'.[32]

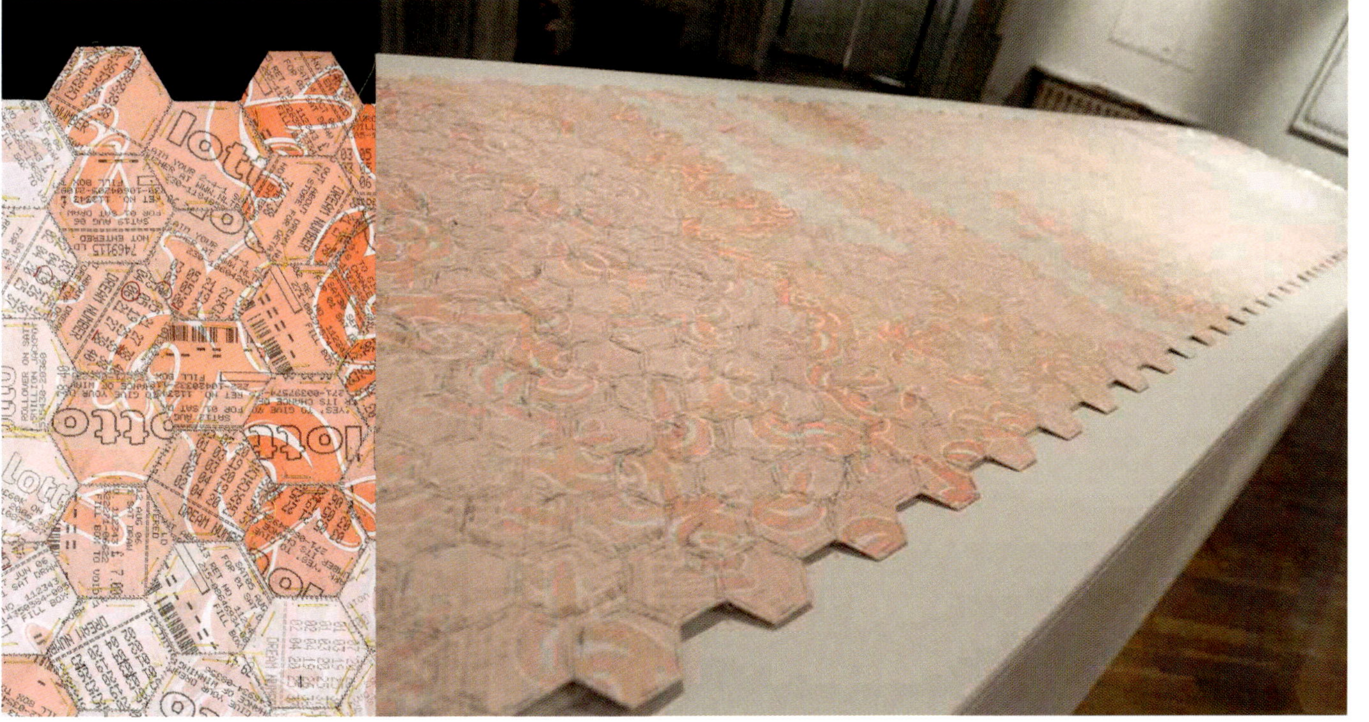

Figures 6 and 7

Rhiannon Williams, *My Loss Is My Loss* (2001–11). Paper patchwork hand-stitched from used lottery tickets, cotton, adhesive interface with card backing, 500 x 80cm.

Image courtesy of the artist.

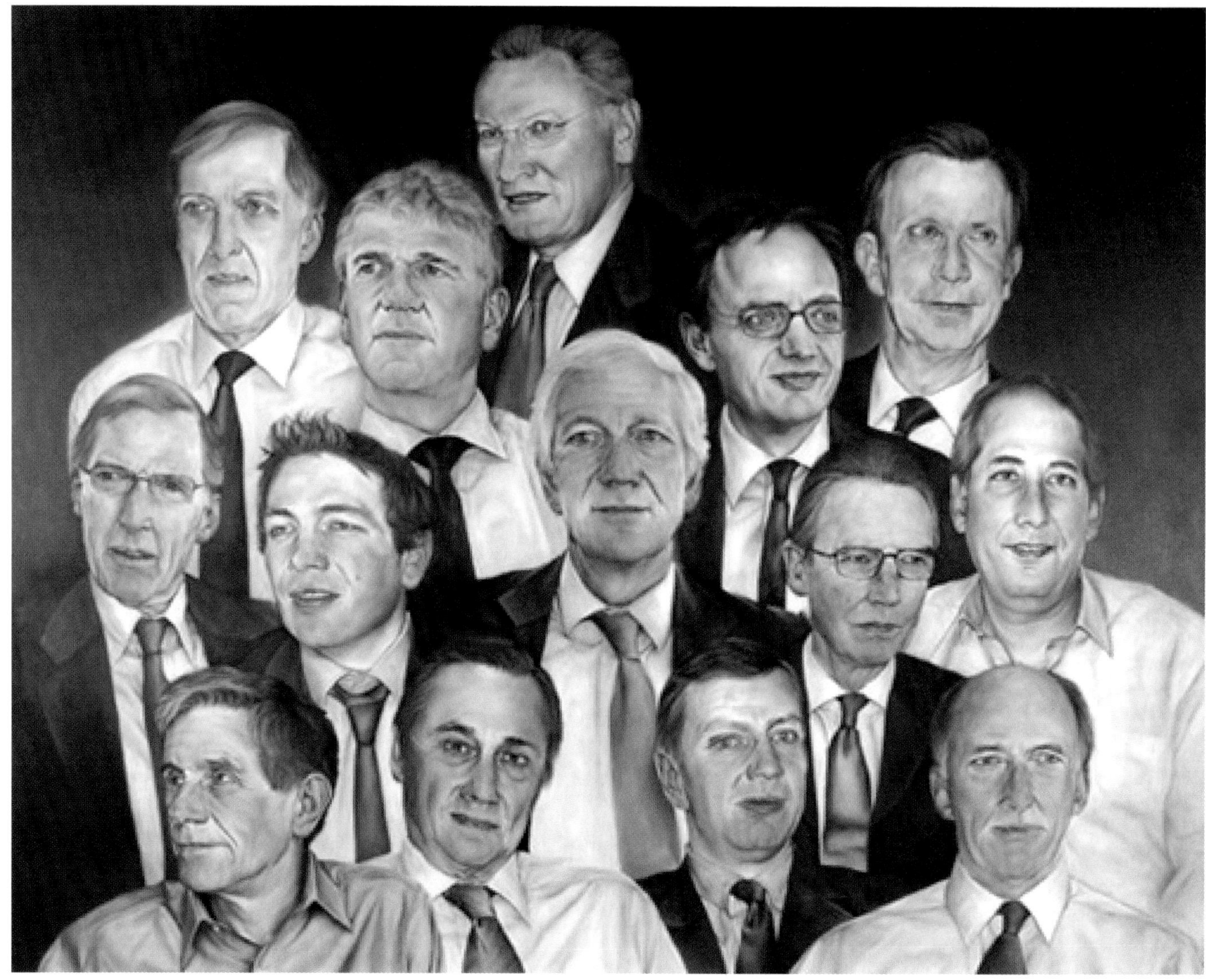

Figure 8

Adam Hahn, *The Salz Servants* (2006). Oil on canvas, 130 x 160cm.

Image courtesy of the artist.

Williams's methodical collection of paper invokes not only archives and the tropes of collections, but a thousand cinematic echoes of banknotes stuffed into bags, thrown into the air, or securely stacked in bank vaults. The scale of this loss-quilt with its fraying and disintegrating edges, allows us to imagine what it might be like to walk upon a carpet of money, or on a floor of our own squandered dreams.

Adam Hahn's *The Salz Servants* tells us a very different story. Hahn's portrait provides an intriguing gloss on Shell's notion that art and money are essentially the same thing, and it can be read as a very particular symbol of the banking crisis of 2008. Here I should note that the larger story in which Hahn's image became caught up finds an uncanny foreshadowing in Ian Rankin's 2008 novel *Doors Open*, a fiction that imagines an unusual heist involving a Scottish bank's art collection.[33]

In 2007, Lord (Dennis) Stevenson, former chairman of HBOS, commissioned a £9,000 group portrait from Adam Hahn, in the style of the 1750 masterpiece *Heads of Six of Hogarth's Servants*. Stevenson – who The Parliamentary Commission on Banking's Fourth Report concluded in April 2013 was responsible for the failure of HBOS alongside former chief executives James Crosby and Andy Hornby – appears amongst the fourteen city grandees, gazing thoughtfully off-frame in a casual position, dressed in an open-necked shirt, in the front left-hand corner of the painting. Taking proud centre stage is his chief scourge, banker-basher number one in this post-Libor-rigging, post-bailout era, lawyer Anthony Salz (by then the Executive Vice Chairman of Rothschild, and soon to be appointed to review Barclay's business practices in the wake of the Libor scandal). It is just the sort of thing to amuse the *Telegraph*'s Dashwood column. And Harriet Denny did indeed have a good long laugh, merrily pointing out that art experts now designate the portrait's inclusion of both Stevenson and Salz as 'priceless'.[34] Stevenson and Salz are of course well known as supporters of the arts, and are both former Trustees of the Tate Foundation.

I was interested to learn that Hahn had also painted Crosby, and that portraits of Stevenson, Crosby and Fred 'The Shred' Goodwin had been made in copper coins. We anticipated that this would be a powerful contemporary statement for this exhibition, and it seemed important to attempt to secure a loan. It was easy enough to find the artist who had pointedly constructed these controversial moneymen in the most material kind of money possible, namely low-denomination copper coins. I also found it simple to track down Adam Hahn, in whose portraiture practice this prescient collision had taken place. But the owner of the painting – possibly the Royal Bank of Scotland Collection, given the identity of the commissioner – proved more difficult to find.

As the RBS collection is well-known, I assumed it would be a quick job to find contact details for the curator. I confidently typed my search terms into the browser. My dematerialised search engine did its thing, and I waited for the swift spike of the 'aha moment' as the RBS collection web site turned up as the first entry. I was confident, fairly sure that I could remember accessing the information before. But this time, the first search term was a news item from the *Guardian*, trumpeting a forthcoming exhibition of this hitherto private collection. I scrolled impatiently down the page, ready to click. But, like the priceless painting in Rankin's art heist novel, it was gone. The only trace of the RBS collection now appeared to be little more than an exhibition flyer. Rather than vanishings and reappearances as artistic strategies, I had become enthralled by the disappearance of an entire collection.

In December 2009, RBS unveiled its plan to exhibit its multi-million pound corporate art collection for the first time. The collection, estimated to comprise some 4,000 items, is thought to be worth in the region of £20 million, and dates back some 250 years. Additionally, during its acquisition of the National Westminster Bank in 2000, RBS had come into ownership of the NatWest's illustrious collection, believed to include works by Reynolds, Riley and Hockney. No catalogue of the collection exists, though it seems that the Department of Culture, Media and Sport (DCMS) did instigate discussions about the production of one for reasons of access.[35]

The exhibition is thought to have been mooted in response to extensive demands for the collection to be used as a public asset, after banking failures led to 70 per cent public ownership. It never took place, although some of the key pieces from the collection have been offered to the National Galleries of Scotland, Art In Healthcare, Dundee WestFest, Kelvingrove Art Gallery and Museum, and the Royal Academy in London, and around forty works of national or historical importance are said to have been exempted from any future sales.

What is certain, however, is that RBS did sell some of the major paintings of the NatWest collection, including pieces by Gilbert & George, Frank Auerbach and Patrick Caulfield.[36] An auction also took place in Sydney, Australia on 26 November 2012 at the Shapiro Gallery. The auction brochure *Sale SH082 – Australian and International Art including Contemporary Art from The RBS Collection* included twenty-three lots from the mysterious collection and generated $127,000 (in addition to $292,500 of sales from artists not attributed to the collection but whose works were sited in that designated section of the sales brochure: without a catalogue of the collection it is impossible to clarify).

Of course many art collections are private and un-catalogued, some are indeed missing, and some – spectacularly – return. The recent reappearance in November 2013 of the Gurlitt hoard (comprising more than 1,400 art works including works by Chagall, Picasso, Matisse and Dix, with an estimated value – that is a key factor in the attraction – of £846 million) has fired the public imagination; moreover, the art heist is a familiar tale in literature and film. Many questions about the constituency and location of the collection remain unanswered at the time of writing, and I am still pursuing leads that I have no doubt will locate a collection 'hiding' in plain sight. What is abundantly clear, though, is the powerful thrill of the staging of a disappearance and the lure of the myth of the absence as presence – and the opportunity this offers artists for the construction of fictions.[37]

Promises and lies: Victoria Bradbury, Superflex, Bill Balaskas, J.S.G. Boggs

The promise and its counterpart, the broken contract, provide a rich seam of material for artists. The British banknotes that 'promise to pay the bearer' are substitutes for their own worth, exerting a complex power as objects.[38] It is generally conceived to be aberrant to destroy them past the point of their functional use, though there is a distinct tradition of self-generated currencies. It seems that remaindered and shredded banknotes or scrapped coins do not retain the power status of the still-functional equivalents. As equally problematic as using valid currency are the artistic renderings of money, whether designed as counterfeit or not. Historically, artists have been punished by the full force of law for *trompe l'oeil* works based on banknotes and coins, even when the work is explicitly not intended to deceive (and has no real power to do so, as no attempt at replication has been made).

The story of J.S.G. Boggs, long pursued by the US authorities, is a prime example. It might seem perverse to include Boggs in this section, as he is so closely associated with *trompe l'oeil* and the discourse of counterfeiting, but I suggest that his work should also be considered through the prism of relational aesthetics due to its connection with the contractual and the social.[39] Boggs, who is arguably the most famous 'money artist' due to the extensive press attention surrounding his trials, makes drawings of banknotes which he then attempts to spend in a range of establishments. It is crucial to note, however, that Boggs does not copy banknotes, or attempt to pass his works off as legal tender. Boggs considers the art of his work not as the detailed drawings, but as the social relationships constructed around his attempt to exchange his drawings for goods or services. This is explicitly his area of research – persuading people to make a conscious choice to accept art rather than money – and results in his banknotes being hard to track and harder still to collect as he refuses to sell notes to collectors, only hinting at where the note was spent, leaving them to track and acquire their object of desire.[40]

Boggs has faced prosecution for counterfeiting in both the UK and Australia, though legal proceedings have not been brought against him in the United States, where the US Counterfeiting Division has been unable to establish a legal opinion. In fact, Boggs's prosecution in the UK led directly to the introduction of the now familiar copyright notice on Bank of England notes – an interesting conflation of counterfeiting and copyright as the legislature seeks to control all possible contracts.[41]

Max Haiven is the author of a detailed survey of artists who have invented their own money (including Andy Warhol and Robert Rauschenburg); who have defaced money as an artistic strategy; who have made works from money; and whose engagement with money as material and subject goes beyond these gestures. In his 2013 essay 'The Art and Money Project: Exploring The Nexus of Creativity and Capitalism' he focuses on a number of relational works, and describes in detail Mel Chin's *Fundred Dollar Bill* project, which encourages school-aged children to design their own money and send it in to the US Treasury to try to influence the US government's policy relating to lead-contaminated soil in some communities. Haiven also describes some of the many artist-designed banknotes that aim to support alternative economies (in the spirit of Boggs, perhaps), as they aim to have a practical use while undermining the Disney Dollar. Finally, he turns to the Amsterdam-based *Exchangibition Bank*, 'a sort of itinerant art-financial institution which pops up on street corners, art international festivals and … other financial institutions' and the project of artist Dadara (Daniel Rozenberg).[42] Dadara has taken this work to festivals including 'Burning Man' in the United States, for instance, which foregrounds the gift economy, where he gifted a zero banknote in exchange for a Spiritual Karma Laundering Contract. Recent appearances of the *Exchangibition* include the 2013 Glastonbury festival, where conversation, storytelling and mud were swapped for zero denomination notes. Although not a household name like the Cattelans, Höllers and

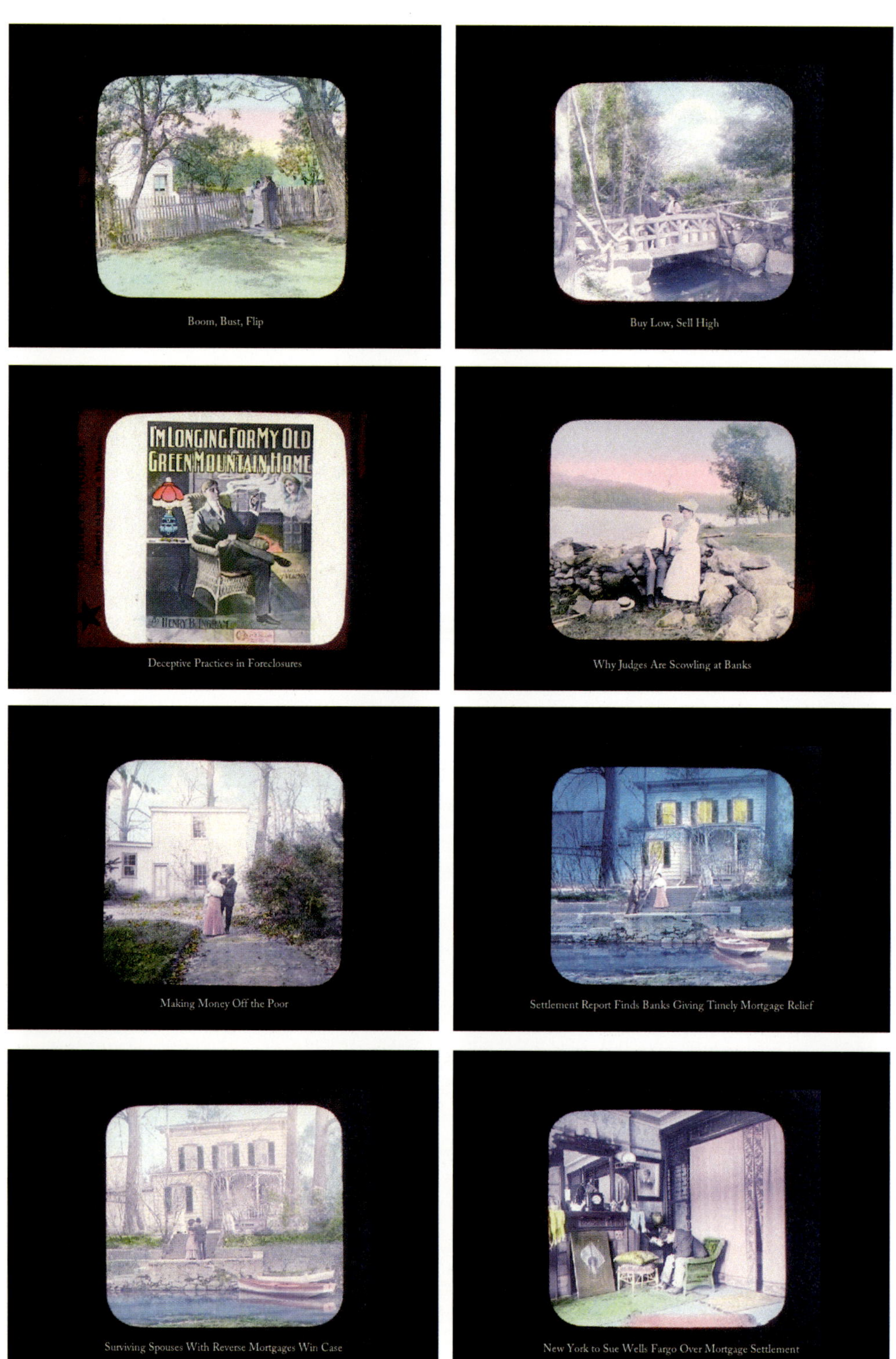

Figure 9

Victoria Bradbury, *Foreclosures 2.0* (2011). Single channel projection of a processing sketch.

Courtesy of the artist.

Tirivanijas that usually illustrate discussions of Bourriaud's concept, Dadara's work 'models possible universes' through the social contract.[43]

It is the reappearance of this contract that seems contextually specific, as individuals and organisations have sought legal redress to resolve perceived contractual breakdowns relating to the 2008 crash. The artists in the next section work with the concept implied in money – the concept of a promise to be realised – and with the consequences of the failures of promises. Dealing with issues such as the correlation of insubstantiality and house value, and the failure of the legislature in the face of systemic inability to understand the implications of financial instruments and practices, Victoria Bradbury, Bill Balaskas and Superflex all question the promises implied and lies suggested by contractual relationships.

American artist Victoria Bradbury, who learnt to code as she learnt to draw, collides the pre-cinema culture of magic lantern slides with continuously and instantly accessible, up-to-the-minute *New York Times* headlines from the 'foreclosures' section. The luscious colouration of Henry Ingram's nineteenth-century slides evokes the Golden Age's idyllic upper-class model of American domestic life in the decade in which home sales were first officially recorded. Bradbury treats the dematerialised code as though it has the materiality of the original glass slides – both heavy and fragile simultaneously – while the evanescent digitised slides draw attention to the easily shattered dream of home ownership. This cunning play of material and immaterial immaculately prefigures the slippage of the two in the context of mortgage loans, contracts and repossession orders. One minute it's arguably the most material thing possible – bricks and mortar – but if the market shifts just a fraction, it can evaporate like steam. The home is forfeited, and the contracted debit relationship is the only thing evidently present, solid, impossible to renegotiate.

London-based, Greek-born Bill Balaskas has been preoccupied with the global economic crisis and the nature of capitalism for a decade. In his works *The Market Will Save Us* and *The Vision of The Market*, Balaskas presents the market as a new god: dogmatic, unassailable, capricious. Originally part of an event developing interventions between London and Istanbul (making a link between the traditional and historical site of financial markets, and the emergent markets of Istanbul), *The Market Will Save Us* comprised a 23 metre banner on the façade of the Royal College of Art and a full-page advert in *Frieze* (edition of March 2013) displaying the same text.

Balaskas asks some unsettling questions. Will society be 'saved' by the art market? Is art to be called to save our souls? His banner evokes something of not only War Office propaganda posters – to paraphrase: 'What did you do in the [culture] war[s], Daddy?' – and echoes of religious billboards typically found outside churches with their claim that 'Jesus will save us', but also of the 'Keep Calm And Carry On' branded products that

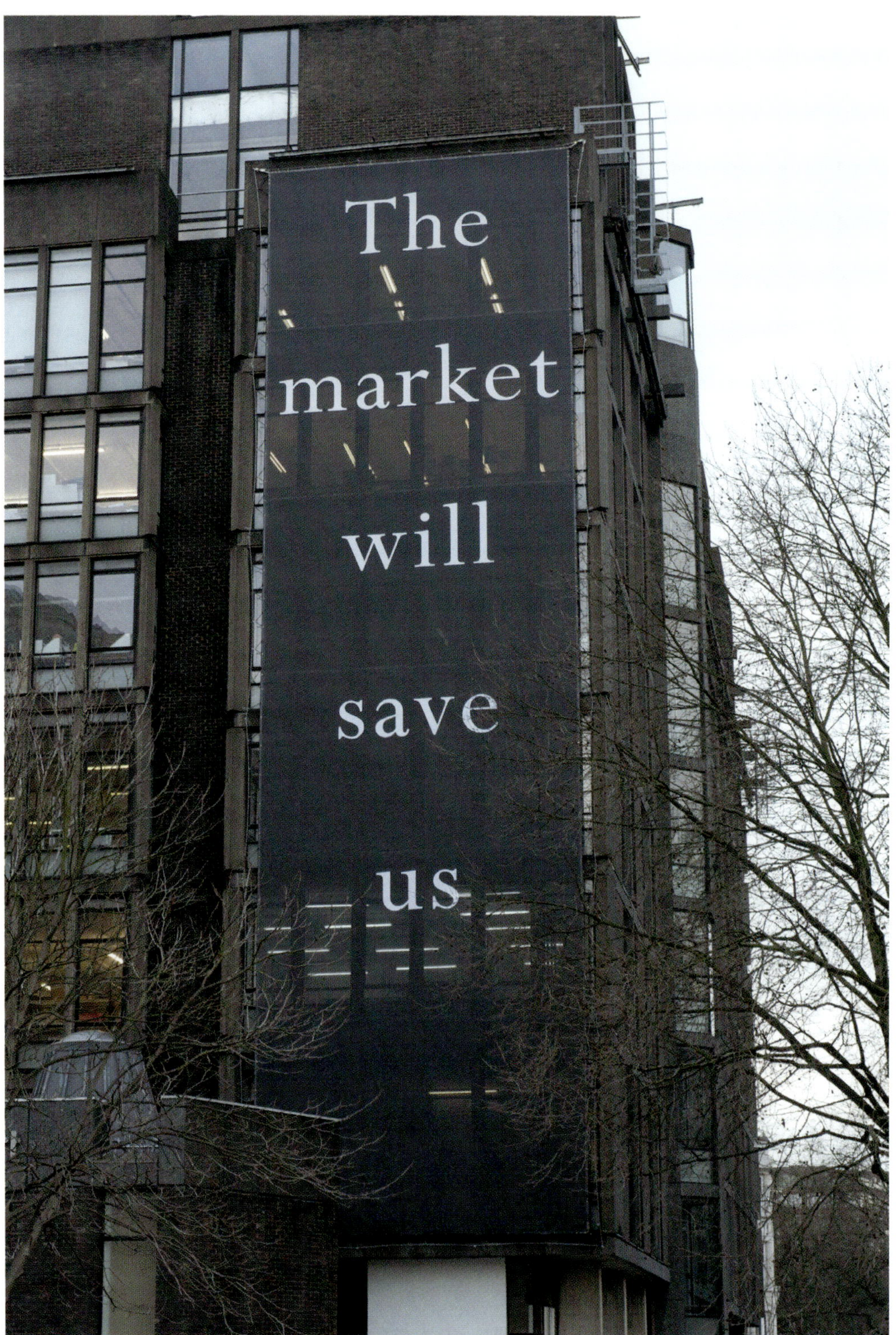

Figure 10

Bill Balaskas, *The Market Will Save Us* (2013). Banner on the facade of the Royal College of Art, 2340 x 680 cm.

Courtesy of the artist and Kalfayan Galleries, Athens–Thessaloniki. Photo by Dominic Tschudin.

are synonymous with 'all being in it together'. Balaskas's banner is monumental in scale, referring perhaps to his assessment of the size of our need for salvation. In common with Bradbury, he inverts the logic of dematerialisation. The scale, weight and complex structural requirements of the work belie the ease with which we carry it away with us, and the power of the work lies not in its phraseology, but in the promises it implies: somewhere, something has promised to save us. Following the financial scandals that have emerged into the public domain since the crash of 2008, many of us are all too painfully aware of the value of our various contracts and the paucity of their worth. We are far from reassured by Balaskas's declaration; rather, we are unsettled and destabilised by it.

The contract as the site for art – whether a social promise for salvation from a religious standpoint or a remedy of law – is certainly not new. There is an argument to be made that the present context demands keen questioning not only of the power relations inherent in our legal arrangements, but also of the weary cynical acceptance that all contractual agreements are inherently corrupted.

In 2009, Danish art collective Superflex, whose modus operandi predominantly fixates on interventions into legal contracts (often challenging copyright laws, a practice it shares with the K Foundation and Geraldine Juárez), entered into a contract with the ANZ Bank. The work *Today We Do Not Use The Word Dollar* established that during trading hours (9am until 4.30pm) on one particular day (27 May 2009) any staff member using the word 'dollar' would be obligated to pay one dollar into the employees' social fund. The contract set out the conditions for the undertaking, and recorded the amount of 'slippages' or 'fines' that needed to be paid. In his critical response to the work, Jon Bywater proposes that the use of the inclusive pronoun 'we' in the title has the dual task of creating the space of a party game while simultaneously recognising the politics of language.[44] As a range of minority groups have demonstrated, 'we' is a word pregnant with privileges, and its repeated use indicates that the 'we' of the title needs to be considered very carefully indeed.

Superflex uses the same mechanism and some of the same process in their subsequent work, illustrated here in *Today We Don't Use The Word Recession* (2010). Responding to the demise of the 'Celtic Tiger' economy (once the fastest growing in the world, but currently one of the most severely affected by the economic downturn) Superflex suggests that it is due to 'liberal bank regulation, bad political governance and a reliance on speculative property development'. They go on to note that 'the average Irish family has lost half its financial assets and unemployment has risen faster than anywhere else in Europe'.[45]

Superflex invited the citizens of Cork in Ireland to partake in a new agreement, invoking the power of language to stave off unhappy events. For the 2010 Midsummer Festival, Superflex proposed an intervention into Irish law: the banning of the word 'recession' in the hopes of lifting the spirits of the citizens and to initiate Cork's emergence from recession. Superflex worked with Lord Mayor Councillor Dara Murphy to craft a proposal to the city council that outlawed the use of the word 'recession'. Superflex puts our belief systems to the test as we are forced to question whether an event can be brought about or staved off by the use of specific words. Here, the term 'recession' (from the Latin *recedere*, to go back) operates as a word of magical power, with the implied ability to crumble economies as it slips from unwitting lips. If no longer using the word will make us feel better, could we in fact talk ourselves into recession simply through the repetition of the term?

From Superflex's original proposition – an intervention into the laws of a sovereign state is an ambitious artwork in any assessment – a compromise agreement was reached, and it was democratically agreed that the Council would issue a decree advocating that on one specific day, citizens should not use the word 'recession'. The decree was issued and states:

> DECREE
>
> TODAY WE DON'T USE THE WORD 'RECESSION'
>
> Through the power of positive thought and collective action, Lord Mayor Cllr. Dara Murphy decrees that for one day, to lift ourselves out of the doom and gloom the citizens of Cork should refrain from using the word
>
> 'Recession'
>
> The citizens of Cork are invited to join with the Lord Mayor in the collective ambition to help drive Cork out of recession and into recovery from this day forward. To kickstart this recovery the lord mayor requests on Thursday 17th June, 2010, that the people of Cork shall in all public utterances, statements and communications, replace the word 'recession' with alternative words or phrases. Citizens are asked to create their own new alternatives, thus contributing to re-imagining the future of the City of Cork. And so recommend to the people of Cork under the Common Seal of the Lord Mayor.[46]

In considering how contemporary artists continue to reflect and challenge the imagery of finance, I have – to borrow terminology from the banking world – speculated upon some of their strategies of action, metaphor and appropriation. I have sought to mirror their fragmentation of the grand narratives of finance and circulation with a text that is itself part of the currency of those strategies. The art works under discussion are not objects as they once might have been. For all of their seductive rematerialisation, their power lies in their activation:

> while the commodities produced by our civilisation circulate on the global markets according to their monetary and symbolic value – with their pure materiality manifesting, at best, through their private consumption – it is contemporary art alone that is able to demonstrate the materiality of the things of this world beyond their exchange value.[47]

Figure 11

Superflex, *Today We Don't Use The Word Recession* (2010). Legal decree.

Courtesy of the artists and Nils Staerk Gallery. Photo: Superflex.

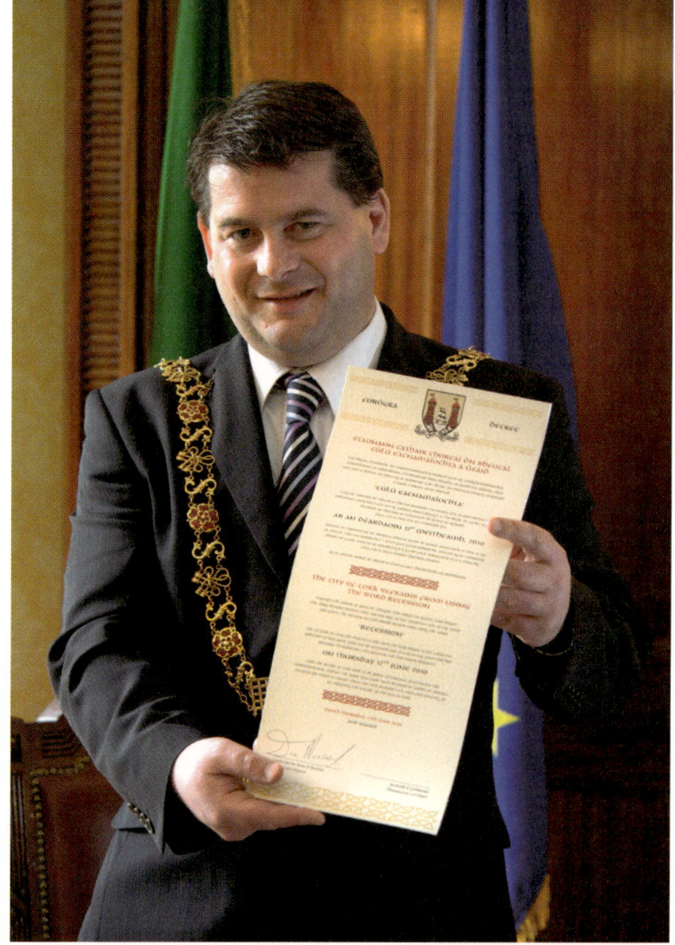

Figure 12

John Haberle, *Imitation* (1887). Oil on canvas, 10 x 14 inches.

Courtesy of the National Gallery of Art, Washington DC and New Century Fund, Gift of the Amon G. Carter Foundation.

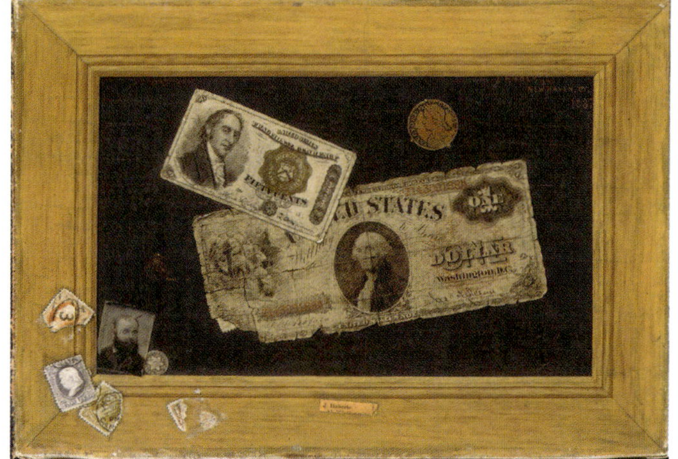

Notes

1 Actually, you can't buy a Richter for a million pounds. Richter's 1968 painting *Domplatz, Mailand* sold in 2013 for a stratospheric $37 million.

2 Andrea Fraser, *Untitled*, 60m video (2003) described in Gary Trebay, 'The way we live now: 6-13-04: ENCOUNTER; sex, art and videotape', *New York Times*, 13 June 2004, www.nytimes.com/2004/06/13/magazine/the-way-we-live-now-6-13-04-encounter-sex-art-and-videotape.html, accessed 12 October 2013.

3 This was the premise of Unlimited Theatre's *Money: The Gameshow*, written and directed by Clare Duffy (2013).

4 Max Haiven, 'The Art and Money Project: Exploring the nexus of creativity and capitalism', 4 June 2013, http://maxhaiven.com/2013/06/04/the-art-and-money-project-exploring-the-nexus-of-creativity-and-capitalism/, accessed 12 October 2013.

5 Peter Schjeldahl, 'The Circus', *New Yorker*, 13 November 2013, www.newyorker.com/online/blogs/culture/2013/11/record-auction-sale-of-francis-bacons-three-studies-of-lucian-freud.html, accessed 14 November 2013.

6 Marc Shell, *Art and Money* (Chicago: Chicago University Press, 1994), pp. 8, 10.

7 Ibid., p. 7.

8 Mark C. Taylor, *Confidence Games: Money and Markets in a World Without Redemption* (Chicago: Chicago University Press, 2004), p. 25.

9 Paulo Herkenhoff, Gerardo Mosquera, and Dan Cameron, *Cildo Meireles* (London: Phaidon, 1999), pp. 10–12, cited on the Tate website, www.tate.org.uk/art/artworks/meireles-insertions-into-ideological-circuits-2-banknote-project-t12526/text-summary, accessed 30 June 2013.

10 Cildo Meireles and Frederico Morais, 'Material language', *Tate Etc* 14 (Autumn 2008): 100.

11 Kynaston McShine was Associate Curator in the Department of Painting and Sculpture at MoMA from 1968–71.

12 Kynaston McShine, Introduction to 'Information' (1970), in Alexander Alberro and Blake Stimson, *Conceptual Art: A Critical Anthology* (Cambridge, MA: MIT Press, 1999), pp. 212–14.

13 Hito Steyerl, 'In Free Fall: A thought experiment on vertical perspective', *e-flux online journal* #24 (April 2011), www.e-flux.com/journal/in-free-fall-a-thought-experiment-on-vertical-perspective/, accessed 1 September 2013.

14 Jim Reid, 'Money to burn', *Observer*, 25 September 1994, cited in www.libraryofmu.org/display-resource.php?id=387, accessed 16 October 2013.

15 www.libraryofmu.org/display-resource.php?id=387, comment number 3 (anonymous) on 14 March 2007, accessed 16 October 2013.

16 Joseph Stiglitz, 'The roaring nineties', *Atlantic Monthly* 290:3 (October 2002), 75–89.

17 Reid, 'Money to burn'.

18 Chris Brooke and Alan Goodrick, *K Foundation Burn A Million Quid* (London: Ellipsis, 1997). All views cited are recorded in the book, many unattributed.

19 Ibid.

20 The Free Art and Technology Lab is an organisation dedicated to enriching the public domain through the research and development of creative technologies and media. The network is committed to the values of open entrepreneurship and licences and the abolition of secrecy, copyright monopolies and patents. Their website is http://fffff.at/.

21 Felix Martin, 'The list: Felix Martin on alternative currencies', *Financial Times*, 6 June 2013.

22 Felix Martin, *Money: The Unauthorised Biography* (London: Random House, 2013). This reference from the Kindle edition, loc 237.

23 Angus Cameron, 'Bitcoin vs. art', *Xenotopia* weblog, 31 July 2013, http://xenotopia.wordpress.com/2013/07/31/bitcoin-vs-art/, accessed 1 August 2013.

24 Lisa Autogena and Joshua Portway, *Black Shoals Stock Market Planetarium*, installation (2003). *Black Shoals Stock Market Planetarium* is a live representation of the world's stock markets in the form of an animated night sky (see Chapter 2 for a description of this work).

25 'We Make Money Not Art' , Interview with Forays: Geraldine Juárez and Adam Bobbette, 19 December 2009, http://we-make-money-not-art.com/archives/2007/12/i-read-about-yo.php#.UpaLQGRHCC4, accessed 1 November 2013.

26 Freeganism is defined as alternative strategies for living based on limited participation in the conventional economy: 'strategies for living beyond capitalism' according to http://freegan.info, accessed 1 November 2013.

27 *Risk Society: Individualisation in Young Contemporary Art from Germany* exhibition, September–November 2013, Museum of Contemporary Art Taipei, www.mocataipei.org.tw/blog/category/1524588 , accessed 1 November 2013.

28 *Im/Possible Community* exhibition, November 2009–January 2010, Shedhalle Zurich http://archiv2012.shedhalle.ch/en/ulf-aminde-pressure-pudency, accessed 1 November 2013.

29 *Im/Possible Community* exhibition.

30 *9/11*, dir. Jules and Gedeon Naudet (CBS Television, 10 March 2002). See also Tom Junod, 'The falling man', *Esquire*, 8 September 2009, www.esquire.com/features/ESQ0903-SEP_FALLINGMAN, accessed 1 October 2013.

31 Jean Baudrillard, *Why Hasn't Everything Already Disappeared?* trans. Alan Turner (Kolkata, India: Seagull, 2009).

32 Nottingham Castle Museum and Art Gallery, *Critical Cloth* (Nottingham: NCMAG, 2011), p. 2.

33 Ian Rankin, *Doors Open* (London: Orion, 2008).

34 Harriet Dennys, 'Dashwood: Picture of Anthony Salz and HBOS chairman Lord Stevenson tells a thousand words', *Daily Telegraph*, 7 April 2013.

35 Author interview with Bridget McKenzie, Michael Savage, Tiffany Jenkins and Francesca Baseby, 22 October 2013.

36 Tim Cornwell, 'RBS art: A bank loan worth millions', *Scotsman*, 10 December 2009, www.martinfrost.ws/htmlfiles/scotnews09/091210-rbsart.html, accessed 1 November 2013.

37 Hahn's The Salz Servants is in the private collection of Anthony Salz.

38 Marc Shell, *Art and Money* (Chicago: University of Chicago Press, 1994).

39 A theory of art in which people come together to take part in a shared activity, producing intersubjective encounters. The theory is articulated by critic and curator Nicolas Bourriaud in *Relational Aesthetics*, trans. Simon Pleasance and Fronza Woods (Dijon, France: les presses de reel, 2002).

40 Lawrence Wechsler, *Boggs: A Comedy of Values*. (Chicago: University of Chicago Press, 1999).

41 Geoffrey Robertson, *The Justice Game* (London: Chatto & Windus, 1998), pp. 263–82.

42 Haiven, 'The Art and Money Project'.

43 Bourriaud, *Relational Aesthetics*, p. 13.

44 Jon Bywater, '*Today We Don't Use The Word Dollars*, a critical response', 2009, http://superflex.net/texts/superflex_today_we_dont_use_the_word_dollars_a_critical_response, accessed 1 November 2013.

45 The 'Celtic Tiger' refers to the economy of the Republic of Ireland between 1995–2000, which expanded at an average annual rate of 9.4 per cent fuelled by foreign direct investment and a subsequent property price bubble.

46 Superflex, *Today We Don't Use The Word Recession*, Decree (2010).

47 Boris Groys, 'Art and money', *e-flux on-line journal* #24 (April 2011), www.e-flux.com/journal/art-and-money-2/, accessed 1 November 2013.

Trollope, the State of the Nation novel and the good banker

Alex Preston

It's still a painful thing to revisit the only hatchet-job carved on my young writing career. I remember very clearly the evening, early spring, waiting for the *Evening Standard* to arrive outside Great Portland Street station. I held off until I was sitting on the bus – top floor, front left – before opening the paper. A moment of *surely some mistake* before it sank in. The novel that I'd written to hold a mirror to the bloated face of the City, that I'd expected to raise the ire of the few friends I had left in finance, was being attacked for something quite different. I felt paternally towards my book, a book that was born the very same day as my daughter, and it was physically painful to read the words. 'Bankers asking the rest of us to feel sorry for them smacks of self-absorption', the piece, by a hack called Rosamund, began, 'yet this is the reaction that financier Alex Preston seems to want from his debut novel, *This Bleeding City*, one of the first fictionalised accounts of the financial crisis to be written by an insider'.[1] I stood up on the bus, swaying slightly, and let out a long howl.

Other reviewers were kinder, and understood that far from wanting to exculpate the bankers, *This Bleeding City* was intended to lift the cloth of secrecy and obscurity that the financiers pulled over their world. I didn't present them as pantomime villains – this seemed to be Rosamund's principal grievance – but that was because it was not their villainy, but their humanity, that rendered these creatures terrifying. I hoped that, by showing the brief instances when the carapaces of obscene wealth and enormous power slipped, I'd start us on the way to understanding why the great catastrophe happened.

In the wake of the credit crisis came a wave of dry, factual investigations by scrupulous and worthy economists that seemed to me, trapped as I was in the heart of the thing, to miss the point entirely. It wasn't Credit Default Swap (CDS) or Collateralised Debt Obligation (CDO) or even sub-prime mortgages that caused the crash; at worst these things were neutral, sub-prime was positively benevolent, a way of extending the (admittedly fishy) American dream of home-ownership to a greater proportion of the population. The evil came from the people who manipulated these financial instruments, it was brewed in their hearts and I wanted to hack a path into those hearts, to show their intricate workings.

In an October 2008 article in the Observer, books editor William Skidelsky noted that 'it seems odd ... that the financial haymaking that has been going on in recent times has largely escaped the attention of writers. The wealth accumulation of the past few years has been considerably more spectacular than that of any previous era, yet the 21st-century Masters of the Universe have remained stubbornly absent from fiction'. He went on to lament that there was no Trollope, and no Augustus Melmotte (the banker villain of *The Way We Live Now)* for our times. He suggested that this was because 'so few of us can understand, let alone sympathise with, the issues that cause bankers to break out in sweats. The drama surrounding a fine adjustment in the value of a derivative, or a 10-point fall in the Dow Jones, is not something that can be easily captured on the page'.[2]

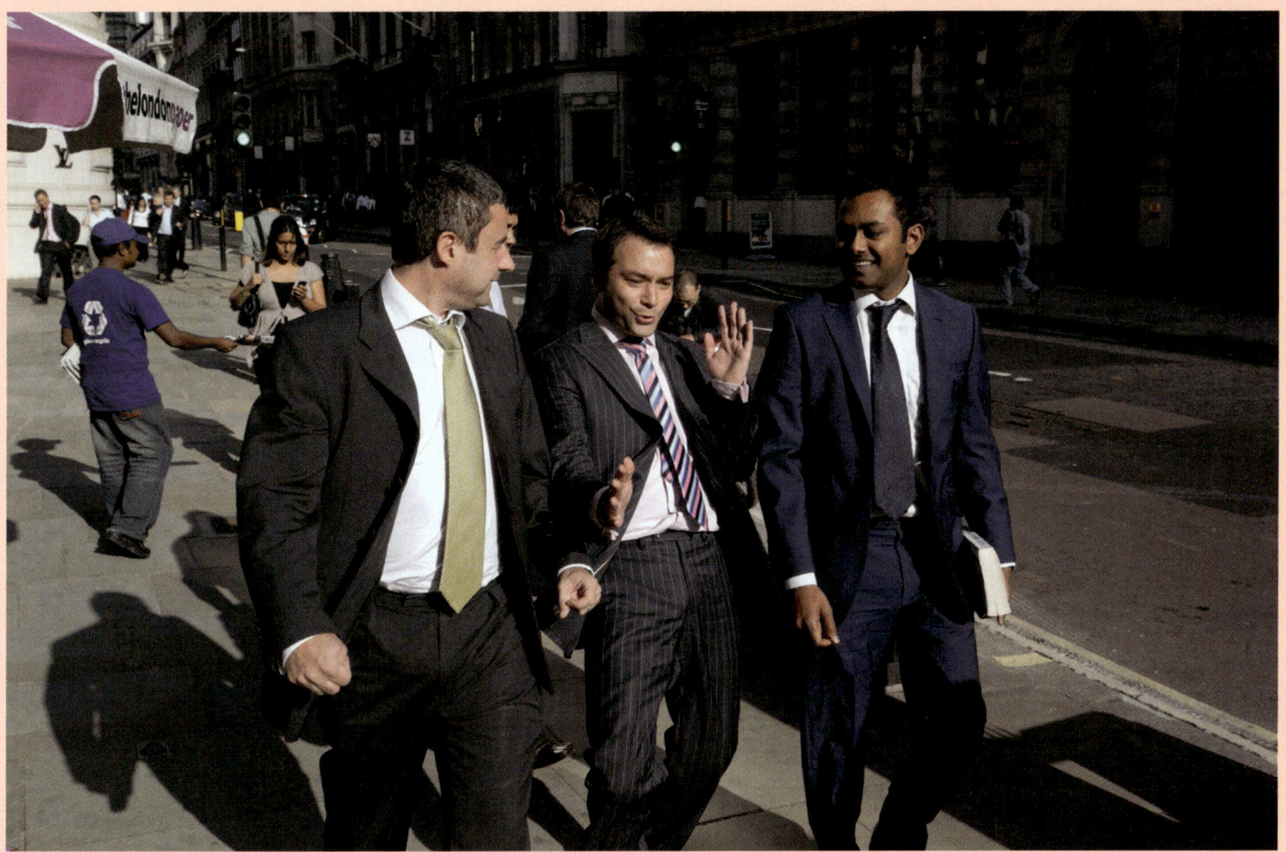

Figure 1

Stephen McLaren, 'Structured Investment Vehicle', from the series *Moral Hazard*.

Courtesy of the artist.

As if answering Skidelsky's rallying cry, a wave of State of the Nation novels began to appear at the end of the last decade, none of them complete without an intricately researched financier. Anthony Trollope's *The Way We Live Now* appeared to still provide one paradigm for the state of the nation novel, a sprawling tour de force with a huge cast of characters and a labyrinthine plot. The shifting viewpoints, keen engagement with contemporary themes, and use of London as a microcosm: this is the model upon which a number of important recent novels have drawn. The first of these was Sebastian Faulks, with *A Week in December*, whose hedge funder antihero, John Veals, is just the Melmotte-ish Machiavelli Skidelsky was calling for.[3] He's described as 'a creature whose heart only beat to market movements', and moves lizard-like through the London of December 2007, accumulating vast riches and destroying innocent lives. The novel finishes with Veals surveying his domain, the capitalist victorious. 'A rare surge of feeling, of something like vindication, came from the pit of his belly and spread out until it sang in his veins. As he stood with his hands in his pockets, staring out over the sleeping city, over its darkened wheels and spires and domes, Veals laughed.'[4]

It might have been thought that John Veals, the modern Melmotte, would provide the model for the portrayal of the twenty-first-century banker. We were living, after all, in the age of

'Sir' Fred Goodwin, of a credit crisis engineered by unscrupulous moneymen that was seeing people thrown out of their homes. The morality of the situation was clear, just as it was to Trollope when he returned from Australia to compose *The Way We Live Now* and surveyed a London that looked and, we understand, felt, not that different from the London of 2007, when I began *This Bleeding City*. The city was awash with financial speculation, floating on a tide of easy credit, buzzing with rumours of takeovers and fast money and commercial adventure. Trollope saw that, he said, 'a certain class of dishonesty, dishonesty magnificent in its proportions, and climbing into high places, has become at the same time so rampant and so splendid that there seems to be reason for fearing that men and women will be taught to feel that dishonesty, if it can become splendid, will cease to be abominable. If dishonesty can live in a gorgeous palace with pictures on all its walls, and gems in all its cupboards, with marble and ivory in all its corners, and can give Apician dinners, and get into Parliament, and deal in millions, then dishonesty is not disgraceful, and the man dishonest after such a fashion is not a low scoundrel. Instigated, I say, by some such reflections as these, I sat down in my new house to write *The Way We Live Now*.'[5]

The malevolent Veals finds reflection in Robert Harris's pacy *The Fear Index*, whose emotionally stunted mathematical genius protagonist, Alex Hoffmann, is a slightly less malignant Veals, while the VIXAL-4 computer trading programme is as amoral and as profit-hungry as Faulks's villain. But then something strange begins to happen. Rather than finding fictional representations of Dick Fuld or Fred Goodwin, puffed-up princes of Wall Street and Canary Wharf preening themselves while the stock markets burn, we begin to find something human, even something sympathetic in the State of the Nation bankers. Far from being latter-day Augustus Melmottes, these figures are closer to the derivative speculating hero of Frank Norris's unjustly forgotten novel *The Pit*, Curtis Jadwin. It is their humanity rather than their inhumanity that emerges.

In Justin Cartwright's *Other People's Money* the leading banker figure, Julian Trevelyan-Tubal, is far from Melmotte-ian malevolence. Rather than a scheming Master of the Universe, he is a bungling throwback, at sea in the world of derivatives and fast money. He loves his children deeply and touchingly. When he sleeps, he dreams that his childhood pony speaks to him comforting words of forgiveness. I asked Cartwright about his protagonist in an email. He said in reply that *The Way We Live Now* was a major influence on the novel, but that 'I did not regard Julian, chairman of Tubal and Co, as a crook. Although, of course, he was. But it struck me that certain ancient loyalties probably would have come into play, and his was to his family, particularly his young children. Not considerations that troubled August Melmotte.'

Similarly, and indeed rather more strikingly, Roger Yount, the banker hero of John Lanchester's sprawling novel of London life, is a genuinely sympathetic character, at the mercy of his acquisitive, manipulative wife. He is described early on in the novel as 'not personally ambitious; he mainly wanted life not to make too many demands on him'.

Yount's moral journey sees him, over the course of the novel, find solace in the love of his children, and the goodness of a Hungarian nanny. He, like Julian Trevelyan-Tubal, is fragile, compassionate and essentially good – far from the Melmotte model.

The most recent author to take on the State of the Nation novel, and one who makes explicit reference to Trollope, is Mark Lawson.[6] *The Deaths* is a novel of wealth and greed in a semi-fictionalised 2011, charting the rise and precipitous fall of four families living in neighbouring Buckinghamshire mansions. There are few likeable characters in the novel, polluted as they are by their ill-gotten gains, but the closest we come is Nicky Mortimer, a banker – 'well, more corporate finance, really'. He is outside the group who are the main subjects of Lawson's satire, and we the readers find ourselves yoking our perspective to his, an interested interloper, surveying the horrors of these gruesome yuppies. Again, the banker is one of the novel's more sympathetic characters. I asked Lawson whether this was a deliberate strategy: 'I remember thinking early on that to have a "good" banker in a contemporary novel would be some kind of modern equivalent of the "good German" in war films. And, certainly, I wanted to avoid the obvious cliché. For the same reason, a jolly nice doctor in the book may, on closer examination, have been responsible for the deaths of several patients. Also, because the structure depends on readers knowing that five people have been murdered, but not which ones – I wanted to tempt people into thinking that certain people might deserve to die because they were: rich, adulterous, addicted to porn, or, indeed, a banker.'[7]

My own novel came out in 2010, and Charlie Wales, the hero, was never supposed to be likeable, he *is* human (much to the *Evening Standard* reviewer's chagrin). It perhaps should not surprise us that authors have attempted a kind of stuttering rehabilitation of the bankers in these State of the Nation novels. Trollope gave us a financier of thoroughgoing iniquity, and Faulks's Veals was equally bad; we usually ask more from our novelists. Great novels engage sympathetically with their characters, looking for the engines of motivation that drive even the wickedest characters. There is a challenge provided to the novelist by the pantomime portrayal of the banker in the popular press: imagine your way into this existence, prove that, even for Fred Goodwin, *tout comprendre, c'est tout pardoner.*

Notes

1 Rosamund Irwin, 'A City of Built of Cliches' (review of Alex Preston, This Bleeding City), *Evening Standard*, 25 February 2010.

2 William Skidelsky, 'Great wealth leads to great art. Where is the Dickens for our times?', *Observer*, 5 October 2008, http://www.theguardian.com/business/2008/oct/05/savings.martinamis, accessed 22 October 2013.

3 Although Faulks admitted to me in an email in February 2012: 'I have not read *The Way We Live Now*, though I was a bit wistful that the title was taken. I did re-read *Bleak House* and *Our Mutual Friend* to see how Dickens connected the different social strata and districts of London. But in the end I wanted to tell my own story. There are no precedents for the crimes, misdemeanours, greed, blindness and stupidity of the modern financial era. To say nothing of the scale of the effrontery and theft'.

4 Sebastian Faulks, *A Week in December* (London: Vintage, 2010), p. 390.

5 Anthony Trollope, *Autobiography of Anthony Trollope* (London: Serenity Publishers, 2009), p. 249 (first published 1857).

6 One piece of dialogue in Lawson's *The Deaths* runs: 'The way we live now' / 'What?' / 'Rebuilding and redecorating houses', (Lawson, *The Deaths* (London: Picador, 2013)), p. 176.

7 Author interview with Mark Lawson, September 2013.

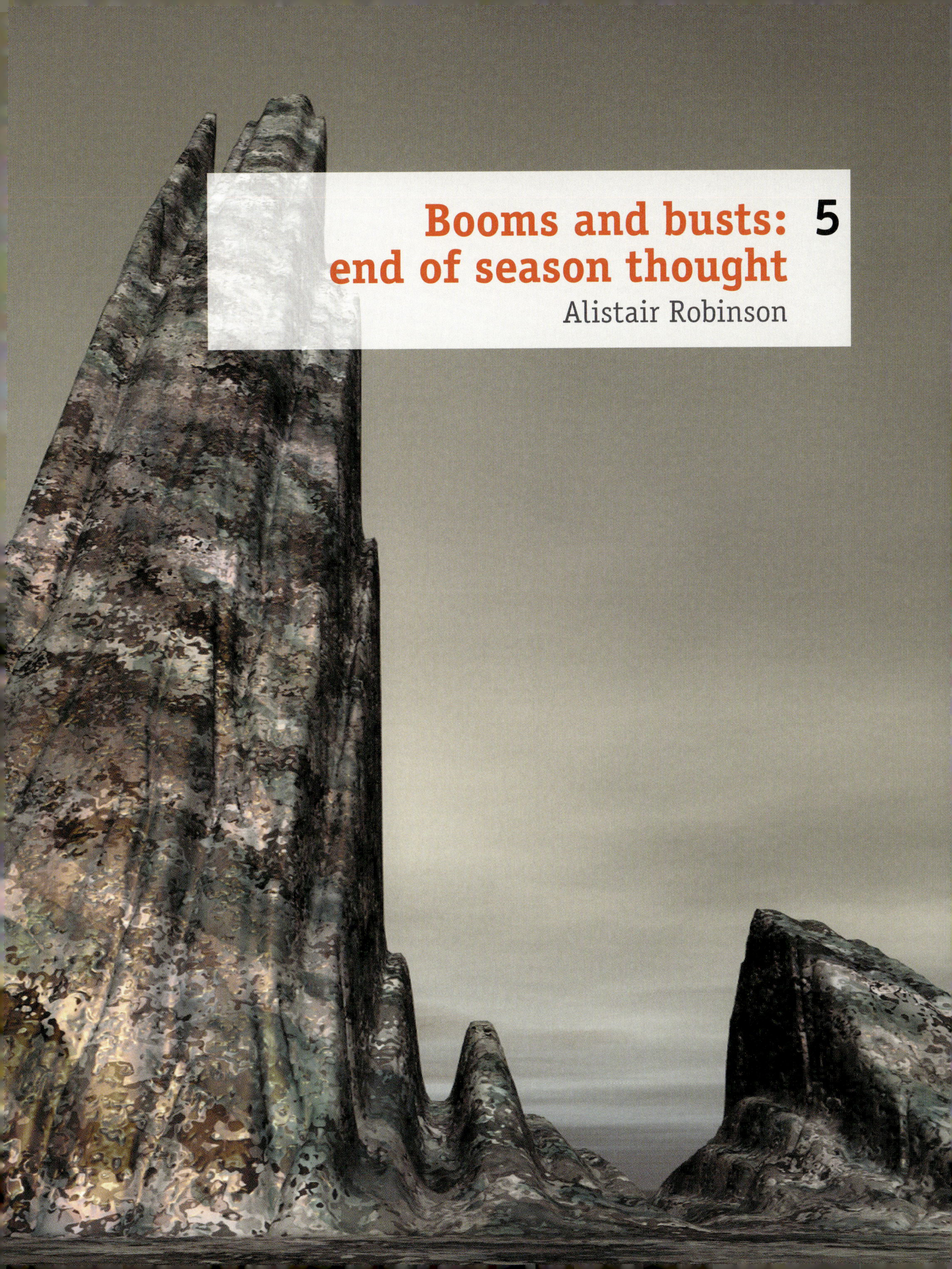

5 Booms and busts: end of season thought

Alistair Robinson

Booms and busts: end of season thought

Alistair Robinson

> The day will come when corporations will cease to consider themselves greater than the country which created them. (William Jennings Bryan, 1896)[1]
>
> Bazaar – Grand Sale of ideas – end of season thoughts – Genuine bargains – Unheard of prices. (Francis Picabia, 1919)[2]

Imagining the workings of the financial markets, or their failure to work, might be thought to necessitate conceptualising their extreme states and contrasting fortunes, even how their very basis leads from 'boom' to 'bust' and back again. The popular experience of the markets is, at present, arguably enthralled by this image of cycles of boom and bust, and the half-truth it presents. The expectation or anticipation of 'extreme' states – which are seemingly unstoppable or akin to natural events – is simply accepted, and acceptable. Both parts of that equation have been put under pressure and queried by artists in quite unexpected ways.

There is a long historical pedigree to alternative ways of picturing the market as the product of collective madness rather than individual economic rationality, whose booms and busts are part of normal business rather than unforeseeable irruptions, as it girates between extremes rather than tending towards equilibrium. The trope of finance as a dizzying fairground ride can be found, for example, in *Des waerelds oen en doolen, is maar een mallemoolen* ('The actions and designs of the world go round as if in a mill') from *Het groote Tafereel der Dwaasheid* ('The Great Mirror of Folly'), produced in the wake of the South Sea Bubble of 1720 (Figure 1). Likewise in William Hogarth's *The South Sea Scheme* social types from contemporary London society ride a merry-go-round, conjuring up the idea of finance as a devilish wheel of fortune (Figure 2). The women crowding the rickety balcony in the background suggest traditional fears about the association between irrationality and femininity in general, as well as particular anxieties about the way that the unregulated nature of the stock market allowed Jews, dissenters and women to participate without regulation in the public sphere.[3]

These satirical prints on the South Sea Bubble rely on an allegorical or emblematic approach to representation, echoing in their form the idea that finance itself worked through the exchange of imaginary, fantastical beings for more tangible and 'real' things. In Hogarth's allegorical vision of finance, for instance, trade is caught napping while the devil dispatches pieces of the body of a prostrate Fortune to a frenzied crowd. The caption on the monument compares the effects of the South Sea crash to the Great Fire of London with both leading to 'the destruction of the City', begging the question of whether financial panics are man-made or a natural disaster.

How to conceive of the violent mechanisms of the market remained as much a problem – of both aesthetics and politics – in the wake of the 2008 crisis as it did in the aftermath of the South Sea Bubble in 1720. Economists have since the beginning of their discipline described and conceptualised distinct phases of speculation, often in terms of 'cycles' or

Figure 1

Des waerelds oen en doolen, is maar een mallemoolen ('The actions and designs of the world go round as if in a mill') from *Het groote Tafereel der Dwaasheid* ('The Great Mirror of Folly') (Amsterdam, 1720).

Figure 2

William Hogarth, *The South Sea Scheme* (1721).

SEE FOLLOWING SPREAD ALSO

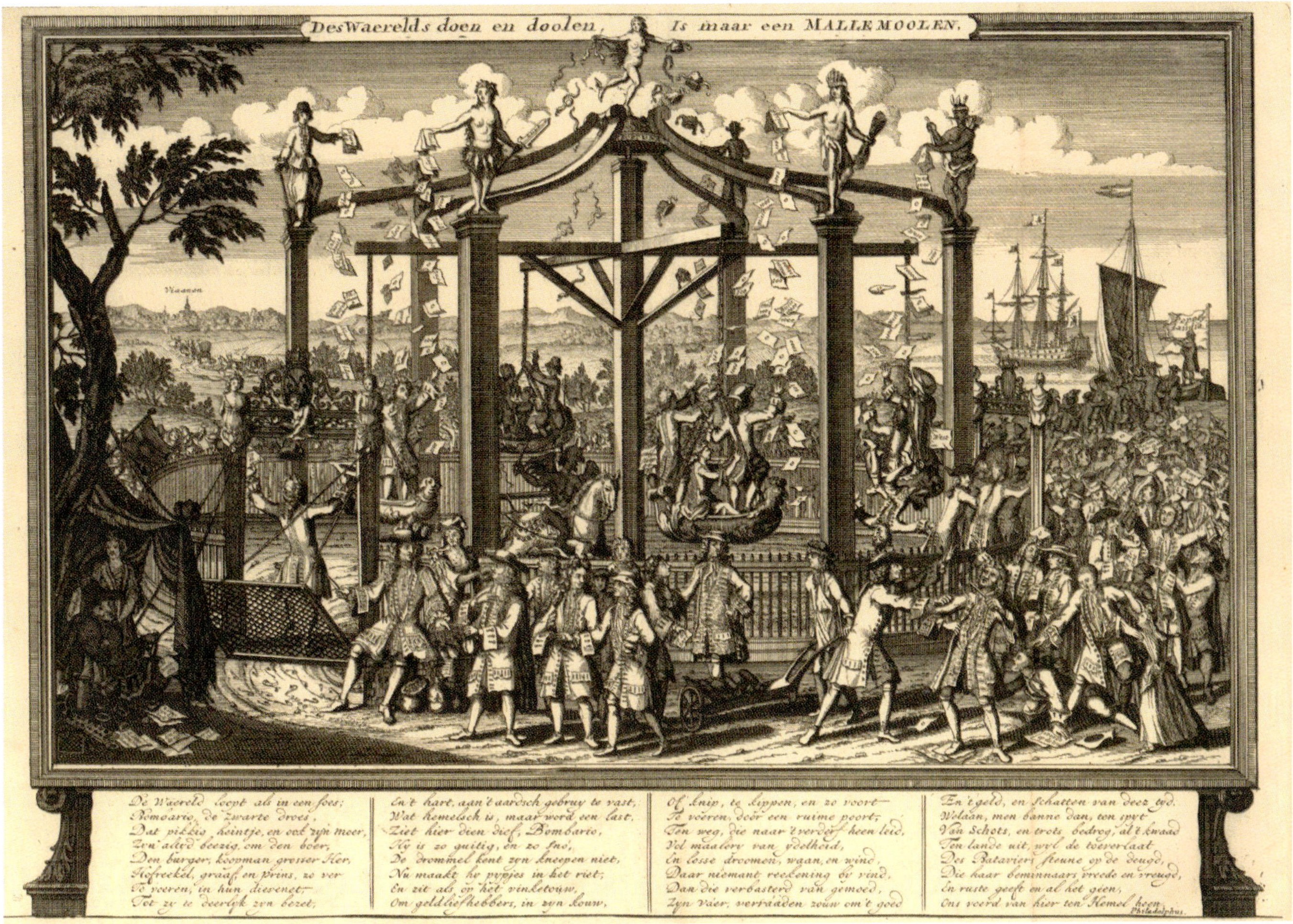

Des Waerelds doen en doolen, Is maar een MALLEMOOLEN.

Vlaanen

De Waereld loopt als in een foes;
Bomoario, de zwarte droes,
Dat pikkis, heintje, en ook zyn meer,
Zyn altyd beezig, om den boer,
Den burger, koopman grosser Her,
Hofreekel, graaf, en prins, zo ver
Te voeren, in hun dievenet,
Tot zy te deerlyk zyn bezet,

En't hart, aan't aardsch gebruy te vast,
Wat hemelsch is, maar word een last,
Ziet hier dien dief, Bombario,
Hy is zo quitig, en zo fnó,
De drommel kent zyn kneepen niet,
Nu maakt hy pypjes in het riet;
En zit als op het vinketouw,
Om geldliefhebbers, in zyn louw,

Of knip, te lippen, en zo voort
Te vöeren, door een ruime poort,
Ten weg, die naar 't verderf heen leid,
Vol maalery van ydelheid,
En losse droomen, waan, en wind,
Daar niemant reekening by vind,
Dan die verbasterd van gemoed,
Zyn vaer, verraaden zouw om't goed

En 't geld, en schatten van deez tyd.
Welaan, men banne dan, ten spyt
Van Schots, en trots bedrog, al 't kwaad
Ten lande uit, wyl de toeverlaat
Des Bataviers steune op de deugd,
Die haar beminnaars vrede en vreugd,
En ruste geeft en al het geen,
Ons voerd van hier ten Hemel heen.

Philadelphus.

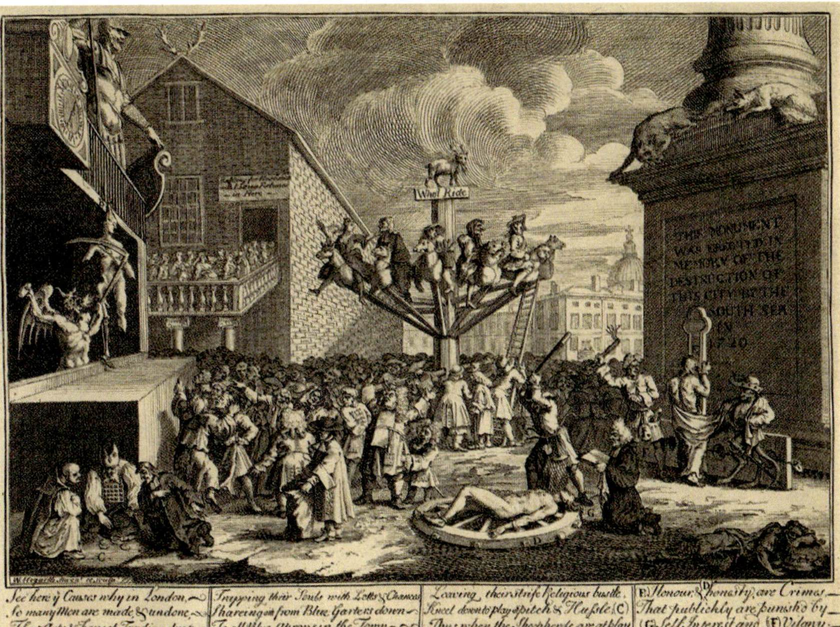

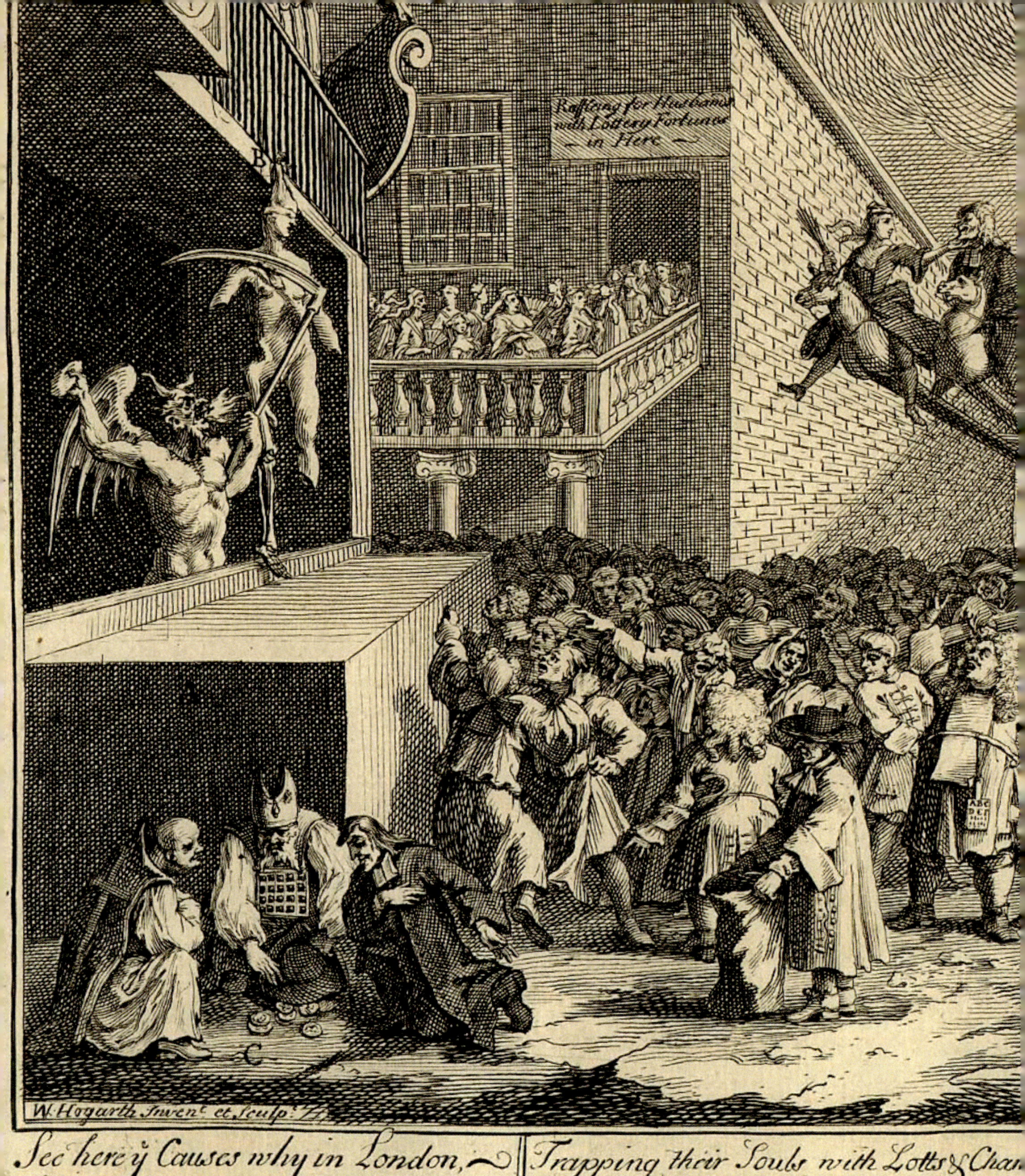

See here y^e Causes why in London,
So many Men are made, & undone,
That Arts, & honest Trading drop,
To Swarm about y^e Devils Shop (A)
Who Cuts out (B) Fortunes Golden Haunches

Trapping their Souls with Lotts & Chan
Shareing em from Blue Garters down
To all Blue Aprons in the Town.
Here all Religions flock together,
Like Tame & Wild Fowl of a Feathe

Printed for John Bowles at N.º 13, in Cornhill

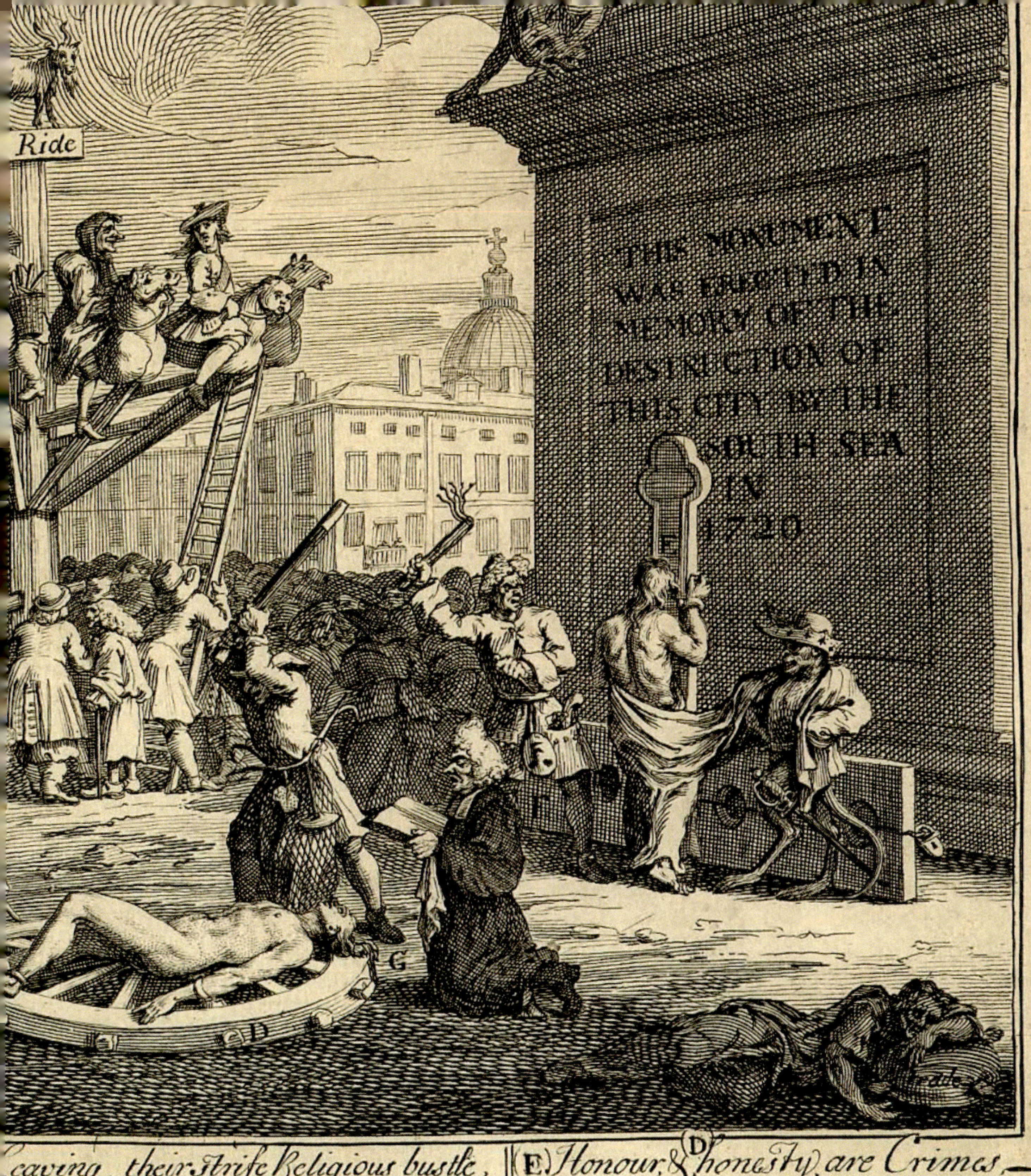

eaving their strife Religious bustle,
neel down to play at pitch & Hussle; (C)
hus when the Sheepherds are at play,
heir flocks must surely go Astray;
he woeful Cause yt in these Times,

(E) Honour, & (D) honesty, are Crimes,
That publickly are punish'd by
(G) Self Interest, and (F) Vilany;
So much for Monys magick powe
Guess at the Rest you find out more

'waves'. Such terms draw on either natural or mechanical imagery for their metaphorical power (and have the added bonus of their associations of imperial rise and decline).[4] There is, though, little consensus as to how 'cycles' can be anticipated, or how long or regular 'cycles' should be. The ways in which they have been represented both by financial professionals and in visual culture draw on figurative imagery that can be examined critically. Even the idea of a 'cycle' that recurs encompasses everything from that identified by Joseph Kitchin (over three to four years) to the 'long waves' of investment (over half-centuries) characterised by Nicolai Kondratiev.[5] The latter's idea of a 'boom', then, lies in the total consequences of an entire technological revolution, such as that initiated by steam power and rail, with the 'bubble' contrasted as a short-term effect. The parameters of market activity are not obvious, but are always seen in relation to both the historical and political vantage point we imagine we occupy.

Furthermore, the terms of representation available are not solely limited to the dramatic extremes of 'boom' and 'bust' – though these clearly have some purchase with regards to the financial crisis of 2008 to the present.[6] The terms are based on a simple binary model, and plot a simplistic dramatic arc. Yet such terms have their uses: they are lodged in the popular imagination, are the mainstay of journalists' terms of description, and have been adapted by economists in innumerable ways. One recent text, for example, refigures waves of investment as 'irruptions', with the subsequent years being an 'ascent' or a 'frenzy', eventually becoming a 'mature' market where values are stable and secure.[7] The combination of imagery from natural processes ('irruptions') and from crowd behaviour ('frenzy') is typical, yet the two are irreconcilable. Placing them as adjacent elides the two registers, implicitly presenting irrational behaviours as being unstoppable forces of nature or acts of God. Such frameworks of understanding, or misunderstanding, have provided considerable scope for artists to intervene. After all, if the majority of mainstream economists (and political figures) in the Anglo-American world were unable to even conceive of the years immediately prior to 2008 as a 'boom', the discipline's claim to knowledge is insecure. By definition there are alternative ways of imagining and showing how we are all implicated in the workings of finance.

Many of the ways in which the recent financial crisis has been represented by artists are surprising. The artists might initially seem to concur with neo-classical economists' own terms and values, rather than offer radical critiques or hostile counter-claims. They avoid outright protest, or often even any direct commentary. We might say that the limits of discourse in our own time are such that to be heard at all outside of the specialist art market, one must occupy a kind of *terra cognita*. We might also say that many artists of note have therefore recognised that in order to act in the financial markets one must necessarily have internalised a set of hypotheses and assumptions about credit, about the predictability of the future, and the nature of our financial relationships. Their areas of contestation *are* these assumptions. I will examine three case studies of how individual artists have approached these problems. In each instance, the dominant terms by which discourse is conducted are placed under pressure, by being re-presented, re-iterated and re-enacted respectively.[8] (The latter two terms are salient: in recent years, the idea of the artist as a 'semionaut' has been supplanted by one in which artists act out, or re-enact situations and scenarios as kinds of social experiments. As here, these social experiments are also ones in popular finance.)

The background to the practices in each of the three artists' bodies of work has been the new 'social contract' that has existed since 2008 between the state, the citizen-taxpayer, and the financial system in both the UK and United States. There is no shortage of literature about such a complex and vast topic, though contemporary artists have some surprising advantages in being able to address it. In contrast to their predecessors, the artists here are not limited to *pictorial* representations, but can recreate or restage some of the market's own processes and operations by working with 'found' material from the world at large. Artists are able to create performative versions of how modern finance works, rather than merely describing it. In working between visual and verbal languages, they have been able to test our conventionalised figures of speech, often by literalising them – by translating verbal coinages that are imagistic into visual images themselves. By placing pressure upon the store of metaphors that have become the stock in trade of journalists describing the financial crisis since 2008, the artists allow us to identify their limits and inadequacies.

One example of the latter way of working is David Cornford and Matthew Cross's work *The Lost Horizon*. Cornford & Cross's modus operandi might, roughly speaking, be described as feeding the hand that bites them. To create *The Lost Horizon* they worked with American Express, who provided *Financial Times* Stock Exchange data, and with the London School of Economics and Political Science (LSE) to find ways to interpret it for both 'lay' audiences and LSE staff and students. Accordingly, the work presents a graphic representation of real statistics, with each day giving rise to a new image. The 'cycle' that we encounter in the work is that of a single day of trading.

Cornford & Cross began their investigation of the dominant or normative ways in which market activity is pictured by working with LSE staff to see what kinds of visual images were most familiar, and could be immediately and readily interpreted. The overwhelming consensus was that the simplest, most universally comprehensible images were graphic ones, with line graphs proving most immediately graspable. Adapting this type of image, and working with the grain of preferences became their starting point to trying to rethink how our financial markets are imagined.

The Lost Horizon adapts the familiar graphs featured in newspapers and other media by drawing into play the metaphors associated with market highs and lows. The artists observe that the workings of high finance have been habitually described as almost

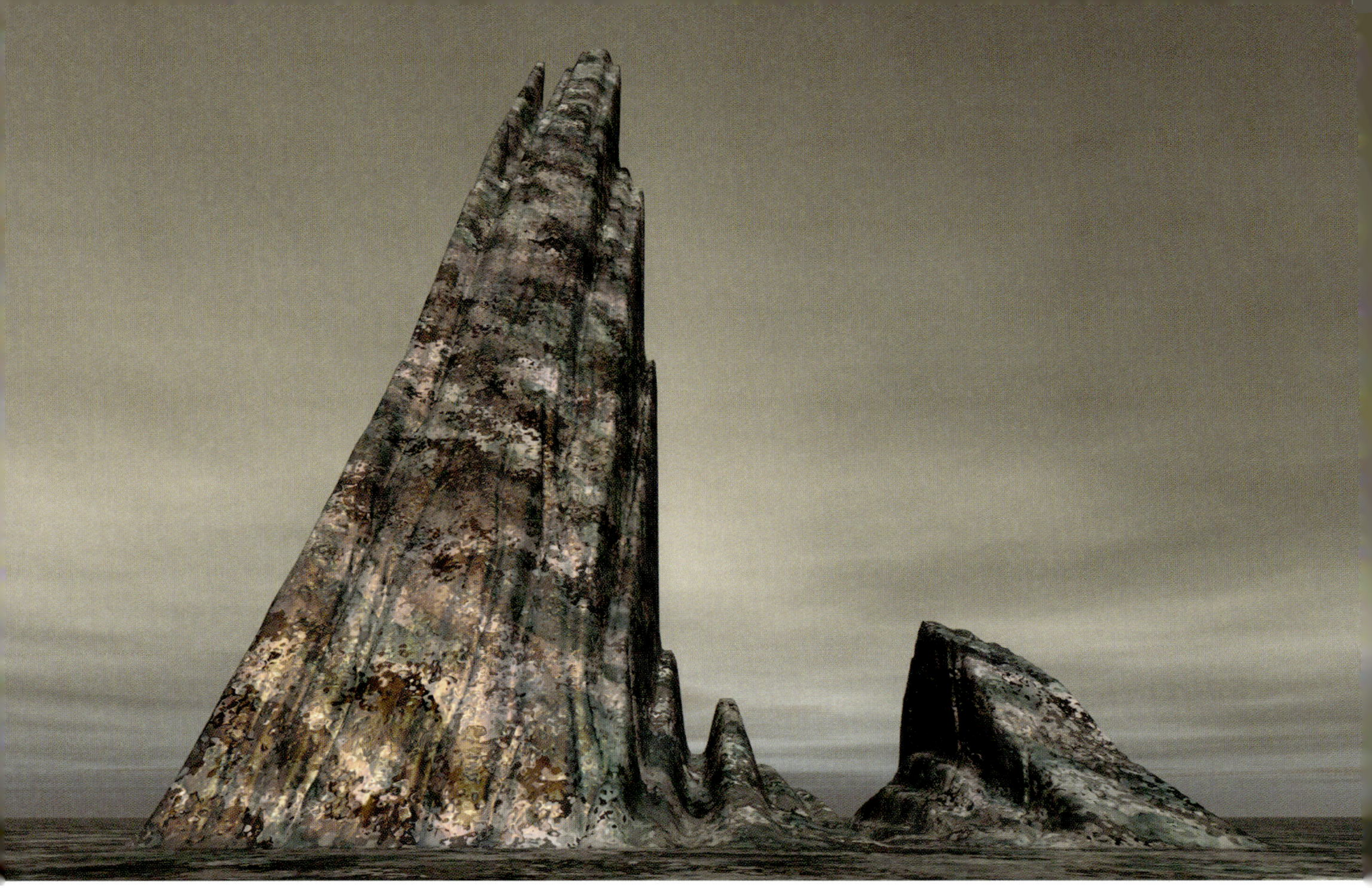

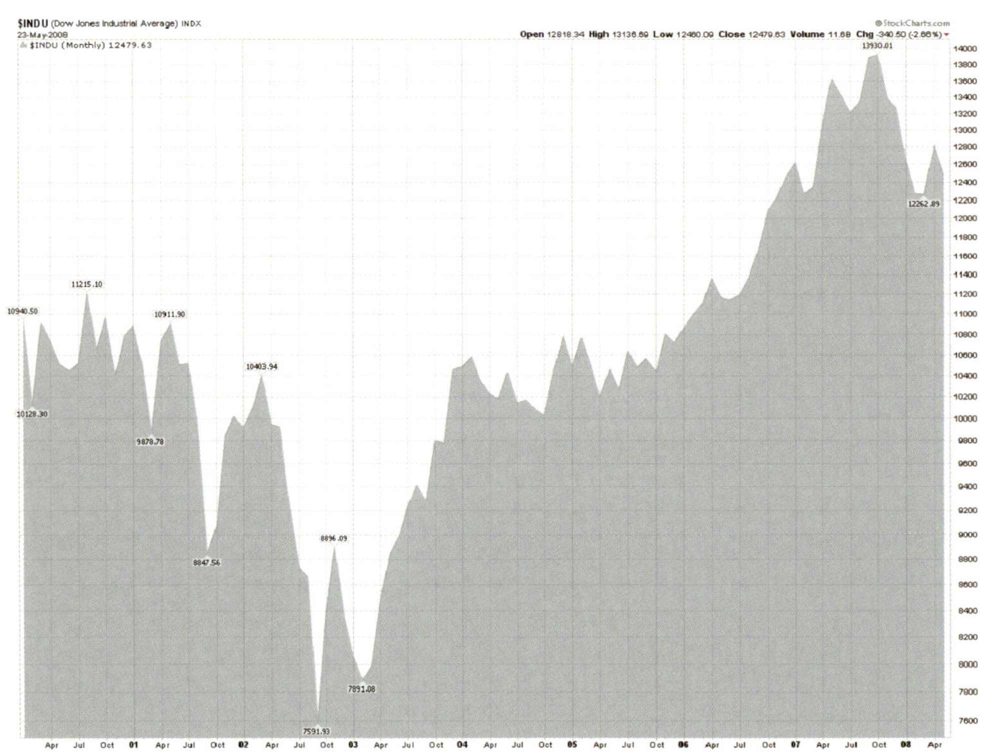

Figure 3

Matthew Cornford & David Cross, *The Lost Horizon* (detail) (2003). Computer-generated image: screensaver generated from financial data. First realised at the London School of Economics.

Courtesy the artists.

Figure 4

Dow Jones Industrial Average, 2000–2008: financial market graph.

Courtesy Stock Charts, New York.

sublime in their ability to defy the comprehension of ordinary educated citizens. In this ideological model, financial literacy is, by definition, restricted to an elite, whose vested interests happen to coincide fully with their abilities to comprehend the market's workings. By contrast *The Lost Horizon* aims to provide even the most financially illiterate person with a guide to the financial world's operations on any particular day. It makes tangible – paradoxically, through virtual forms – all of the movements of the market over the previous day's trading. Cornford & Cross deliberately take the dominant images or terms of reference to describe the market in order to reveal them as ideologically loaded constructions. The artists note that their images and terms of description are taken directly from the field: 'the language and imagery of business is rich with metaphoric references to mountain landscapes ... the concepts of risk and security in commerce are often visualised in images of climbers scaling the heights of an unspoilt wilderness'.[9] Each rise and fall is represented as a part of a landscape that pushes and pulls at the earth, with market movements becoming monstrous forces being unleashed from under the earth's crust.[10]

The Lost Horizon, in other words, transforms FTSE statistics into landscape imagery, and in particular into jagged mountain ranges that offer both a sense of threat or danger, and a sense of hope that these peaks can be safely conquered. One part of their research entailed discovering how information and ideas are communicated between traders – their group behaviour. The artists observe that the markets are mostly observed from the safety and isolation of a computer screen, but as each trader uses real-time software, any amendment in their peers' behaviour is instantly transmitted to all the other participants. At the moment one or more traders betray merely an inkling of fear or of hope through their actions, that has repercussions worldwide, despite the apparent abstraction of their actions.

The artists also develop their works so that they reshape the context out of which they are created. The artists act as participant-observers in the financial landscapes they depict, in a quasi-ethnographic fashion. As traders' worlds are imagined through screens, so *The Lost Horizon* was created on and for computer screens. Traders exchange data, never encountering physical commodities or tangible forms of currencies. No physical manifestation of capital is ever seen. Accordingly the artists employed CGI software ordinarily used in cinema or computer gaming to visualise fantasy landscapes (or, as here, landscapes of fantasy). The artists argue that screens act as *both* windows onto 'virtual' space *and* a means of immediate access to data from across the world. They are both escapist and the most advanced form of global data-capture network. They 'might equally represent a point of entry into or exit from the system: the screen is an ambiguous threshold between lived experience and information space'.[11]

Cornford & Cross's means of presentation equally draws on the context that a work is created from, in this case both the LSE and markets' own self-representations. In one realisation, the work is presented in the form of monumental landscape images that deliberately resemble paintings by Caspar David Friedrich. In Friedrich's key works an onlooker surveys the entirety of the 'horizon' beneath him from an unassailable position of commanding power. We imaginatively occupy that position in *The Lost Horizon*: the stand-in spectator is absent, and we enter into his or her role, as a surrogate 'master of the universe' with an imagined omniscience. Furthermore, the work was installed as a screensaver throughout the LSE for a whole year, being updated daily in response to new FTSE figures. Each student and member of staff was able to immediately gauge the last day's trading, and to experience the artwork (wittingly or unwittingly), notwithstanding the irony that the screensaver is only operative when the computer itself is not. Such a situation 'corresponds to a daydream' that users can project their fantasies onto.[12] Users are invited to idly gaze at the screensaver and lose themselves within it, as though the imagined landscape could subsume them, and their imagination, wholly. As the title infers, *The Lost Horizon* reminds us that a poststructuralist revolution in capital has taken place: there is no external point of reference or guarantee, no ultimate ground of value.[13]

As the artists put it, their role is 'playful' in staging oppositions within a single work. It contains an elision between graphic and geological systems. Data and nature are rendered as equivalents: market 'forces' and geological 'forces' are conflated. Incompatible timescales are made commensurate. The minute-by-minute responses of traders are made akin to thousand-year movements of the earth's crust. As the artists remark, 'envisioning numerical abstractions in this way generated a landscape of alienation: a parallel world where reality [itself] was determined by abstraction'.[14] 'The market' is represented as a distant, remote place, a mountain range entirely external to human agency. As Cornford & Cross know, those who wish to see their own (ideological) propositions 'naturalised' do so through figurative speech. Making an idea into an idiom, a common figure of speech, places it above contention. The artists' role is to reverse that process, transforming commonly held notions into 'concrete', if virtual visual imagery.

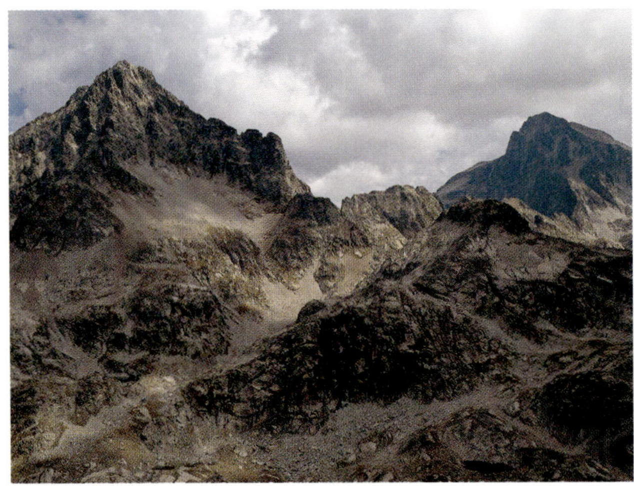

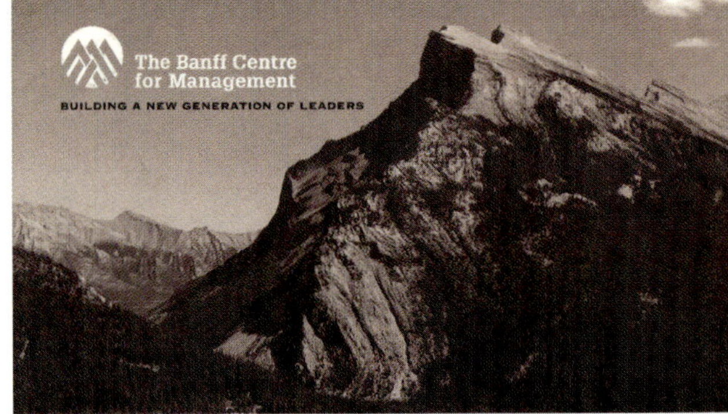

If Cornford & Cross make 'literal' the default terms of description for the market 'from within', as if they were 'embedded' journalists in a financial war zone, Simon Roberts looks at the terms that journalists themselves have coined. He queries the media's failure to represent 'market failure', despite producing alarming quantities of verbiage. His work asks what is excluded from representation by attempting to re-present the *entirety* of the field of representations. Roberts's project *Credit Crunch Lexicon* combines three related forms of representation and understanding: textual, graphic and photographic. The term 'lexicon' is apposite: his work constitutes a compendium of all of the common terms that have coloured the way the Anglo-Saxon world has seen the financial crisis since 2008. Roberts believes language – whether visual and verbal – never merely conveys, but conjures into being that which it purports to describe. Like Cornford & Cross, he has undertaken a kind of 'fieldwork', albeit with his field being the news media across print, the internet and television. As with Cornford & Cross, he has found that simple line graphs are all but ubiquitous in attempts to 'explain', or rather present the idea of the financial crisis to a broad audience. They are, as Roberts describes, almost a 'meme': an idea that primes us in how to behave, and which acts like a viral contagion so that the idea becomes near-universal. As he argues, they are amongst the principal ways in which 'knowledge is used and misused. Graphs are employed as badges, as a kind of shorthand denoting what the dynamics of a situation supposedly consist of. But almost invariably the graphs distort (if not falsify) through their choice of timescale or their frame of reference'.[15] The graphs that 'rolling' news programmes feature magnify changes by presenting them on a daily or hourly basis (as Cornford & Cross also discovered). The news 'cycle' supplants the market 'cycle' as what is knowable, while reporting the process with apparent neutrality. Roberts's strategy, like that of Cornford & Cross, is one of sly defamiliarisation. Rather than presenting explicitly oppositional imagery, or presenting clear counter-arguments, Roberts merely collates what is already 'out there'.

Figure 5

South-Western Pyrenees, France (1993).

Figure 6

'Building a New Generation of Leaders' (1997). Brochure cover artwork. Published by Banff Centre for Management, Alberta, Canada.

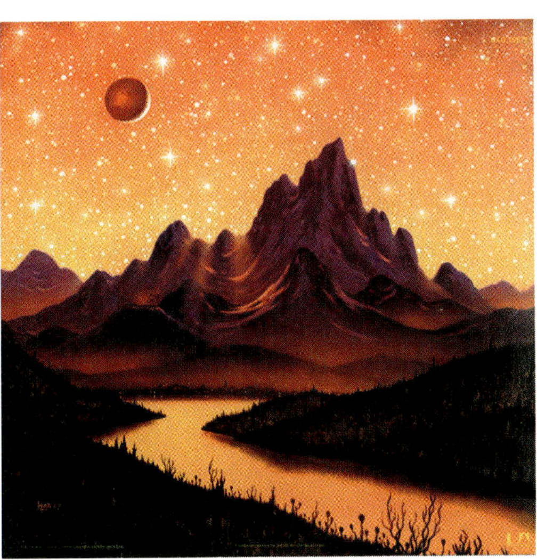

Figure 7

David A. Hardy, 'Hall of the Mountain Grill' (1974). Artwork for Hawkwind album cover.

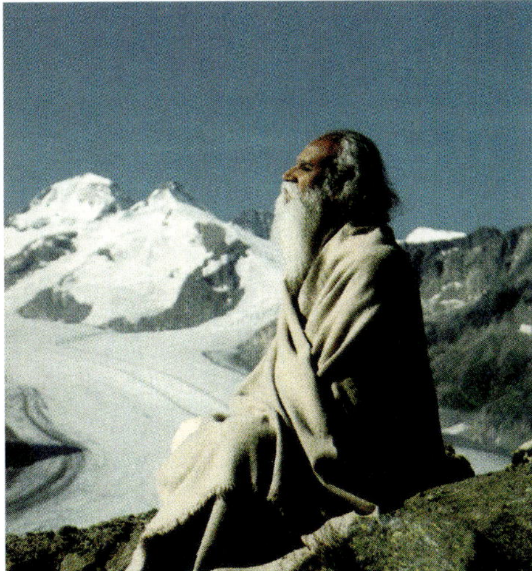

Figure 8

'Guided Meditation' (1987). Artwork for audio cassette pubished by Integral Yoga Distribution, Virginia, USA.

DEXIA DIAMETRICALLY OPPOSITE DIAMOND AND DYBVIG'S MODEL OF BANK RUNS DIKTATS OF AU
JLL TAX DODGY LOANS DOING NOTHING IS NOT AN OPTION DOLE QUEUES DOLLAR DOLDRUM DOL
D DOWN BY UNCERTAINTY DRAMATIC SHARE-PRICE SLIDE DRAW DOWN CREDIT LINES DRIVING DO
CHISM ECONOMIC STORM ECONOMIC SUICIDE ECONOMIC TURMOIL ECONOMIC WORLD WAR ECONO
SCUE ELIMINATE BANKING ELIMINATE STRUCTURAL DEFICIT ELITE BONDS EMBATTLED EMBEZZLED
BARELY IMPLEMENTED REFORMS ENGULFED IN CRISIS ENSURE RICHER PEOPLE PAY TAX ENTRENCH
N COMMISSION EUROPEAN FINANCIAL STABILITY FACILITY EUROPEAN INVESTMENT BANK EUROPEA
DED FUNDS EXECUTIVE REMUNERATION RISING EXIT STRATEGY EXOGENOUS CHANGE EXPANDING I
NG EXTRA BORROWING EXTRAORDINARY REGULATORY LAXITY EXTRAORDINARY SQUEEZE EYE-WAT
TH FALTERING FAMILY BUDGETS FAR MORE DANGEROUS PHASE FAST-RISING EXECUTIVE PAY FATTE
TY FINANCIAL ARMIES FINANCIAL COMPUTING CENTRE FINANCIAL CONVULSIONS FINANCIAL ENG
DE FINANCIAL SYSTEM FREEZING UP FINANCIAL TRANSACTION TAX FINANCIALISATION FIREPOWER
FLIGHT TO SAFETY FLIP FLOP FLOATING EXCHANGE RATES FLOOD THE FINANCIAL SYSTEM FOG IN TH
IAC AND FANNIE MAE FREE LUNCH FREE RIDING FREEZING RECRUITMENT FRENCH CAC FRENZIED
FUNDING WOES FURTHER TURMOIL FUTURE LOSES FUTURE SHOCKS FUTURES G7 G8 G10 G20 G21 G22 (
ECATED TAX GLOBAL PERMA-CRISIS GLOBALISATION GLOOM OF THE JOB MARKET GLOOMIER THAN
ECASTS GRIM-FACED GROSS DOMESTIC PRODUCT GROSS FAILURES OF THE REGULATORY REGIME GR(
MPTS HAMSTRUNG BY AUDITED STATEMENTS HAND-OUTS HANG SENG HARD TIMES HARD-NOSED
OMMISSION HIGH STREET WOES HIGH UNEMPLOYMENT HIGH-OCTANE FINANCE HIGH-STAKES GAM
OF LOAN PACKAGES HOUSEHOLD BUDGETS HOUSEHOLD ECONOMIC ACTIVITY TRACKER HOUSING I
RAL POLITICIANS IDIOT HEADLINES IDOLATRY OF THE MARKET IGNOMINIOUS END ILL-DISCIPLINED
NCUMBENT ADVANTAGE INDEBTEDNESS INDEPENDENT COMMISSION ON BANKING INDIVIDUALIST C
JDIES INSTITUTE OF INTERNATIONAL FINANCE INSURMOUNTABLE HURDLES INTENSE ECONOMIC HA
BLY BUST IRRESPONSIBLE CAPITALISM IS AUSTERITY THE ANSWER ISLAND SPIRIT IT MIGHT LEAD TO W
IAN ECONOMICS KEYNESIAN LOGIC REAFFIRMED KICK START THE ECONOMY KLEPTOCRACY KNIFE
RGER SLUG LARGER THAN PREVIOUSLY EXPECTED LAST HURRAH LAST WAKE-UP CALL LASTING DIV
IEAD CHOP LESSONS HAVE BEEN LEARNED LET'S CHANGE THIS SYSTEM LEVERAGE EXPLODES LEVER
BIG EUROPE LITTLE REGARD FOR APPROPRIATE CAPITAL BUFFERS LIVING BEYOND ITS MEANS LIVINC
TRIPLE-A CREDIT RATING LOSS OF CONFIDENCE CAN BE FATAL LOSS OF INVESTOR CONFIDENCE LOSS
F MONETARISM MADE BILLIONS BETTING AGAINST CDO'S MADOFF INVESTMENT SECURITIES MAGIC
NIPULATION MARKET MELTDOWN MARKET TENSIONS WILL PERSIST MARKETS ARE NOT THE MONSTE
A-BUCKS INC MELTDOWN MESSY WAVE OF DEFAULTS MIB INDEX MILITANTS ITCHING FOR A FIGHT M
RANCE MONOPOLISED BY A MINORITY MONTI'S MEDICINE MONUMENTAL DEBTS MOOD IS UGLY MO
OST-FAVOURED NATION MSCI ALL COUNTRY WORLD INDEX MUCH MORE NEEDS TO BE DONE MUDDL
TIVE FUTURES NEGATIVE IMPACT NEGATIVE INCOME TAX NEGATIVE INFLATION NEGATIVE MARKET S
S OF THE GAME ARE THE OLD RULES OF THE GAME NEW TURMOIL NIGHTMARE SCENARIO NIKKEI NO
ODY RESPONSIBLE PAYS ANY PRICE NON-PRICE COMPETITION NON-RECOVERY NORTHERN ROCK NOT
FLOADING ON BORROWED TIME ONCE-IN-A-CENTURY CREDIT TSUNAMI OPEN CLASS WAR OPEN TH
S OVERHEATING OVERINFLATED OVERSHOOTING OVERVALUED CURRENCIES PAID FOR BY A POUND S
ARLIAMENTARY BLAME-GAME PASTY TAX PATH DEPENDENCE PAWNBROKERS THRIVING PAY BACK DE
S PERILOUS STATE OF BRITISH ECONOMY PERILOUSLY PERCHED ON THE CUSP PERPETUAL ACCUMUL
QUENCES POLITICAL IDEOLOGY POLITICAL WILL POLITICS OF WAGE REPRESSION PONIES UP FOR DE
CING PREDICTED PREFERENCE SHARES PREPARE FOR MORE PAIN PRESENT DILEMMA PRESSURE FROM T
NYMOUS WITH DISASTER PROJECT MERLIN PROJECTED DEBT PATH PROLONGED BOND-BUYING SPREE
BLIC MONEY IS TIGHT PUBLIC SECTOR PUBLIC SERVANTS PUMPING MORE MONEY PUNISH PROFLIGAC
JINTUPLE FUND FIREPOWER QUIT THE EURO RACE TO THE BOTTOM RACING AWAY RACKED BY UNCE
PAY CUTS REALLOCATION OF PAIN REALTY RECESSION REBALANCE THE ECONOMY RECAPITALISATION

DIRE CONSEQUENCES DIRE FINANCES DIRE SALES FIGURES DIRECT ACTION DISAPPOINTING UPDAT
NS DOMESTICALLY GENERATED INFLATION DOMINO DEFAULT DOMINO EFFECT DON'T WANT TO PA
GES DROP LIKE A STONE DROP THE DEBT DRUM BEAT OF GRIM NEWS DRUNK ON ARTIFICIAL PROSPE
UNFIT ECONOMIES OF SCALE ECONOMY FACES MAJOR HEADWINDS ECONOMY HITS CHOPPY WATER
ING RADICAL STRUCTURAL REFORM EMERGENCY AID EMERGING REALITY OF CUTS EMU BLOC END O
ROZONE ENVIRONMENT OF UNCERTAINTY EQUITY ERODE HOUSEHOLD REAL INCOMES ESCHERIAN C
LATIONS EUROPEAN STABILITY MECHANISM EUROPEANS ARE LAZY SPENDTHRIFTS EUROPEANS KEE
C DEMAND EXPANSIONARY FISCAL CONTRACTION EXPERIAN FOOTFALL EXPLICIT FISCAL REDISTRI
EVELS OF PERIPHERAL DEBT EYE-WATERINGLY LARGE NUMBERS FACING DOWN PUBLIC-SECTOR UNIC
TS FEDERAL RESERVE FEEBLE REBOUND FEEBLE RECOVERY FEEL-BAD FACTOR FELL FEROCIOUS SQU
G FINANCIAL FILIBUSTER FINANCIAL FORTUNES FALL FINANCIAL FRICTION THEORY FINANCIAL G
L FISCAL ASPHYXIATION FISCAL BASKET-CASE FISCAL CONSOLIDATION FISCAL CREDIBILITY FISCAL I
NEL FOOD PRICE INFLATION FOOTLOOSE CAPITAL FOOTNOTE IN HISTORY FOR THE LOVE OF GOD FOR
TITIVE LEVERAGED BIDDING FRESH LOW FRESH PANIC FRESH RETREAT FRESH STIMULUS FRESH TRAN
BLE GAME CHANGER GAME OF CHICKEN GEARING RATIOS GENERAL ABSTRACT EQUIVALENT GENER
D GLOOMY OUTLOOK GLOOMY STATISTICS GLOOMY SURVEY GMB UNION GOING BUST GOING WITH
VERESTIMATE ASSET VALUES GROTESQUE IMBALANCE GROUP OF DEBT GROWING INCOME GAP GRO
S HARD-PRESSED FAMILIES HARDLINE APPROACH HARDLINE EUROSCEPTICS HEAD-SCRATCHING H
RINKMANSHIP HIGHER RATIOS OF DEBT TO REVENUES HIRE AND FIRE HIRE ME HISTORIC LOWS HIT
OUSING BUST HOW MUCH IS ENOUGH HOW TO STIMULATE GROWTH HUGE DROP HUGE LOSES HUGE
TARY UNION ILLEGALLY KEPT CASH IMMORAL CAPITALISM RUN AMOK IMPAIRMENT CHARGE IMPLO
NDUSTRIAL ECONOMY HAS BEEN DISASTROUSLY HOLLOWED OUT INDUSTRIAL RELATIONS INDUSTRI
INTENSE VOLATILITY INTERDEPENDENCE INTEREST ON DEBTS INTEREST-FREE CREDIT INTERIM FOR
IT'S ALL ABOUT SPENDING IT'S BACK TO THE THIRTIES IT'S HURTING IT'S NOT FATAL BUT IT'S PAINFU
YBOSH THE PAYOUT LABOUR LAWS LABOUR MOVEMENT LABOUR'S FAULT LABOUR'S LAX REGULAT
ATE CAPITALIST EXCESS LAW OF THE TENDENCY FOR THE RATE OF PROFIT TO FALL LAYING STAFF O
UNT LEVERAGED UP LEVERAGING LEVY LIABILITY LIBOR LIFE-CYCLE HYPOTHESIS LIGHT TOUCH REC
TERITY BRITAIN LOAN DELINQUENCY LOANS TO DEPOSIT RATIO LOBBYING CHINA LOCK-IN LONDON
ER WEALTH LOSS-ABSORBING CAPITAL LOSSES LOST CONTROL LOST DECADE LOST GENERATION LOW
MAJOR SELL OFF MAJOR SLUMP MAKE THE TRADE-OFF MAKE-OR BREAK MAKING CONCESSIONS MA
ETS BELLY-FLOP MARKETS HIT THE PANIC BUTTON MARKETS RALLYING MARKOZY MARMITE WORKER
M WAGE MINSKY MOMENT MIRED IN DEBT MIS-SELLING TOXIC SUB PRIME MORTGAGES MISERY INDEX
DISMAY MOODY'S MORAL HAZARD MORALLY BANKRUPT MORALLY REPUGNANT MORE AUSTERITY M
UGH MUDSLIDE OF GLOOMY NUMBERS MUPPETS MUSHROOM CLOUD OF UNREGULATED DERIVATIVE
NT NEGATIVE NUMBERS ARE NOT GOOD NEGATIVE OUTLOOK NEGATIVE WATCH NEO-LIBERAL CAPIT
UNTABILITY NO AFFORDABLE CREDIT AVAILABLE NO CONVINCING CONSUMERS NO EASY REMEDY NO
GH TO DO A FISCAL FIX NOT SINCE THE CALLAGHAN GOVERNMENT NOT WEALTH CREATION BUT W
EY TAPS OPPORTUNISTIC LOOTING OPTIONS OSBORNOMICS OSBOURNE IN DENIAL OSSIFYING SOCIET
ERMANENTLY PAIN FOR SAVERS PAIN NOW GAIN LATER PAINFUL FISCAL CONSOLIDATION PAINFUL RE
BY STEALTH PAY DISPARITIES PAY DOWN DEBTS PAY FREEZE PAY MORE AND WORK LONGER PAY RESTRA
PESSIMISTIC PICTURE PICKET LINES PICK UP THE BILL PIE IN THE SKY ECONOMICS PIGS PILING AUSTE
LLING PONZI SCHEME POOREST ARE HARDEST HIT PORTFOLIOS DROP SHARELY POSSIBLE DOWNGRA
RKETS PRESSURE ON MARGINS PREVAILING GLOOM PREVAILING WEAKNESS OF PRODUCTIVITY PREVA
ONGED FINANCIAL MELTDOWN PROLONGED MARKET BATTERING PROP UP PROPAGANDA WAR PROPH
EXCESS PUNISHED BY AUSTERITY PUNITIVE TERMS PUNITIVELY UNAFFORDABLE PURCHASING MANA
Y RACKED UP DEBTS RAIDING THE COOKIE JAR RAIDING THE GOLD RESERVES RAIDING THE PIGGY BA
SSION BLAMED FOR DIVORCE SPIKE RECESSION CONTINUES RECKLESS LENDING RECLAIM THE STATE I

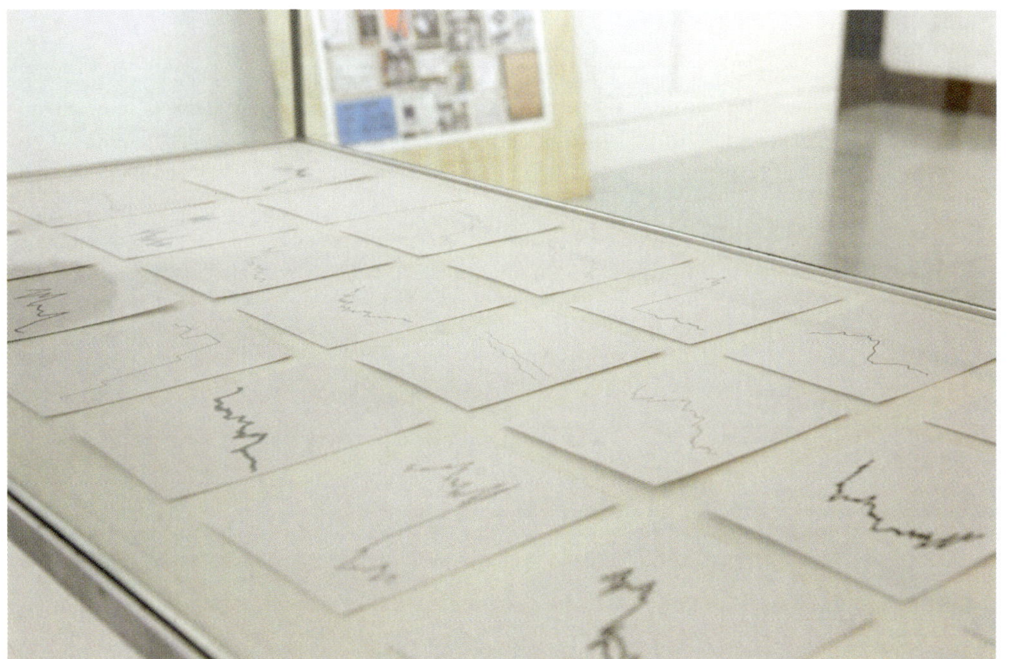

PREVIOUS SPREAD

Figure 9

Simon Roberts, *Credit Crunch Lexicon* (2012). Installation in the exhibition *Let This Be a Sign* at Swiss Cottage Gallery (June 2012).

Courtesy the artist.

Figure 10

Simon Roberts, *Credit Crunch Lexicon* (detail) (2012). Installation in the exhibition *Let This Be a Sign* at Swiss Cottage Gallery (June 2012).

Courtesy the artist.

He adopts the very 'repetition, insistence, and hyperbole' that characterises mainstream discussions.[16]

In exhibition, the graphic element of *Credit Crunch Lexicon* is composed of dozens of line graphs either presented adjacent to one another, in a single line, or in a museum-style case. The sheer massing of material suggests that the world is in the middle of an unstoppable disaster. Roberts's principal intervention is to remove the labelling of the axes, so that 'understanding' of any kind is impossible. All that we see are endless numbers of downward-moving lines. Roberts argues that these graphs could, even in their original format, only ever loosely illustrate an assumption rather than forge an argument. Roberts has, on one occasion, laid out the graphs flat inside a case – again, unlabelled. If one approaches from the left side, all are reversed: bust becomes boom becomes bust. Set out in this way, the work provides a dynamic enactment of the cyclical nature of speculation, and the binary either/or format of the narrative. Such simple processes – logical inversions, the use of 'found' material and visual puns – are all ultimately indebted to Surrealism.

As outlined above, *Credit Crunch Lexicon* consists solely of quotations of other authors' words and images. A second component of the work is a vast, wall-sized sequence of written phrases similarly extracted from media coverage, and rendered in a style that makes them appear akin to signage. The 'signs' provide an endless stream of exhortations or directions that contain manifest contradictions. The work is, then, a kind of 'library' collated over a five-year period: a monumental collage of twenty-first century news about the financial crisis that distantly echoes Walter Benjamin's 'Arcades Project'. Benjamin attempted to encapsulate the movement of capital in the nineteenth century into a single volume composed only from quotations.

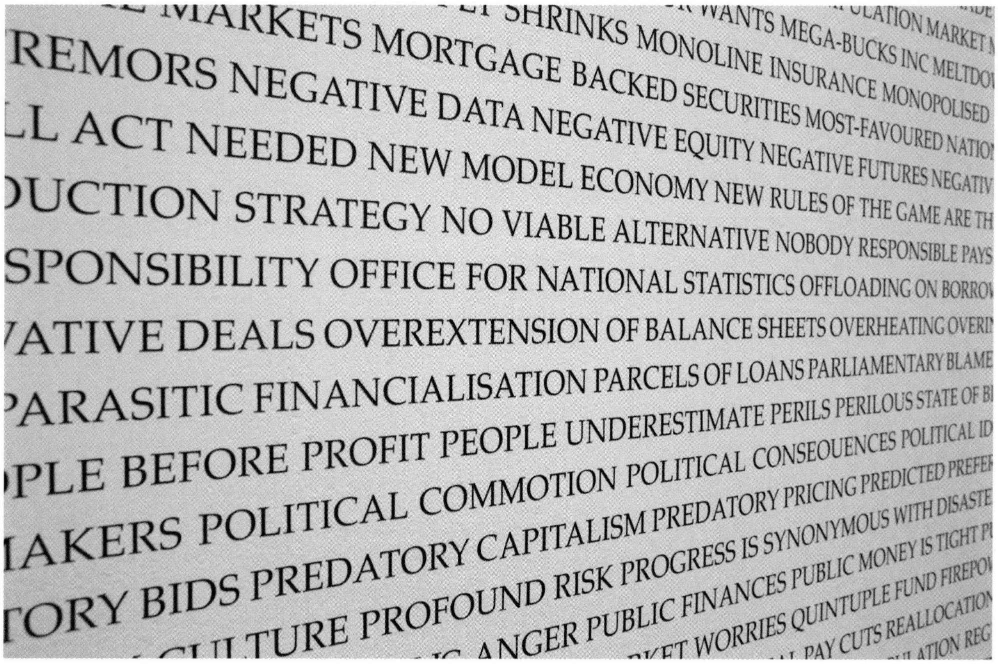

Figure 11

Simon Roberts, *Credit Crunch Lexicon* (detail) (2012). Installation in the exhibition *Let This Be a Sign* at Swiss Cottage Gallery (June 2012).

Courtesy the artist.

Like Benjamin, Roberts sees himself as an archivist of the present, and the recent past. He attempts to achieve the same end for our own century and the financial crisis that has defined it since 2008 using similar means. The effect is of hearing a radio tuned to all channels simultaneously, cacophonous and alarming: we encounter a seemingly continuous stream of sound-bites literally writ large. The volume of words is a kind of monstrous assemblage, rendering the language employed ridiculous and frightening at the same time.

Roberts remarks that while the consequences of the crisis are novel, its very predictability and that it arose from structural features of the market have been effectively suppressed. Instead, the media have merely replicated the financial markets' own impenetrable language and the opacity of their processes.[17] He argues:

> From 2008 we all had to learn a new language: a new sequence of terms that had made no impression on our consciousness before then. Coinages like 'derivatives' and 'default swaps' still remain opaque to the majority of the population but are repeated in print or online ad nauseum. The sheer strangeness of the terms lends them to being read as a kind of 'concrete poetry' in a gallery.[18]

Roberts's work extrapolates the idea that the very language already used to represent the financial crisis is artificial, or even artistic. Gobbets of language are extracted from their context and re-presented as though they were historical artefacts. *Credit Crunch Lexicon* is based on the aim of creating a sense of *ostranenie* – of distancing ourselves from our own language, and generating a sense of alienation from our existing moral universe. The terms in which Susan Buck-Morss has described Benjamin's uses of 'found' text also characterise Roberts's 'concrete poetry': 'It makes little difference ... whether the "images" of the nineteenth century were pictorially or verbally represented. Whichever form they took, such images were the concrete, "small, particular moments" in which the "total historical event" was to be discovered'.[19]

Roberts's quasi-surrealist tactics invite us to register the present as a historical moment, and in doing so render tangible the historical forces that brought about another 'crisis'. This is best achieved not by coining new, vivid images, but by a kind of sedimental accretion of the opaque technical terms and wilfully clichéd images that characterise our existing linguistic field. Roberts subscribes to Stefan Collini's argument that we can only imagine each field and debate through the 'image-clusters' that they offer up.[20] To paraphrase Collini, the relationship between high finance and the entire economy is graspable through the 'range of idioms ... [in which that] political argument [i]s conducted', and by grasping 'how these idioms derive from or [a]re mutations of other established intellectual standards'.[21] Roberts's role is to present the entirety of the 'image-cluster' that the media have created, to test them against 'established intellectual standards'.

Roberts also takes Collini's line that 'clichés can be revealing of what a culture takes for granted' as axiomatic.[22] The third component of *Credit Crunch Lexicon* is a 'found' photographic archive in which the images present a litany of visual clichés. We encounter photographs from the financial markets of traders and others in moments of apparent despair, rage, or frustration. Their gestures and facial expressions are often almost identical. It is as though they were playing out a finite range of roles from the theatrical repertoire, as if they are 'actors' in their field who can only 'play to type', or self-stereotype.[23] To adapt Collini's argument again, the repetition of such images provides an ironic 'reassurance that ... the forces at work are few and simple, that "complexity" is a dodge created by pedants'.[24] Roberts's position is not merely that the media simplify matters into monocausal explanations. Nor is it that they simply personalise structural issues, making 'market failure' a matter of individuals' failings and closing off any possibility of wider debate or analysis. These are well established. Rather, Roberts sees that our 'image-clusters', pictorially, verbally and graphically trap us, constituting the limits of what can legitimately be said, rather than what is sayable. Again, Roberts takes Benjamin's 'Arcades Project' as exemplary, his position echoing the idea that 'the debris of mass culture [i]s the source of philosophical truth'.[25] In the last instance he believes, as Max Ernst and Picabia did before him, that we are known by the ephemera that we keep.

If Roberts has made manifest what the symbolic consequences of the 2008 crash have been, Wolfgang Weileder has perhaps been the one artist able to positively re-enact its financial consequences, albeit in microscopic form, and in negative. His work *Cashpoint* was conceived in 2008 and realised as a public installation in Australia the following year. It has yet to be realised in Europe, perhaps for understandable reasons, despite being on initial inspection a simple proposition. We encounter an abstracted but functioning full-scale version of an ATM (Automatic Teller Machine), created in stainless steel. Weileder insists that it is shown only in public, and only in a city's regeneration area/s. In other words, it becomes almost invisible, and part of the city's ordinary street furniture. Indeed as an object, *Cashpoint* is also a piece of perfectly honed minimalist sculpture: austere,

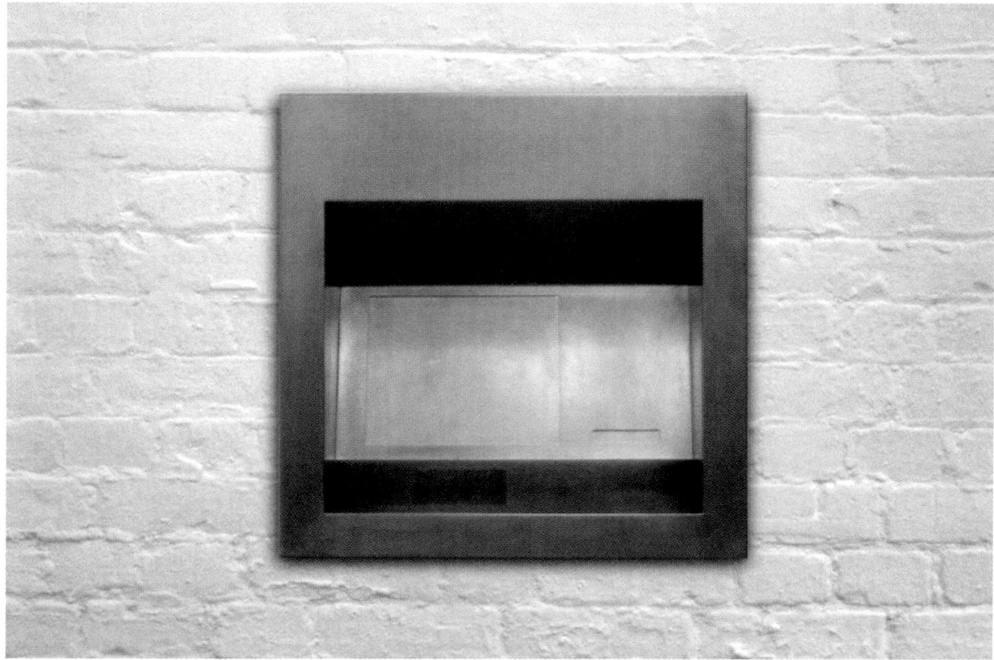

Figure 12

Wolfgang Weileder, *Cashpoint* (2008). Stainless steel, computer, cash dispensing mechanism. 60 x 40 x 60cm. Installation as part of the project 'Back to the City' in Newcastle, Australia, 2008, with Michael Tawa.

Courtesy the artist.

geometric, and industrially manufactured. Depending on our framework of reference, we might read its appearance as either akin to something that the minimalist Donald Judd might have made, or equally as an object intended to fit, comfortably and unobtrusively, into a corporate façade.

However, *Cashpoint* is not merely a 'sculpture'. It only functions in relation to a public context, in which it 're-directs the expected and habitual flow of people through the city'. More provocatively, it achieves this by redirecting the flows of capital which both banks and the state usually organise. The originality of *Cashpoint* lies in the unexpected situations and relationships it generates. We might say that it exists only in the narratives it creates in those who see it, or hear about it. The existence of the work is intended to be revealed gradually, as it becomes a story told by word of mouth throughout its city. (It is secreted into the city: unlike most public sculpture, there is no accompanying publicity, unveiling ceremony, or accompanying information.)

The principal noteworthy feature of this cashpoint is that it dispenses a banknote of the smallest denomination available, once a day every day, at a random, computer-chosen interval. Behind the façade sits a computer, programmed to choose one second from the 86,400 in each day to release a £5 (or 5 Euro) note. The process repeats for as long as the work is funded, as the source of its capital is central to its working and meaning. Weileder insists that *Cashpoint* only distributes *public* money. In doing so, he has created an inverted image of the public philanthropy towards the banking sector that is itself an inverted image of progressive redistribution. Since 2008, the UK government has

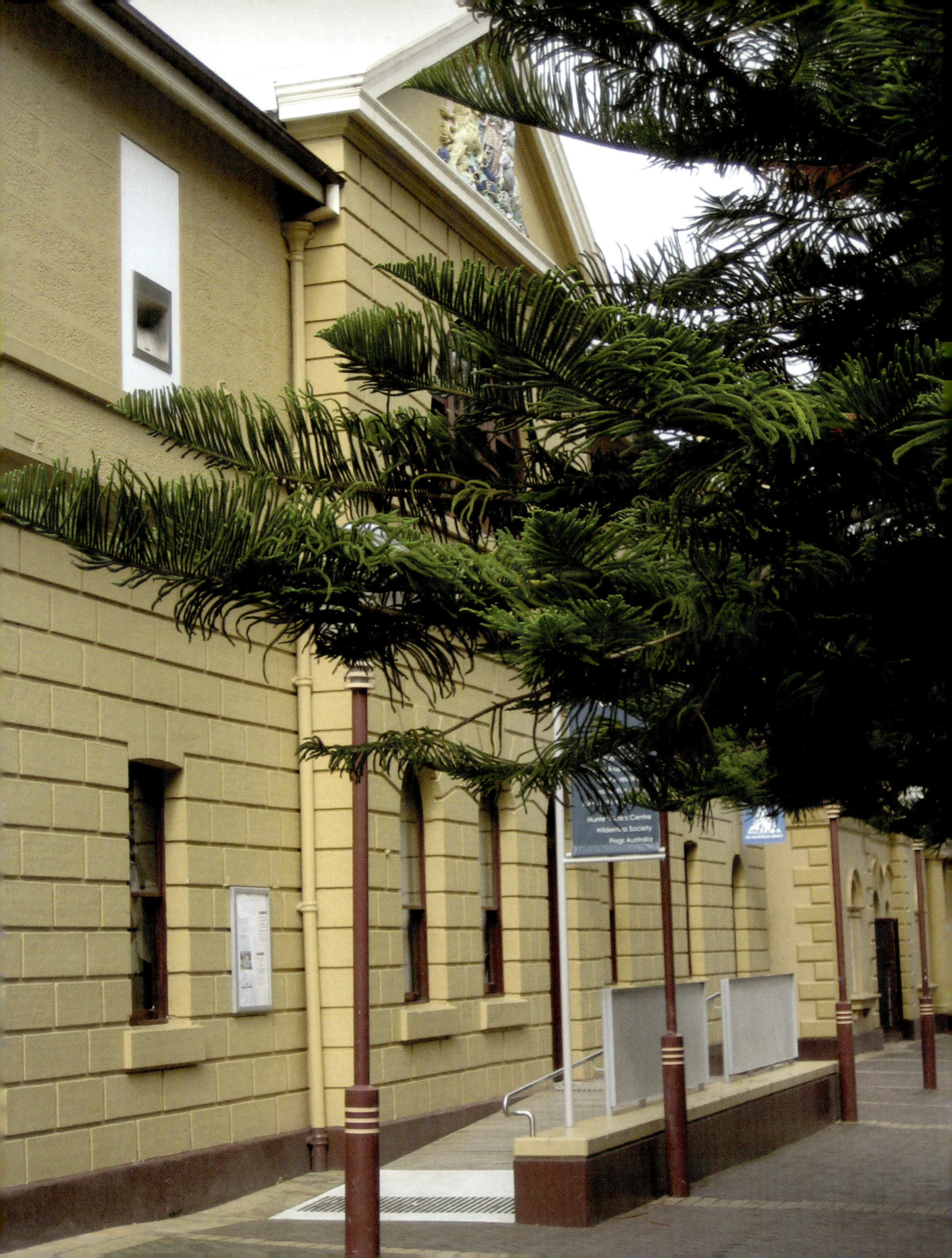
Flags Australia

Figures 13 and 14

Wolfgang Weileder, *Cashpoint* (street views) (2008).

Courtesy the artist.

deployed £66 billion in underwriting the financial sector.[26] Weileder's work returns a tiny proportion back to the public, amongst other tasks, by establishing a publicly funded, free bank that 'gifts' cash to members of the public. One (classic Surrealist) means of picturing the-world-turned-upside-down is to re-invert it back again.

Cashpoint also recalls Robert Tressell's novel *The Ragged Trousered Philanthropists*, published in 1914. Its centenary is painfully apt: once again, the beneficiaries of public generosity have been the most privileged private individuals. Entire citizenries have become philanthropists towards capital-rich institutions (and their employees) in almost exactly the model that Tressell outlined. *Cashpoint* exists, then, principally in relation to the idea that we ordinarily refer to 'the economy'. Weileder suggests that we inhabit *an* economy rather than the (only) economy possible, and that other forms of exchange exist.

For neoliberal governments to socialise debts accrued by organisations that were critical of state intervention is, of course, something that would have delighted the Surrealists in its absurdity and outright improbability. André Breton maintained that his modus operandi was, simply, 'to outplay the probable'.[27] It would appear that many financial leaders' attitude to risk in recent years was similar, and that in 'outplaying' the markets, they outplayed entire governments and populations inadvertently. Rather than being based on infallible algorithms and data capture, 'outplaying the probable' has been the basis of what was punitively called wealth creation by many.

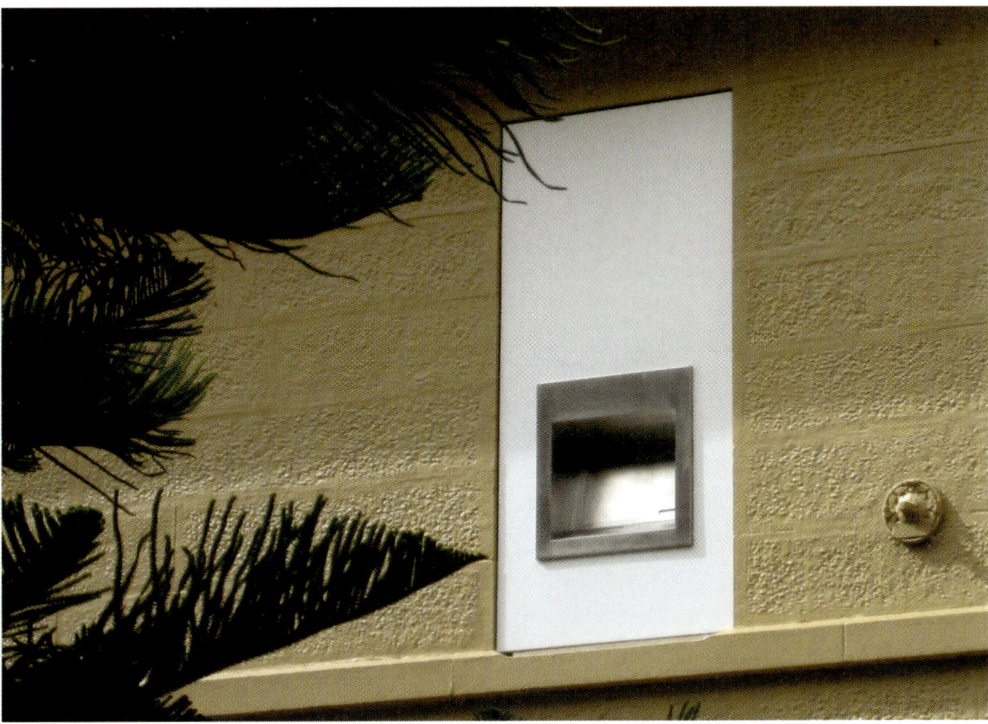

For Weileder *Cashpoint* exists in part to create a bank that disregards or inverts all usual logics. It disperses capital rather than accumulates it. It rewards people at random, rather than in proportion to their efforts or their place in the economy. It creates an alternative gift economy that cannot be reduced to cost-benefit analysis. It inverts the roles of public and private, or at the very least confuses them. While *Cashpoint* is 'pointed' in its purposes, it is generous in its actions. It echoes Picabia's thoughts above. The small, fragile paper objects – credit notes – that are circulated are 'genuine bargains' at 'unheard of prices'.[28] But more importantly, Weileder invites us to speculate whether whole constellations of ideas – or even an entire worldview – have seen their stock fallen since 2008. He queries if our own values have themselves become unexpectedly devalued.

For the three artists here, there remain other possible financial worlds beyond that defined by polar opposites of excess and retrenchment, of a rush to credit and an accompanying crash. As this chapter has outlined, they do this precisely by re-introducing us to the world we already inhabit. Each asks, if only implicitly, how we might imagine other ways of circulating capital and creating value beyond recycling and repackaging debts. In doing so they take it as a given that history, rather than merely capital, is 'liquid'.

Notes

1 Quoted in Philip Coggan, *Paper Promises: Money, Debt and the New World Order* (London: Allen Lane, 2011), p. 2.

2 Quoted in Ruth Brandon, *Surreal Lives: The Surrealists 1917–1945* (New York: Grove Press, 2000), p. 165.

3 Helen Paul, *The South Sea Bubble: An Economic History of Its Origins and Consequences* (London: Routledge, 2011), p. 10.

4 For a detailed discussion of the way that economics has historically turned to the other sciences for its metaphors and theoretical framework, see Philip Mirowski, *More Heat than Light: Economics as Social Physics, Physics as Nature's Economics* (Cambridge: Cambridge University Press, 1989), and *Machine Dreams: Economics Becomes a Cyborg Science* (Cambridge: Cambridge University Press, 2001).

5 Nikolai Kondratiev, *The Major Economic Cycles* (Moscow: Voprosy Koniunktury 1925).

6 The classic analysis of financial crises as an identifiable part of the business cycle is provided in Charles P. Kindleberger, *Manias, Panics, and Crashes: A History of Financial Crises*, 4th edn (Basingstoke: Palgrave Macmillan, 2000).

7 Carlota Perez, *Technological Revolutions and Financial Capital: The Dynamics of Bubbles and Golden Ages* (Cheltenham: Edward Elgar Publishing, 2002).

8 Nicolas Bourriaud's seminal text *Relational Aesthetics* (Paris: Les Presses Du Reel, 1998) popularised the idea that, 'The contemporary artist is a semionaut, he invents trajectories between signs'. A decade later, exhibitions and texts on re-enactment coincided across Europe and America. See for example, http://atc.berkeley.edu/201/readings/Blackson.pdf, accessed 18 October 2013.

9 Interview with the author, August 2013.

10 In the photographic series 'High altitude' (2008–10) the German artist Michael Najjar provided a similar rendition of the stock market graph as a digitally manipulated mountain range.

11 Interview with the author, August 2013.

12 Interview with the author, August 2013.

13 For an account of the links between postmodern finance and postmodern theory, see Mark C. Taylor, *Confidence Games: Money and Markets in a World Without Redemption* (Chicago: University of Chicago Press, 2004).

14 Interview with the author, August 2013.

15 Interview with the author, October 2013.

16 Ibid.

17 As part of the exhibition *To Have and To Owe* (New York, 2012) the artist Cassie Thornton and academic Leigh Claire La Berge created a wall-sized infographic charting the interconnections between the stock market crash and the incidence of words such as 'complex' in financial journalism (http://to-have-and-to-owe.tumblr.com/, accessed 18 October 2013).

18 Interview with the author, October 2013.

19 Susan Buck-Morss, *The Dialectic of Seeing* (Cambridge, MA: MIT Press, 1991), p. 71.

20 Stefan Collini, *Public Moralists: Political Thought and Intellectual Life in Britain, 1850–1930* (Oxford: Oxford University Press, 1993), p. 153.

21 Ibid., p. 153.

22 Ibid., p. 357.

23 http://brokershandsontheirfacesblog.tumblr.com/, accessed 18 October 2013.

24 Collini, *Public Moralists*, pp. 230, 358.

25 Buck-Morss, *The Dialectic of Seeing*, p. ix.

26 http://uk.reuters.com/article/2013/06/10/uk-britain-banks-privatisations-idUKBRE9580JB20130610.

27 Brandon, *Surreal Lives*, p. 214.

28 'There is a fundamental difference between the paper money system and the metallic standard it replaced. Gold is no-one else's liability: you can own it outright. Paper or electronic money is always *a claim on someone else* whether a bank or a government. Modern money is debt and debt is money'. Coggan, *Paper Promises*, p. 3.

The only way is up baby

Ben Lewis

An imagined argument between a contemporary art dealer and an art critic.

In the last ten years I have had scores of arguments with people who think there is nothing suspicious or incredible about the contemporary art market. I have been able to hone my answers to their criticisms over many encounters. Here I present my arguments in the form of a dialogue.

In 2008–09 you made a film called *The Great Contemporary Art Bubble* which purported to investigate the contemporary art market, alleging widespread market manipulation.

Yes, did you like it?

No. It was the work of a man who hates contemporary art and wants to destroy it.

It was the work of someone who loves contemporary art – and wants to save it.

Do you still get any work as an art critic?

Not much. Within 6 months of the release of that film, my commissions as an art critic were reduced by over 80 per cent – roughly the same percentage as the crash in the contemporary art market worldwide.

Ha! You ended that film with the words, 'The Great Contemporary Art Bubble will go down in history as the epitome of the vanity and folly of our age'. How much more wrong could you be?

I was right in several ways. The market did crash that year, 2008–09, and only began picking up again in 2010. Volumes of sales went down by 50–75 per cent, depending on how you calculate it. Prices for many artists have crashed and not recovered. Take Hirst for example. According to Artnet, Hirst works bought between 2005 and 2008 have since resold at an average loss of 30 per cent.

Hirst will recover. People are very funny, because they like buying things when they're expensive. They don't like buying things when they're inexpensive.

That is the classic sales pitch of the dealer. But if that were the case there would be no ups and downs in prices.

Yes, but the big art market is back: in May 2013 Christie's set a global record for a contemporary art sale with a figure of $495m.

Make your mind up – are people not buying art because it is too cheap, or is everyone buying because prices are going up? It is true that I did not anticipate the art market would reassemble itself more powerfully than ever, like the last scene in *Terminator Two*, when the robot reconstitutes itself from its liquid fragments. However, we should question how real the price rises really are. America is printing $85bn new dollars a month in its 'quantitative easing' programme. As one art market commentator observed in the 1980s, 'It's not the art that's not worth the money; the money isn't worth the money'.

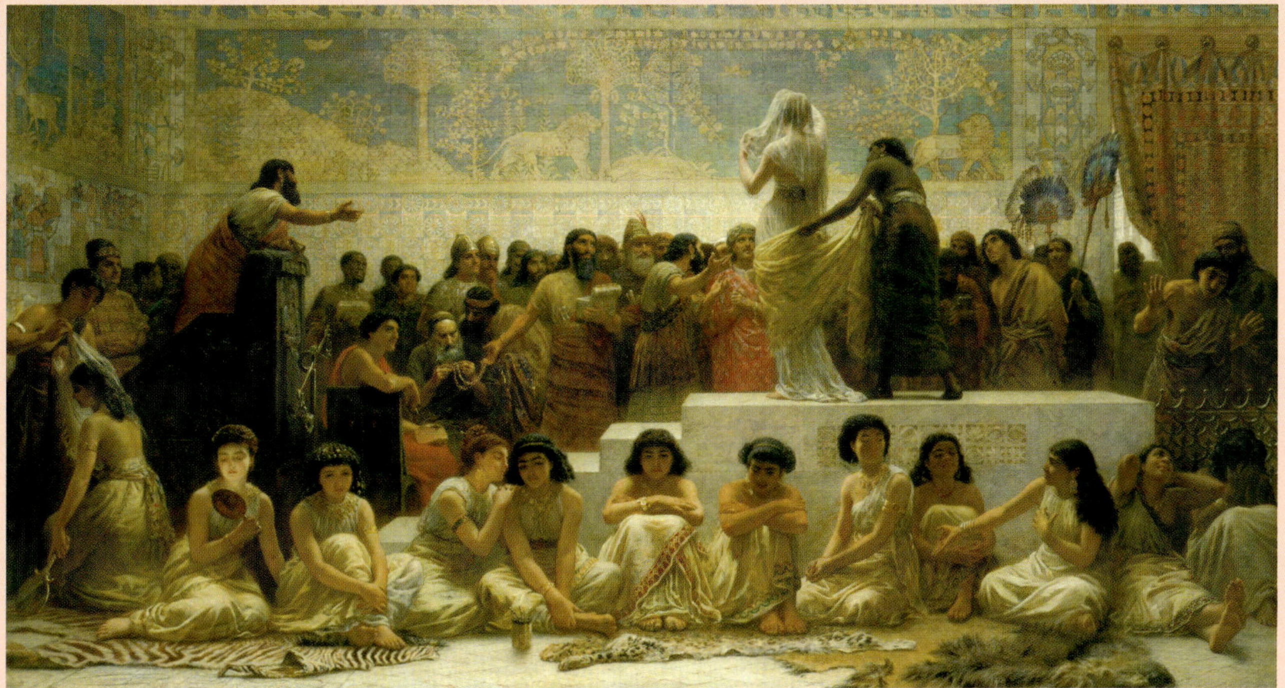

Figure 1

Edwin Longsden Long, *The Babylonian Marriage Market* (1875).

Royal Holloway, University of London.

As a fan of contemporary art you should surely applaud the rise in prices paid for it over the last ten years. There are thousands more collectors coming from new markets like Russia, Latin America and Asia.

What has been happening in recent years is that the market has actually stifled innovation. Artists who arguably started out full of original ideas, simply recycled the same ones over and over again on an ever bigger scale because there was a market for them – as in Hirst's Spots and Prince's Nurse Paintings. The good ideas of the art of the 1970s have become gimmicks that have led to endless product ranges. Even much of the work of Ai Wei Wei takes European conceptual art formulae and applies them to Chinese content – a load of chairs or bicycles turned into a geometric shape etc.

Fortunately, your views are irrelevant today. Critics don't matter. The collectors and the museums decide.

True. One problem is the collectors are often the museums. Public money has shrunk dramatically in real terms as a percentage of the budget of public institutions. Museums need billionaire collectors to help them build new wings and buy new art.

'Twas ever thus. There have always been rich collectors buying and selling art. Look at the Medicis. And artists have always made work for a market. Look at Rembrandt.

We no longer live in a feudal system. We can expect a more up-to-date art market today than existed five hundred years ago.

There is a famous joke. Why do pop stars go out with models? Because they can. HNWIs (High Net Worth Individuals) buy art because they can too.

The relationship between the world of the rich and the world of art is more complex than that. When Roman Abramovich pays $80m for a Francis Bacon he is only paying $1m of that because it is a great work of art, and $2m because it enhances his social status. The remaining $77m is because of other features of this market.

Like what?

Today the core of the art market is controlled by a handful of key American and occasionally British players. Did you know that in the May 2011 contemporary art auctions in New York, 52 per cent of all lots in Christie's evening sale consisted of artists exhibited by Gagosian Gallery. At Sotheby's this number was exactly half. Sotheby's, Christie's, Gagosian, White Cube and a handful of dealer-collectors such as Peter Brant, Aby Rosen and the Mugrabis control the heart of the art market. They maintain prices most of the time in a premier league of artists (and there is a trickle-down effect through the whole art market). Anyone else who wants to join the club – a Russian oligarch, a newly minted Chinese multi-millionaire or Qatari Sheikh – can, but they have to pay a premium price for it, often bidding against these core group of dealers who all know each other. The new money is made to pay more by the old money. Is it a cartel-like economy? Depends on your definition of that word.

That is a conspiracy theory.

Perhaps, or more like a system with a few different people sharing the same objectives.

There's nothing illegal about that. It's just supply and demand.

No, it's not just that. Above all, these values are produced by market practices that are rare in other fields. Dealers maintain the prices of their artists at auction, to make sure they don't fall below a certain level, or to set new record levels. This seems to me to have been acceptable in a much smaller art market, where artists' careers were so fragile. Now the same strategies fuel a highly speculative market.

The auction market is used as a loss leader: a place where dealers parade their wealth and power, while the sale of works of art is not as simple as it appears. To give you an abstract example: you are a successful gallerist, with a number of artists whose work has grown in value over the last five years and a number of collectors who have bought frequently from your gallery. You wish to launch the career of a new artist. What kind of influence can you exert on your collectors? You might offer to sell them a work by your new artist with the verbal agreement you will buy the work back in a year's time, if they don't like it. Then once you have persuaded a few of your 'inner circle' of collectors to invest in your new artist's work, you can approach an outer circle, and tell them you have sold x number of works to important collectors such as Mr Y and Mrs Z...

That is all theoretical. What evidence do you have of market manipulation?

There have been some interesting incidents that have recently come to light that suggest conflicts of interest.

In the past year, two major collectors have also filed lawsuits against Larry Gagosian, the world's most successful art dealer. In one instance, the gallery took on a work for sale from a collector, and then offered it to a potential buyer in an email that read, 'Seller now in terrible straits and needs cash. Are you interested in making a cruel and offensive offer? Come on, want to try?'

In November 2010 the renowned art adviser and dealer Philippe Segalot 'curated' an auction at Philips de Pury, which was – amazingly – titled 'Carte Blanche'. Segalot picked the works in the auction. He and staff from his company were seen bidding against each other in the auction, and they purchased many works of art in the auction, apparently on behalf of different clients.

If there was anything suspect happening then market regulators would investigate.

It is rumoured that the American authorities thought of investigating the Philippe Segalot sale and even contacted some insiders about it. But they decided against it – probably because they think this is just the rich ripping off the rich. They are not as concerned as I am about the cultural impact.

You only have a handful of incidents which you would find in any market. One of the great achievements of the top gallerists and dealers is that they have turned art into a lifestyle – the art fairs, dinners, private jets all go together ...

... together with money laundering for which art is a unique tool, for these reasons: its sale and purchase are rarely public, the market is non-transparent and unregulated, and it's easy to disguise or alter the value of a work of art as you ship it around the world's tax havens – the customs officers are not connoisseurs. It's not a coincidence that the global system of tax havens, now estimated to contain around $20–30 trillion, has grown rapidly simultaneously with the art market.

So basically you think the reason the art market has grown so rapidly is that you can get away with stuff in the art market that you can't do in other financial or commodities markets?

That's what I used to think, but now we are discovering day-by-day that the art market functions much more like the corrupted markets of globalisation. In May 2013 the legendary art dealer Helly Nahmad was charged with running an illegal gambling ring for high-fliers. How appropriate in an age when artworks have become chips in a global casino. Also this same year, the hedge fund of Steve Cohen, the legendary art collector, was fined $616m for insider trading – not so different from the art world.

So what do you think should happen?

The art market should be regulated.

How?

Using the same kind of rules that apply to stocks and shares. There should be an overseeing body empowered to investigate abuses, like the SEC or FTC in America.

Art is a private purchase that an individual makes for his own pleasure. All that would be an invasion of privacy.

No, art is not like a Louis Vuitton handbag, that is used and eventually given away to a thrift store. It is an investment good, not a luxury good.

Even if I was to accept that, you cannot regulate the art market. Dealers have to support the prices of their artists at auction, otherwise the whole market would collapse. Everyone knows the game that is being played.

That's what they said about the financial markets in the 1980s, before insider trading was outlawed.

But there is a difference from the financial markets. The art market is too small to be regulated.

It is not as small as it used to be. All markets should be fair, no matter how small they are. Since I made *The Great Contemporary Art Bubble* several incidents of alleged market manipulation in the art market have come to light.

The market is too big nowadays for manipulations.

One minute you say the market is too small to regulate, the next you say it is too big to manipulate.

Do you think that one day the art market will crash again?

Yes. Definitely.

You will be wrong again. The value of art will never go down from its present levels. There are more HNWI individuals on the planet than ever before. They have accepted contemporary art as part of their lifestyle. There are cyclical movements but the trend is always upwards.

That is what they would have said in the late nineteenth century. At that time there was a huge art market bubble and an insatiable public appetite. Salon painters or Orientalists such as Bouguereau, Gerome, Makart, Meissonier and Sir Frederick Leighton became wealthy celebrities. Half a million people visited the Paris Salon each year. In 1882, a work by Edwin Longsden Long, *The Babylonian Marriage Market*, achieved a record auction price at Christie's for a work by a living artist: £6,500, which in today's money is £4m. Ten years after his death, Long's work had lost 90 per cent of its value. His biographer wrote, 'One of the Victorian art world's most important figures had drifted into relative obscurity. The throngs of visitors who went to see his work at Burlington House or Bond Street had disappeared, his auction house record dismissed as an isolated sensation'.

No. 4880 Southampton Commercial Bank

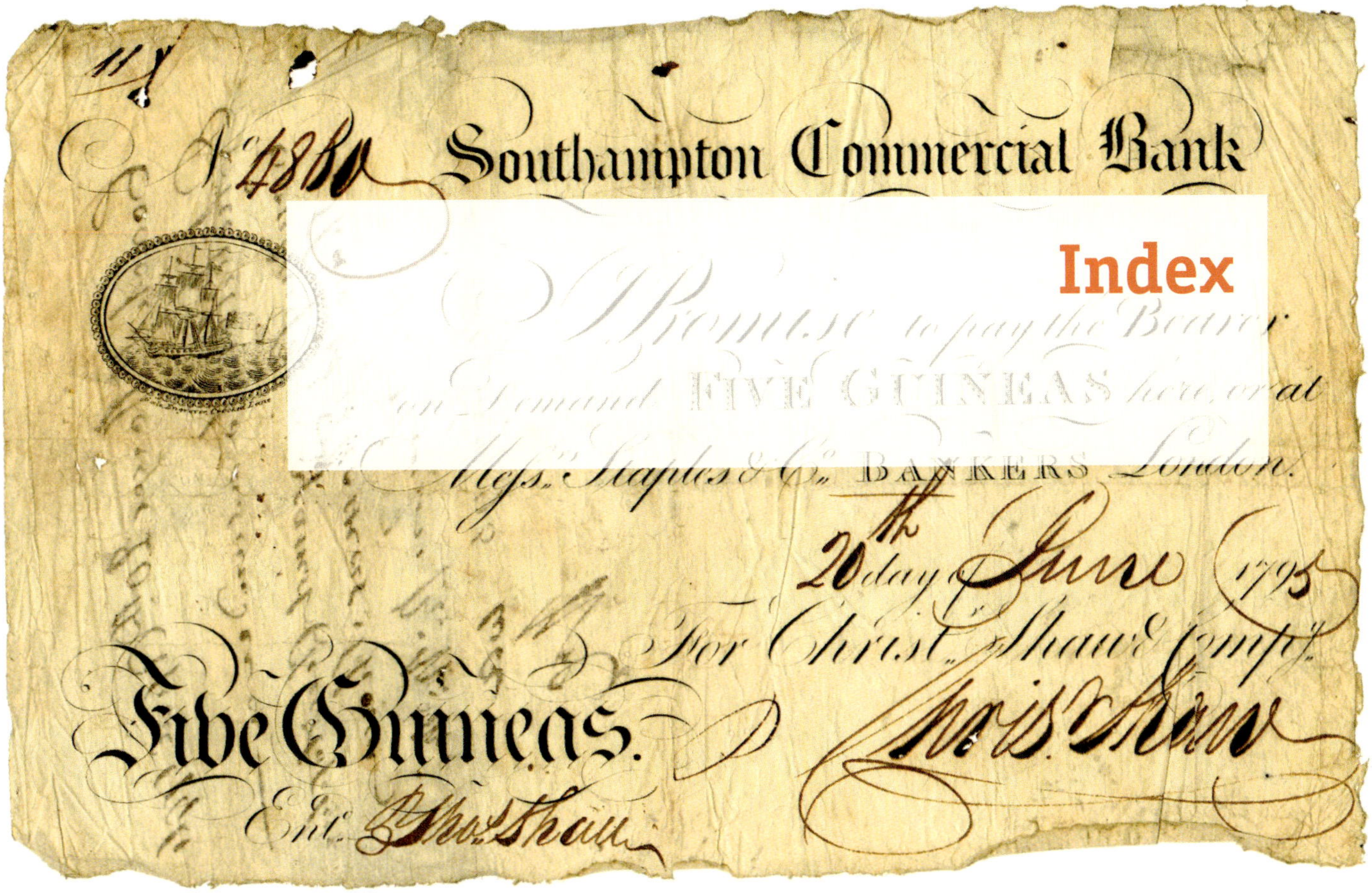

Index

I Promise to pay the Bearer on Demand FIVE GUINEAS here, or at Mess.rs Staples & Co. BANKERS London.

20th day of June 1795

For Christr. Shaw & Compy.

Five Guineas.

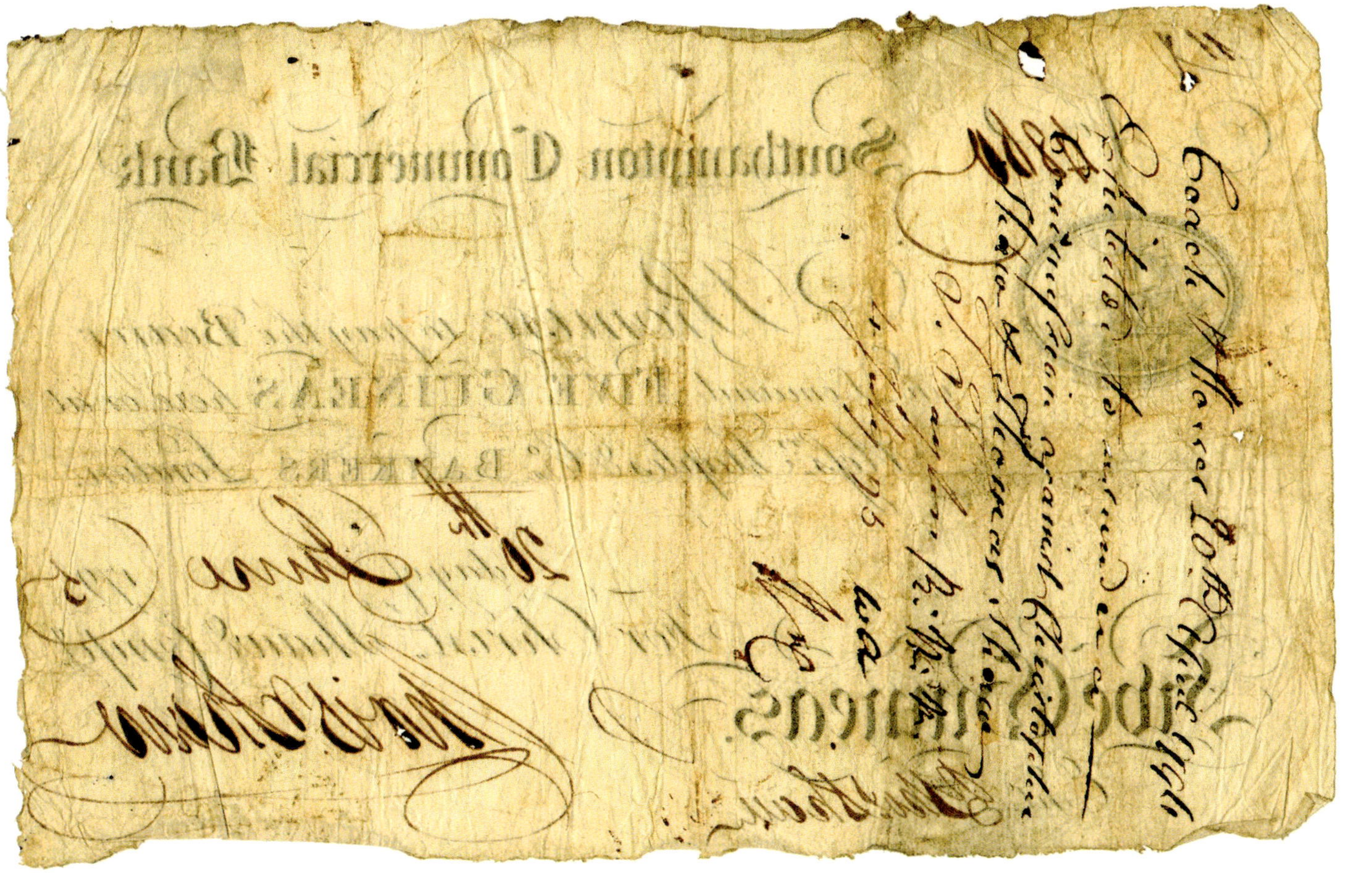

Index

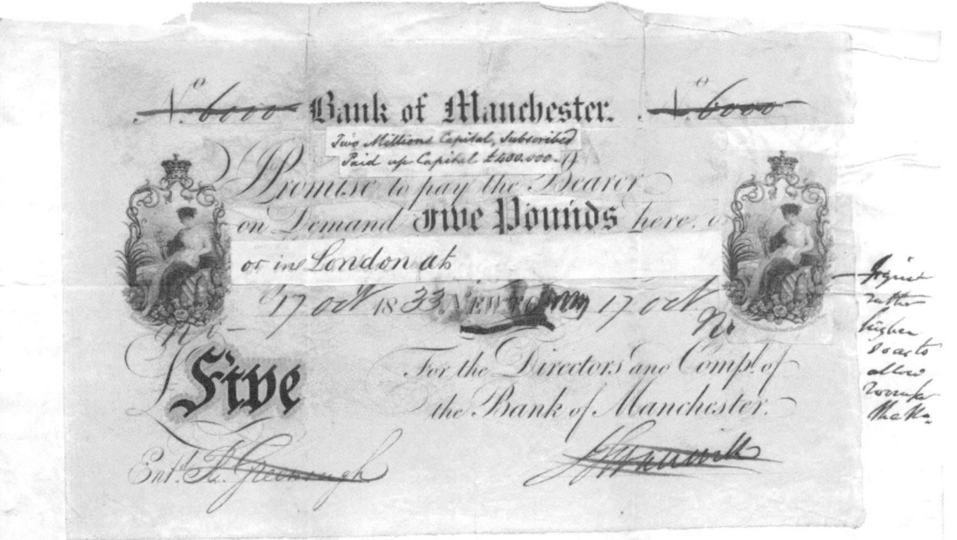
Bank of Manchester.
Two Millions Capital, Subscribed
Promise to pay the Bearer
on Demand Five Pounds
or in London at
17 Oct 1833
17 Oct
Five
For the Directors and Compy. of
the Bank of Manchester.

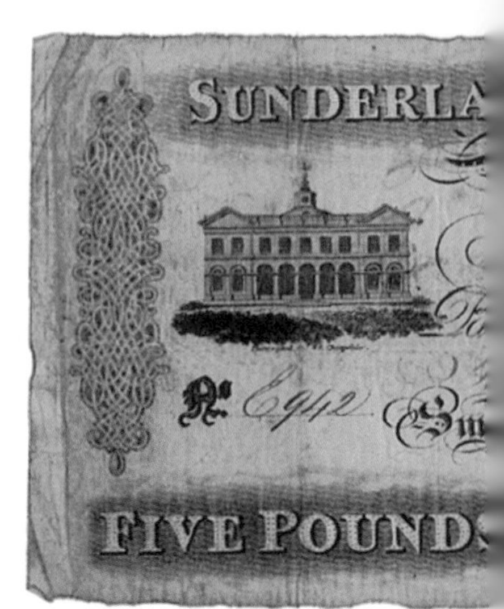

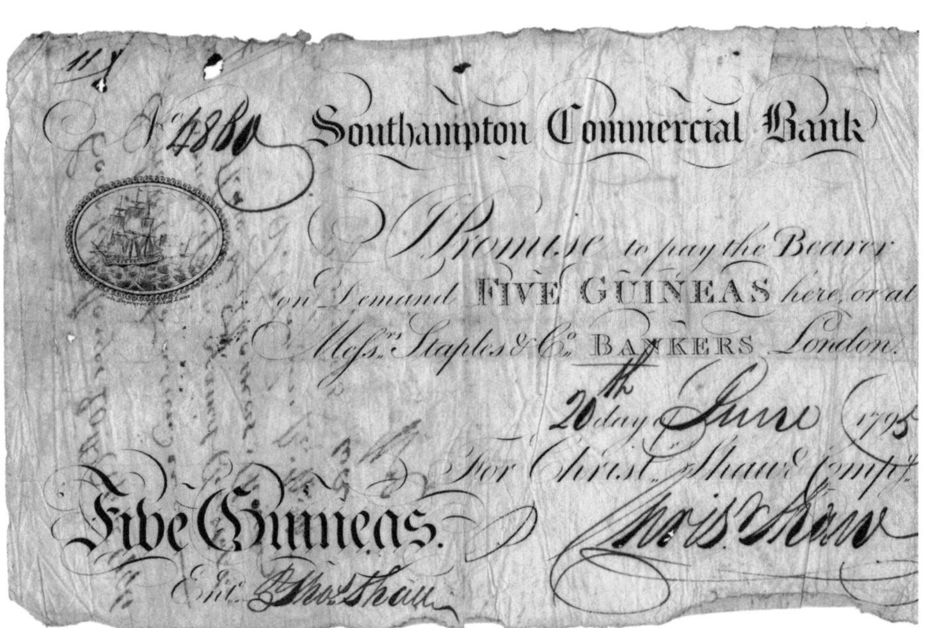
No. 4880
Southampton Commercial Bank
Promise to pay the Bearer
on Demand FIVE GUINEAS here, or at
Messrs. Staples & Co. BANKERS London.
20th day June 1795
For Christ. Shaw & Compy.
Five Guineas.

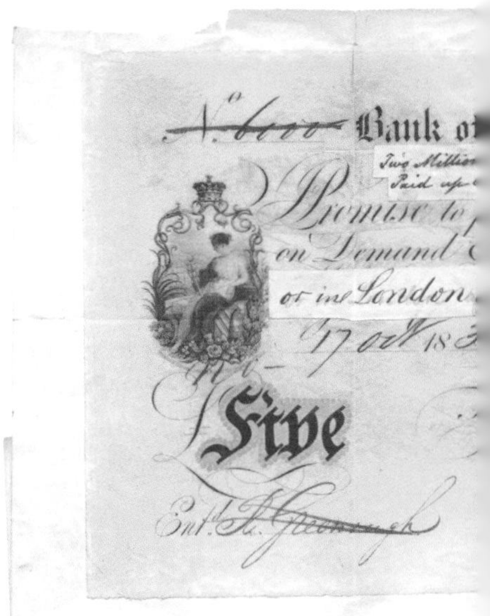
Five

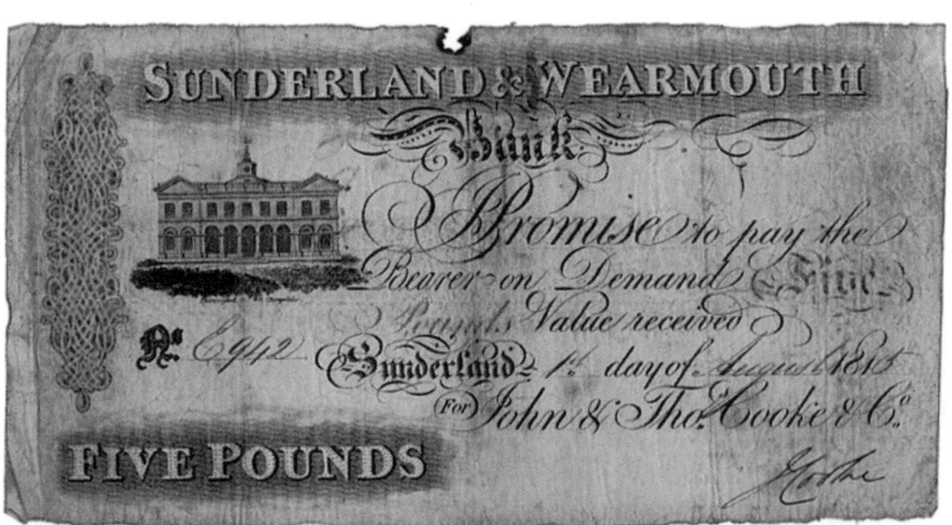
SUNDERLAND & WEARMOUTH
Bank
Promise to pay the
Bearer on Demand Five
Pounds Value received
No. E942
Sunderland 1st day of August 1815
For John & Thos. Cooke & Co.
FIVE POUNDS

No. 4880